DEDICATION

This book is dedicated to Kay Goodnow and Rick Springer who passed away in 2014. They were two great pillars of the Clergy Abuse survivor's movement and apostles in the fight against Clergy Abuse.

About the Author

Vinnie Nauheimer has utilized his talents to expose the Clergy Abuse scandal to the world and to reveal the corrupt hierarchy that, even now, tries to suppress it. He has published two books and a play dealing with the subject of Clergy Abuse. The covers of his three books are his original oil paintings. In addition to the artwok used on the book covers Mr. Nauheimer sponsors a page on Facebook called "The Clergy Abuse Collection" where more of his artwork can be seen. You do not have to be a member of Facebook to view this page.

Epistles on Clergy Abuse, offers a unique historical perspective on one person's fight to rid the church of his son's molester. Vinnie's effort resulted in the most public case of clergy abuse in the NY archdiocese's history. The end result was that the offending priest, Fr. Gennaro Gentile was defrocked. Epistles on Clergy Abuse is a three part book. The first part is a chronological compilation of Vinnie's letters to the archdiocese as well as to other bishops around the country letting them know that there were people who wouldn't believe their lies anymore. The second part contains a selection of published "Letters to the Editor" to newspapers throughout the country. Part Three consist of actual correspondence between the author and survivors from 1999 to 2004; the letters are the inside story of the incredible personal pain and suffering caused by clergy abuse. If he had to revise this work, he would lead with the correspondence to survivors. It is suggested that anyone who reads this book start reading part three, conversations with survivors, first and then read the other sections. It is available in both hard copy and e-book from: http://bookstore.xlibris.com/Products/SKU-0025616049/Epistles-on-Clergy-Abuse.aspx

Silent Screams is selection of poems written on the subject of Clergy Abuse. The poems are heartbreaking, touching and satirical as they deal with all aspects of clergy abuse. It is available in both hard copy and e-book from: http://bookstore.xlibris.com/Products/SKU-0017200017/Silent-Screams.aspx

The Predator Wore a Collar is a play loosely based on my experiences with Clergy Abuse and the NY Archdiocese. Nothing would thrill him more than to see this play produced.

Preface

When it comes to religion, politics and the law, most people can't be bothered to either learn or understand it. Only after it becomes personal will people expend the time and energy to learn about them. I was one of those reluctant people until circumstances dictated I learn. It seemed incomprehensible that a two thousand-year-old church had no laws or prohibitions against priests, bishops, cardinals and popes who have committed clerical sexual abuse. It became perfectly clear that they're there, but no cleric will voluntarily tell you about them.

After delving into both the New and Old Testaments, Canon Law, the Catechism and church history, is that there are plenty of rules for dealing with child abusing clerics. The first record of written church laws, Canons, against clerical child abuse came to us from the Council of Elvira around 312 AD. The laity has never been told about these laws because if they knew, the hierarchy, couldn't manufacture the excuses they use to shield themselves against their failure to remove offending clerics. So God damn priests and bishops for not following their own rules!

The Canons, for sexually abusing children of either sex or pederasty, which is defined as homosexual men having sex with teenaged boys were equal to the crime. The offending prelates were forbidden for the rest of their life from ever receiving communion again. They lost their offices and were excommunicated. These same laws were on the books in the Eleventh Century when St. Peter Damian wrote his treatise, The Book of Gomorrah, which railed against the predatory sexual practices of the clergy of the time. In later centuries however, it was considered ill-mannered to even study the Book of Gomorrah because of the shame it cast upon the clergy. Today's hierarchy has chosen not to punish and encourages the sexual abuse of children because of their failure to follow their own rules. This is a blight upon the church. So for their inaction, god-damn priests, bishops, cardinals and popes for putting up with crimes that so clearly fly in the face of all that Jesus taught.

At the heart of the matter is this question: "Can any pope be a true representative of Jesus Christ on earth who knowingly allows these perverted sexual crimes against children to take place without taking the necessary action to stop it?" The two are polar opposites, irreconcilable and therefore call into question the validity of the pope being the true representative of Christ on earth.

A generation of prophets sprang forth from survivors. Armed with the Internet, survivors of clergy abuse and their families sought the truth. They found it and in doing so were able to call bishops, cardinals and popes liars because according to the churches own precepts, they were liars. By lying to the world, the hierarchy disgraced themselves, their God and all those that believed in them. The hierarchy damned themselves.

Many prophets of the Old Testament were put to death, not because they foretold the future, but because they told the truth. The warnings of dire consequences that eventually came to pass were misconstrued as an ability to foretell the future when in fact, the original message of the prophets, reform, was forgotten. The destruction of evil entities does not require a degree in fortune telling; it merely needs an angry populace armed with a clear vision, common sense and the truth.

Prophets remind those in charge when they are violating God's law. This happens every time men hungry for power try to convince the populace that they speak for God. This is a fundamental character flaw of those who hold power, especially priests, high priests and the hierarchy as they are called. Priests, bishops, cardinals, and popes have developed an overwhelming urge to think themselves: gods, demigods, god's sole representative on earth or superior to the regular folk. This is a tradition that goes back before the Pharaohs and continued through the ages especially in the Roman Catholic Church. This donning of what I call the "God Mantle" leads to all sorts of abuse of power. Among these abuses of power is the unbridled rape, sodomization and molestation of children. For allowing this, the hierarchy should be damned.

In the Roman Catholic Church, clerical cultural inbreeding has wed the "god complex" to hubris. "A person who is said to have a "god complex" does not necessarily believe he is God, but is said to act so arrogantly that he might as well believe he is a god or has been appointed to act by a god." Hubris applies to any outrageous act or exhibition of pride or disregard for basic moral laws." The result of this unholy union has created self-serving monsters that create and change the rules as they are needed to defend the indefensible. Thus the need for prophets!

The outrageous acts and total disregard for moral laws displayed by today's Roman Catholic hierarchy are readily explained in the above paragraph. Now compare what was said above to the passages below and see how easy it is to connect the two. Nowhere is this false ideology of Divine Right more clearly stated than in <u>Vehementer Nos</u> an encyclical promulgated by Pius X in 1905.

> "It follows that the Church is essentially an unequal society, that is, a society comprising two categories of persons, the Pastors and the flock, those who occupy a rank in the different degrees of the hierarchy and the multitude of the faithful. So distinct are these categories that with the pastoral body only rests the necessary right and authority for promoting the end of the society and directing all its members towards that end; the one duty of the multitude is to allow themselves to be led, and, like a docile flock, to follow the Pastors."

Pius X's assumption that priests are on a higher level than the laity did not go unheeded. Consider the arrogance of this title: Conference of Major Superiors of Men. Who but arrogant, self-serving, elitists would give themselves a title that proclaims them superiors of men? Not to worry, this is egoistic attitude has spread to nuns as well. Mother Superiors have their organization also egotistically called: The Conference of Major Superiors of Women Religious.

The following is an excerpt of a letter sent to the members of an organization known as the Conference of the Major Superiors of Men by their then Executive Director. These words, written shortly after Boston's sex scandal broke, were truly prophetic in predicting the demise of the priesthood. The CMSM represents all the religious orders of priests except the diocesan priests. Behold the words of those who believe themselves the divinely appointed betters of the human race.

> "The days of the *pass* or *station house adjustment* for Father or Brother by the Irish cop or prosecutor are over. Either we will learn to become more comfortable in the gaze of the *rude and scoffing multitude* (depending on our attitude) or we will be dragged *kicking and screaming* into a new future for religion and religious life"[10](italics are the author's emphasis)

The thought processes that allow priests to refer to the laity as the "**rude and scoffing multitude**" are the same ones that allow and even encourage priests to use children as sex objects. "**Less than**" is the operative concept because it allows the children to be treated as though they are mere baubles to be used, abused and discarded. This superiority complex became an integral part of the clerical culture because the church was powerful enough over the last millennium to silence most of their critics. Without prophets to keep these men (priests) in line both their power and abuse ran rampant. Without prophets, there was no one to remind the clergy of the words of Jesus, the Holy Scripture, the bible, Canon Law and the Catechism.

The biggest detriment to prophets are the masses who follow like the aforementioned sheep. Regardless of the religion, followers don't want to believe they've been conned because it calls into question their core belief system. It is much easier to kill the prophet than rethink religious values. Cognitive Dissonance, defined as a refusal to believe an unacceptable truth, is a disease that has run rampant throughout the Catholic laity. The sexual abuse of children has become so blatant, so excessive and so vulgar that the wall of cognitive dissonance has started to crumble thanks to the efforts of survivors of clergy abuse. When the burden becomes so onerous, the people will rise up and change will be made. The laity damns bishops and priests.

History repeats itself again as the Clergy Abuse Scandal has made the laity very weary of serving their children up to sate the sexual appetites of priests; hence the prophets from the Clergy Abuse Movement have risen to tell their truth. The people who have risen up to fight clergy abuse can be compared to the Apostles. One by one they spread the word that the sexual abuse of children was intolerable, a sin against the laws of God, Man and Morality. The survivors who found their voices encouraged others to speak their truth. As with the apostles, Rome tried their damnedest to silence these outspoken survivors who decried the sexual abuse of children by clergy. In an effort to continue hiding the truth about clergy abuse, the church used every dirty trick in their arsenal: they filed suits, countersuits, intimidated victims, used their bully pulpit, the church press, the media to denigrate victims. They even stirred up the faithful against anyone who would dare speak the long known, but never verbalized truth about clergy abuse. Fortunately, the days of burning at the stake in the name of God have passed into history; otherwise, many of these outspoken apostles (survivors) would have been silenced.

So it began; one voice brought forth another voice, which brought forth yet another until the multitude of voices could not be ignored. Thus the work of these prophets succeeded in awakening the world to the problem of clerical sexual abuse. I count myself fortunate to be one of those voices. The world needs more voices to shine a bright light on the dark, dank morass of clergy abuse that has been festering in the Roman Catholic Church for centuries. Pass it on!

In a talk to clerics in November of 2014, Pope Francis said this about prophets:

> "Prophets receive from God the ability to scrutinize the times in which they live and to interpret events: they are like sentinels who keep watch in the night and sense the coming of the dawn (cf. Is 21:11-12). Prophets know God and they know the men and women who are their brothers and sisters. They are able to discern and denounce the evil of sin and injustice. Because they are free, they are beholden to no one but God, and they have no interest other than God. Prophets tend to be on the side of the poor and the powerless, for they know that God himself is on their side."

What an apt description of all the wonderful clergy abuse prophets, vocal survivors, who have given their blood, sweat, tears and even their lives in the struggle against a church rife with child abuse.

Forward

Why God Damn: Priests and Bishops? It is very simple. There are 210 cardinals, not one is a public advocate for the victims of clergy abuse. There are over five thousand active bishops. Not one is a public advocate for the victims of clergy abuse. There are over 400,000 priests serving in parishes around the world. Being generous, less than 500 have openly opposed clergy abuse or criticized the hierarchy for their gross incompetence in handling clergy abuse or for bringing scandal down upon the church in a public forum. That's one tenth of one percent! They are all guilty either by their sins of omission or commission. So I repeat, God Damn Both Bishops and Priests.

To publicly decry contraception, divorce or gay marriage while ignoring clergy abuse, the rape, sodomization and molestation of children is nothing short of ludicrous! Yet bishops and priests do it with aplomb! Let this book be testament to their bottomless hypocrisy. It never occurred to me that I would learn as much about how the hierarchy of the Roman Catholic Church has twisted the words of Jesus, their own Canons and even the Catechism as I now know. This was not some herculean effort on my part, it consisted of merely studying what has been available to all of us for years, but we were never told it was available, encouraged to read it, understand it or explore it. As is the case with most human beings, we are quite content to let someone else like a priest, bishop, cardinal or pope interpret the rules for us and never question them. The hierarchy of the RCC knows this and their very existence depends upon the laity remaining dutiful sheep who never question. From personal experience, I can tell you bishops get flustered and angry when called to task by a lay person who knows the rules and questions their authority. Two cases in point are: A bishop, who I'll presume was flustered and unable to answer my arguments. In the last letter of our correspondence, he called me very uncharitable. Another bishop in a fit of pique tried to either belittle me or impress me by writing his final letter back in Latin. "Are these "Men of God?" Hardly!

As I have seen and as you will see, in the following pages, the hierarchy of the RCC has made a mockery of the teachings of Jesus, its own laws and those of civil law. However, it is the laity's inaction that allows the hierarchy to continuously perpetrate their hoax! The laity must condemn priests, bishops and cardinals because they can't serve two masters. If the clergy abuse scandal has done one thing other than the irreparable harm to untold numbers of children, it has proven that these men, priests, do not serve God.

Table of Contents

What is the Language of Clergy Abuse?

I spoke the language of love.
They ignored me like their dove.
The church, I didn't want to bash;
Just put a pedophile in the trash.

I spoke the language of shame
The bishop held me to blame.
"Protect the children," I said.
The words rang hollow in his head.

I spoke the language of parental pain
That will never, ever wane,
But it fell upon deaf ears.
My failure caused more tears.

I spoke the language of priestly abuse.
Long after it was of no use.
Ever downward my head hung;
Is my speech an unknown tongue?

I spoke the language of alarm.
Don't you realize the great harm?
There are abused children everywhere.
Business as usual, the bishop didn't care.

I spoke the language of frustration
About children and molestation.
Might as well talk to the moon;
They treated me like a buffoon!

I spoke the language of scripture,
Went so far as to paint a picture.
Then quoted from Canon Law
And was promptly shown the door!

The Gospels were completely ignored;
Speaking of Jesus left them bored!
Who was I to interpret their boss?
They left me feeling like dross.

Plain language had no meaning;
The whole process was demeaning.
Grief stricken and bereft
There was only one language left.

I used the language of the courts.
Filed a suit regarding the torts.
Now I had the bishop's attention
Suing the church defied convention!

I had found a language they understood
Everything else was simply: no good!
Why had I used sugar and honey
When all they understood was money?

They had more angles than protractors.
"Priests are independent contractors."
Legal terms like "Seal of Confession"
And other tidbits from the legal profession.

Appeals, bankruptcy, lying to the courts,
Utilizing machinations of all sorts.
But the court put us on an even keel
And finally, the bishops had to deal.

Shekels, dollars, dead presidents
The foundation of their residents
Gone would be their lap of luxury
Gone with their depleted treasury.

Money equals power; that they know.
Of neither one could they let go!
Refusing to admit they failed
Bishops from their pulpits railed.

Invoking the name of Christ
Making him part of their heist
Never admitting to their sins
Publicly hiding their secret grins.

There is a new language in the land
They're asking all to give a hand
The new way to promote salvation
Is to change the language of legislation.

They must protect the Catholic religion.
Don't change a lot, just a smidgeon.
Limit the damages to a trivial amount;
Payout sizes that really don't count.

They'll continue their good works
And once again enjoy lavish perks.
To the lawyers, judges, and legislature
Bishops sent this grand nomenclature.

As it was with the Pharisees, so it is now
The God's honest truth they disavow.
You can't stop the seeds of hypocrisy
From thriving in a self-serving theocracy.

There is one language above all others,
Which is truth, my sisters and brothers.
Pray for the day it may come to stay
And blow convoluted language away.

I Accuse!

7/19/08

Have you ever felt like the boy who yelled, "The Emperor has no clothes?" Did you ever scream to yourself, "Damn, this is wrong!"? Have you ever seen something so clear and vividly that you wondered, "How come everyone doesn't see this?" If the same thing happens time and time again, in city after city, in state after state, and in country after country, why do we fail to call it what it is? If the act is a criminal act, perpetrated by members of the same organization, and covered up by the management of said organization, why can't we just call it organized international crime?

We label those dealing in cocaine, the South American Drug Cartels. We label terrorists with cells in multiple counties with names like Al Queda. There is the Golden Triangle that supplies heroin to Southeast Asia and then there is the Illicit Drug Trade that refers to the heroin coming out of Afghanistan. All-encompassing multinational criminal enterprises have names like the Mafia, Triad, Cosa Nostra, Yakuza, etc. Even stand up institutions like banks have been referred to as Money Launderers. So why haven't we labeled and pursued the Catholic Church for their worldwide sexual abuse of children?

The crime of clerical sexual abuse committed by Catholic priests has been publicly documented in the following countries around the globe: Argentina, Australia, Austria, Belgium, Bosnia, Brazil, Canada, Chile, Columbia, Croatia, Czech Republic, England, France, Germany, Greece, Ireland, Italy, Mexico, Malta, Netherlands, New Zealand, Philippines, Poland, Slovenia, South Africa, Trinidad and Tobago, United States and Venezuela.[1] This should put an end to the fallacious argument used by the last pope that clergy sexual abuse was strictly an American phenomenon. Sexual abuse reported in 28 countries can hardly be called an American problem

 The United States, because of its size does deserve a special note. Clergy abuse by Catholic priests has been documented in all of 50 of its states. Most of these states, because of land mass and population, could be a country within itself. Several states in the U.S. have more documented cases of sexual abuse by Catholic priests than most other countries. Does that mean it is a solely a problem in the United States as JPII stated? No, it just means that the size and population of the U.S. offered more opportunity.

Why, with its priests committing the same crime (the sexual abuse of children) on a global scale, hasn't the Roman Catholic Church been named as an international sponsor of child abuse? Why when the hierarchy of the RCC has been compounding sex crimes by aiding and abetting these criminals, hasn't the hierarchy of the RCC been named as an international criminal organization? The priests committing the rape, sodomization and molestation of children are all members of the religious organization known as the Roman Catholic Church. Before becoming priests these men must all go through a rigorous and lengthy indoctrination period. The guidelines established for their seminary formation come from the hierarchy and the leadership in Rome. The Catholic Church sustains its candidates for the priesthood while they go through their training. The RCC will not ordain them as priests unless they have completed their training. Only Rome may defrock a priest once they've been ordained. Therefore, the criminals who have raped, sodomized and molested children are duly trained and ordained priests of the Catholic Church, which is headquartered in the city/state known as the Vatican. These same criminals, who commit vile acts against children, are the responsibility of the RCC headquartered in the Vatican.

If they weren't, why does the hierarchy of the RCC go out of their way to protect these criminals by silencing victims, shifting predator priests from parish to parish, state to state and country to country? The hierarchy is nothing more than the layers of management between priests and the pope called bishops and cardinals. If management is protecting criminals, what does that make the manager and what does that make the hierarchy?

A criminal organization!

 Further proof of the international scope of these criminal activities comes to us in the form of a secret instruction sent to all bishops around the world in 1962. It also cites an 1887 document as seen below. The operative word here is secret. One of the hallmarks of any organized criminal element is their fanatical obsession with secrecy. Why do criminals obsess over secrecy; because it is the key to their ability to operate freely. Mobsters with high public profiles usually wind up with a bullet in their head. Dictators don't disclose the location of killing fields. Bank heists are never advertised in the local paper. Drug dealers don't hold press conferences to announce the arrival of drug shipments. Pedophiles don't wear neon signs proclaiming their proclivity, and the RCC will do everything in their power to keep child sex abuse and the abuser a secret. The instruction Crimen Sollicitationis gives an unprecedented view into the Catholic Church's obsession with secrecy. If nothing else, Crimen Sollicitationis shows how the Church has conspired to keep crimes against children a secret for well over a century as seen in this excerpt from the English translation:

11. Because, however, what is treated in these cases has to have a greater degree of care and observance so that those same matters be pursued in a most secretive way, and, after they have been defined and given over to execution, they are to be restrained by a perpetual silence (Instruction of the Holy Office, February 20, 1867, n. 14), each and every one pertaining to the tribunal in any way or admitted to knowledge of the matters because of their office, is to observe the strictest ++7++ secret, which is commonly regarded as a secret of the Holy Office, in all matters and with all persons, under the penalty of excommunication latae sententiae,[2]

The penalty for breaking secrets (talking) about a priest involved in the sexual abuse of a child is the worst punishment that could be meted out upon a believer of Catholic Doctrine. Their history is replete with examples of people who have chosen to die rather than forfeit their salvation.

This 1962 instruction, called Crimen Sollicitationis, was signed by the Pope John XXIII. According to Fr. Tom Doyle, noted Canon Lawyer and survivor advocate, it is very similar to an instruction issued in 1922. The 1962 instruction was reaffirmed in 2001 under the signature of the current pope who at the time was the head of the Congregation for the Doctrine of Faith, Cardinal Joseph Ratzinger.[3] Why one has to ask, is it necessary to say the same thing three times in less than a century? The logical conclusion is that it has been a long recognized problem

Even though the name Crimen Sollicitationis refers to the crime of soliciting in the confessional, the section marked Title V deals with the sexual abuse of children. Title V of Crimens Sollicitationis is subtitled: "The Worst Crime" as seen from this excerpt:

Title V

The Worst Crime

73. To have the worst crime, for the penal effects, one must do the equivalent of the following: any obscene, external act, gravely sinful, perpetrated in any way by a cleric or attempted by him with youths of either sex or with brute animals (bestiality).

74. Against accused clerics for these crimes, if they are exempt religious, and unless there takes place at the same time the crime of solicitation, even the regular superior can proceed, according to the holy canons and their proper constitutions, either in an administrative or a judicial manner. However, they must communicate the judicial decision pronounced as well as the administrative decision in the more serious cases to the Supreme Congregation of the Holy Office.[4]

The wording of Title V is extremely important as it confirms the Vatican's own knowledge and acceptance of the fact that the sexual abuse of children, regardless of sex, is a crime. The Vatican did not use the words evil, sinful, offensive, lapse of judgment, moment of weakness or illness. They used the word "crime" which is the only word that can adequately describe the act of a priest preying on a child for his own sexual gratification. Therefore, by stating that "the sexual abuse of children is a crime," the Vatican tacitly acknowledges before God and man that priests who commit the crime of having sex with children, are in fact criminals! They also demand that these criminal acts be reported to their international headquarters, the Vatican.

Criminals commit crimes. Sex with children is a crime under both canon and civil law. Therefore, there can be no doubt that priests who commit the crime of sexual abuse with children are criminals! Ipso facto, those who protect these criminals are themselves guilty of aiding and abetting criminals. The Vatican has known for centuries that the sexual abuse of children is a criminal offense. In that, they are in total agreement with the secular law of just about every country on earth.

Not only is the sexual abuse of children considered a crime by the Vatican, but to add emphasis to the matter, the Vatican chose to label it "The Worst Crime." Of all the adjectives that are available to describe a crime, the Vatican chose to call the sexual abuse of children "The Worst." What does that make the men who allow these sexual predators ply their trade unabated? What does this do to the commonly used hierarchal defense, "I didn't know?" What does it say about the hundreds of bishops in 28 known countries around the world who failed to live up to the Vatican's standards? What does it say about a Vatican that tolerated these failures?

Crimen Sollicitationis directs the bishops to prosecute crimes of child sexual abuse? Failing to do so makes them all scofflaws! They scoffed at every indecency perpetrated on the bodies of children around the world. Neither bishops nor the Vatican can claim ignorance of the law anymore! Whether it was an internal or external law, they failed to prosecute the rapists, sodomizers and molesters in their midst; by their own account, the criminal element.

Therefore, I accuse!

Due to the global ongoing sexual abuse and cover-up by the hierarchy of the Catholic Church, it is safe to assume that the only part of Crimen Sollicitationis that was adhered to was the demand for secrecy. Up until 2002 almost every settlement involving sexual abuse by a priest came with an enforceable gag order on the victim. The victims were silenced while most offending priests were moved to new hunting grounds.

The logical question to ask is, "Cui Bono," who benefits? Who benefits from the silence? It could be argued that the priest and his accuser benefit from the silence. However, since there were no remedies for the care, compensation or treatment of the victim, it is hard to see how victims benefited from Crimen instruction. There has never been any proof whatsoever of rampant false charges being brought against innocent priests. Therefore innocent priests haven't benefited. So who are the chief beneficiaries of the document Crimen Sollicitationis? The sexually abusive priest and the Roman Catholic Church are the only beneficiaries.

Therefore, I accuse!

Lest Crimen sidetrack us, the salient points are: 1. The document was sent from the International Headquarters. 2. The document was sent out globally. 3. The document was sent in secrecy. 4. The document demanded secrecy. 5. The penalty for violating secrecy is the harshest penalty the church can mete out: excommunication. 7. It labels the sexual abuse of children as "The Worst Crime" thereby admitting to the world the Vatican's complete understanding of the vile nature of the act of sexually abusing children.

By their own hand they are condemned.

In the 28 countries we know about, the rape, sodomization, and molestation of children are publicly documented. Why then hasn't Interpol gotten involved? Interpol states that the protection of children is one of their primary goals. This is the first paragraph taken from Interpol's page on children:

Crimes against children!

Children are the most vulnerable individuals in our society; they are also the most precious commodity that the world has and have a right to be protected from all forms of abuse. INTERPOL as an organization is also committed to eradicating the sexual abuse of children and has passed several resolutions making crimes against children one of International policing top priorities.[5]

They tell us that, not preventing, but eradicating (wiping out) sexual abuse is one of their top priorities. How can the sexual abuse of children be a top priority when the chief global culprit, the Roman Catholic Church has not been formerly accused by either the UN or Interpol?

I accuse!

The evidence is abundant for any who would make even a cursory examination of the facts. The Dallas Morning News did an entire series on the international scope of both clergy sexual abuse and its cover-up. Central to the series was the theme of hierarchy moving predator priests internationally in order to save them from being tried for crimes committed or to provide new hunting grounds or both.[6]

The facts accuse!

The need to protect children around the world is a global priority of United Nations. The U.N. through its UNICEF organization has put together "The Convention on the Rights of the Child." Here are articles nineteen and thirty-four from that convention, which address the sexual abuse of children.

Article 19

1. States Parties shall take all appropriate legislative, administrative, social and educational measures to protect the child from all forms of physical or mental violence, injury or abuse, neglect or negligent treatment, maltreatment or exploitation, including

sexual abuse, while in the care of parent(s), legal guardian(s) or any other person who has the care of the child.

Article 34

States Parties undertake to protect the child from all forms of sexual exploitation and sexual abuse. For these purposes, States Parties shall in particular take all appropriate national, bilateral and multilateral measures to prevent:
(a) The inducement or coercion of a child to engage in any unlawful sexual activity;
(b) The exploitative use of children in prostitution or other unlawful sexual practices;
(c) The exploitative use of children in pornographic performances and materials.[7]

I accuse the RCC of violating the Convention on the Rights of the Child!

The Holy See, which could be a member of the United Nations by virtue of the fact that the Vatican is a city-state, has elected not to become a member of the UN. Rather it has been granted the nomenclature of permanent observer. This means that they enjoy the full rights of every sovereign member except the right to vote. In this way they can lobby for whatever they desire and not have to go on record as voting for or against an issue.

They chose to not to support "The Convention on the Rights of the Child." The Holy See declared that *"the application of the Convention should be compatible in practice with the particular nature of the Vatican City State and of the sources of its objective law."* in a statement issued when they declined to be a signatory. To date, all members but two have ratified the Convention.[8]

The United Nations through Interpol, its international police agency, and UNICEF, their children's agency recognize the need to police and prevent the sexual abuse of children throughout the world. They state this is a top priority. The Convention on the Rights of the Child, which has been widely accepted by governments around the world, seeks to end the sexual abuse of children. Why then have the UN, UNICEF, and Interpol chosen to totally ignore the most public, international series of sex crimes and cover-ups against children running from the twentieth into the twenty-first century?

I accuse!

Having established that the sexual abuse of children is accepted by the RCC as being a criminal act, it follows that aiding and abetting criminals is also a crime. The international criminal activity of aiding and abetting sexual predators by the RCC is well documented. The award winning newspaper The Dallas Morning News did an excellent series of articles dealing with the international flight of pedophile priests to escape prosecution entitled Runaway Priests. The following are excerpts from some of their articles as listed on the website Bishop-accountability.org.

Dr. Navarro-Valls (chief spokesperson for the pope) previously declined to comment on The News' investigation, which found more than 200 accused priests, brothers and other Catholic workers hiding across international borders and living in unsuspecting communities, often with the church's support. About 30 of the men were wanted by law enforcement in another country.[9]

Where is Interpol? Where is the outcry from UNICEF?

Bishop Thomas V. Daily of the Diocese of Brooklyn, in an exchange of correspondence with a Venezuelan bishop in 1991 about allegations against Father Diaz, praised the priest's work in his diocese even as a 60-count indictment was pending against him in Queens on child sexual abuse charges. Later that year, after pleading guilty to three counts of sexual abuse in the case, Father Diaz was deported to Venezuela, where the pattern of victimizing young boys continued unabated.

And so it went throughout Father Diaz's ministry. Moving from country to country, from parish to parish, from victim to victim, he was often held unaccountable by church officials and was treated delicately by some law enforcement authorities, the interviews and documents show.[10]

How can the above be anything but an international criminal conspiracy?

His order, the Salesians of Don Bosco, has long moved priests accused of sexual abuse from country to country, away from law enforcement and victims. Indeed, it is how many others in the Catholic Church have dealt with the problem, a yearlong Dallas Morning News investigation has found.[11]

The crimes committed by the hierarchy of the RCC against the children of the world have been documented many times in many countries. In each country from Poland, to Ireland, to the United States around and down to Australia, the story is the same. Priests who commit criminal acts of sexual abuse against children are shuffled from country to country with no regard for either local or international law. These priests are shuffled by a complicit hierarchy who are guilty of aiding and abetting criminals. Once transferred, these priests are free to prey upon a fresh population of unsuspecting families who revere the priest as god's representative on earth.

In 2002 Pope John Paul II stated before the world, "There is no room in the priesthood for those who sexually abuse children."[12] But nothing was done; priests were still being shuffled and names of priestly perpetrators are still a closely guarded secret. In April of 2008, while on the plane over to the United States, Benedict XVI said, "I am deeply ashamed"[13] while referring to the Clergy Sex Abuse Scandal. On July 19, 2008, in Australia, he said,

"I ask all of you to support and assist your bishops, and to work together with them in combating this evil. Victims should receive compassion and care, and those responsible for these evils must be brought to justice."[14]

"AND THOSE RESPONSIBLE FOR THESE EVILS MUST BE BROUGHT TO JUSTICE!" Strong words from the pope! The pope is an honorable man; bishops and cardinals are all honorable men and they speak well. Yet nothing was said about revoking Crimen Sollicitationis. Did he forget that as Cardinal Ratzinger in 2001, he reaffirmed its validity? He can say one thing publicly, but as long as he still binds everyone with knowledge of clergy abuse to the absolute law of secrecy under the chapter 11, " a secret of the Holy Office,[15]" the pope is only mouthing words. As long as Cardinals, Law, Mahony, George, Egan and Levada remain in office, he is only mouthing words. As long as bishops and the leaders of religious orders who shuffled pedophiles from country to country remain in the priesthood, the pope is only mouthing words. The pope is the only one who can start bringing those responsible for these evils to justice!

It is time to put an end to the global scourge of clerical child abuse and put these criminal priests behind bars along with the members of the hierarchy who have purposefully aided them. (It seems that Pope Benedict agrees with me.) These crimes are a violation of God's law, Church law, Civil law, and International law (all covered in this treatise). As proven in the United States, the only thing that will change the way the RCC harbors their criminals is a courtroom. Interpol must aid in the capture of these international child-abusing fugitives and the U.N. must bring charges against the Vatican in the World Court. Only the credible threat of listing the Vatican as a criminal organization, making them stand trial for the abuse of tens of thousands of children and covering-up for thousands of priests will force the much needed changes while making the world a safer place for children. Interpol and the UN had every right to get involved in the clergy abuse scandal because it violates their conventions. Now both the UN and Interpol have an invitation to get involved straight from the pope's mouth. Pope Benedict XVI has just asked for "aid and assistance" followed up by "those responsible for these evils must be brought to justice." The Vicar of Christ on earth is asking for help in bringing to justice to those who committed and helped in crimes of sexual abuse against children. What greater invitation can be made?

Note 1. To any lawyers who may represent or have represented survivors of sexual abuse. Crimen Sollicitationis means "crime of solicitation" which refers to crimes of the confessional. Reading this text is extremely difficult because everything up until Title V is about soliciting in the confessional. Title V paragraph 72 states: "Those things that have been stated concerning the crime of solicitation up to this point are also valid, changing only those things necessary to be changed by their very nature, for the worst crime," Take Crimen Sollicitationis (English version) and put it in a Word document. Then do a find/replace with find Solicitation and replace it with child abuse. You will be amazed at how it clarifies the document giving you a clearer understanding of what Crimen Sollicitationis says about the clergy abuse of children.

References

1. http://en.wikipedia.org/wiki/Roman_Catholic_sex_abuse_cases_by_country#See_also July 9, 2008 and http://www.scribd.com/doc/1021887/SEXUAL-ABUSE-IN-THE-CATHOLIC-CHURCH-2002 July 9, 2008

2. http://www.priestsofdarkness.com/crimen.pdf July 10, 2008

3. The 1922 Instruction and the 1962 Instruction "Crimen Sollicitationis," Promulgated by the Vatican: Thomas Doyle, O.P., J.C.D. June 30, 2008

4. http://www.priestsofdarkness.com/crimen.pdf July 10, 2008

5. http://www.interpol.int/Public/Children/Default.asp July 11, 2008

6. http://www.dallasnews.com/sharedcontent/dws/news/longterm/stories/Runaway_

priests_hiding_in_plain_sight.5ee1e9be.html, July 11, 2008

7. http://www.interpol.int/Public/Children/Conventions/unConvCR.asp July 12, 2008

8. http://www.unicef.org/pon95/chil0008.html July 12, 2008

9. http://www.bishop-accountability.org/news/2004_09_12_Dunklin_InThe.htm

July 12, 2008

10. http://www.bishop-accountability.org/resources/resource-files/timeline/2002-04-20-Murphy-Diaz.htm July 13, 2008

11. http://www.bishop-accountability.org/news/2004_06_20_Dunklin_ConvictedSexual.htm July 13, 2008

12. http://www.poynterextra.org/extra/abusetracker/2002_04_21_archive.htm

July 18, 2008

13. http://aftermathnews.wordpress.com/2008/04/15/pope-says-he-is-deeply-ashamed-of-clergy-abuse-scandal/ July 18, 2008

14. http://www.thewest.com.au/default.aspx?MenuID=2&ContentID=85771

July 19, 2008

15. http://www.priestsofdarkness.com/crimen.pdf

20

According to Aquinas' definition, there are heretics in the Vatican

The unmitigated gall along with the exasperating temerity of the Vatican and the pope is nowhere more evident than in the slap in the face that the pope has just delivered to the global survivor community. Just when you thought they couldn't sink any lower than equating the ordination of women with the raping, sodomizing and molesting children; they do this. The mentality that pulled Cardinal Law out of harm's way and rewarded him for covering up criminal acts and the criminals who committed them is flourishing in Rome.

In the first place, the ruling elite of the Vatican along with the pope have lost all their integrity if one supposes that they had any in the first place. Acting holy and deliberately disobeying Sacred Scripture, which is the Word of God, and also the Catechism and Canon Law which are the teaching elements of the Magisterium are the acts of heretics according to St. Thomas Aquinas.

Compounding their crimes against man and God, they tried to convince the world that ordaining a woman is as grave a scandal to the Body of Christ as the raping of a child by a priest. On top of that, the pope reinstates two bishops who allowed children to be abused because they were spineless as well as being unfaithful to the teachings of Christ. The hypocrisy of the leadership of the Roman Catholic Church knows no bounds. In 2009 the pope said, "Victims should receive compassion and care, and those responsible for these evils must be brought to justice." The pope cannot reconcile any of his actions with his deeds. His lies and hypocrisy have brought untold scandal down upon the church. The English language does not have words to describe such an unprecedented display of contempt for Jesus Christ, his people and scripture. The only two words that come even close to describing this bald-faced act of duplicity are Mysterium Iniquitatis.

The job of the Magisterium (the pope and all the bishops) is teaching or interpreting Sacred Scripture. It puts Sacred Scripture on the top after which come all else. For example, if there were a conflict between what Jesus said and what and what a bishop says some five hundred years later, the quoted words of Jesus takes precedent. The Catechism tells us the following in Para. 86: "Yet this Magisterium is not superior to the Word of God, but is its servant." Direct quotes by Jesus on the single subject child abuse are found in all three of the Synoptic Gospels. Jesus himself tells us how the well being of children is of profound importance to him, but the hierarchy hasn't listened.

Here are the direct quotes from Jesus condemning the sexual abuse of minors:
   Matthew 18:6 But whoso shall offend one of these little ones which believe in me, it were better for him that a **millstone** were hanged about his neck, and *that* he were drowned in the depth of the sea.

   Mark 9:42 And whosoever shall offend one of *these* little ones that believe in me, it is better for him that a **millstone** were hanged about his neck, and he were cast into the sea.

Luke 17:2 It were better for him that a **millstone** were hanged about his neck, and he cast into the sea, than that he should offend one of these little ones.

Matthew 18:10: Take heed that ye despise not one of these little ones; for I say unto you, That in heaven their angels do always behold the face of my Father which is in heaven.

Matthew 18:14: In the same way your Father in heaven is not willing that any of these little ones should be lost.

Matthew, Mark and Luke also quote Jesus as saying: "But when Jesus saw it, he was much displeased, and said unto them, Suffer the little children to come unto me, and forbid them not: for of such is the kingdom of God."

The importance of these tracts must be put in perspective. The well regarded concept of the Virgin Birth is in the narrative form which does not carry the same weight as a direct quote from Jesus. Also, it is only found in two of the Gospels whereas admonitions against defiling children are found in all three of the Synoptic Gospels. Jesus stated multiple times that no one should prevent children from coming to him. Yet the hierarchy has steadfastly refused to ignore Him.

What does this mean? It means that if the hierarchy had put just half the belief into the words of Jesus concerning child abuse, as they did to the concept of the Virginal Birth, there would be neither the clergy abuse scandal we have today nor those in previous eras of church history. Next is the gravity of their sins. The current hierarchy right up to the pope has knowingly moved pedophile priests around and then covered up for these monsters in direct violation of Sacred Scripture. The perverted culture of the Vatican is and has been responsible for the rape, sodomization and molestation of children. There has been an ongoing, well documented denial of the words of Jesus. In plain English, they have committed gross acts of heresy by refusing to adhere to Sacred Scripture.

Aquinas defines heresy as: "a species of infidelity in men who, having professed the faith of Christ, corrupt its dogmas." He further states: "Heresy comes from restricting belief to certain points of Christ's doctrine selected and fashioned at pleasure, which is the way of heretics." Aquinas says this of the heretics motives: "The impelling motives are many: intellectual pride or exaggerated reliance on one's own insight; the illusions of religious zeal; the allurements of political or ecclesiastical power; the ties of material interests and personal status; and perhaps others more dishonourable"

If Aquinas were alive today, he would have no problem condemning the current hierarchy for the heretics they are. The hierarchy, men who profess faith in Christ, have

22

created their own dogma which says, "We make decisions for Christ and we will totally ignore anything He has said which will cause us to forfeit our jobs, riches or the priests who make our jobs, power and riches possible." In order to maintain the allurements of ecclesiastical power, not one bishop has ever been laicized in connection with the clergy abuse scandal. That includes both bishops who have personally abused children as well as bishops who have protected the perverted priests who preyed on children. Now, two bishops that have resigned over their involvement with clergy abuse have been reinstated. Every member of the hierarchy has maintained both their personal wealth and power despite numerous transgressions a la Cardinal Law who was whisked out of Boston to insure he maintained both his power and opulence. In short, they have corrupted the Sacred Scripture, thrown our children to the wolves and for what, to maintain the status quo!

However, this heresy does not stop with Sacred Scripture. The heretics have and continue to ignore both the Catechism and Canon Law making their heresy complete. The following paragraphs are from the Catechism:

> **2326** Scandal is a grave offense when by deed or omission it deliberately leads others to sin gravely.

> **2287** Anyone who uses the power at his disposal in such a way that it leads others to do wrong becomes guilty of scandal and responsible for the evil that he has directly or indirectly encouraged. "Temptations to sin are sure to come; but woe to him by whom they come!"

> **2353** Fornication is carnal union between an unmarried man and an unmarried woman. It is gravely contrary to the dignity of persons and of human sexuality which is naturally ordered to the good of spouses and the generation and education of children. **Moreover, it is a grave scandal when there is corruption of the young**. (Emphasis mine)

> **2389** Connected to incest is any sexual abuse perpetrated by adults on children or adolescents entrusted to their care. The offense is compounded by the scandalous harm done to the physical and moral integrity of the young, who will remain scarred by it all their lives; and the violation of responsibility for their upbringing.

The acts of raping, sodomizing and molesting children, allowing them to continue and then covering them up can safely be assumed to be manifestly a grave scandal. The Catechism specifically points out the evils of adults having sex with children. Strike two, the hierarchy has turned their backs on Sacred Scripture and the Catechism. What's next? Next is Canon Law. The current hierarchy has denied, by their failure to remove bishops, Canon Law applies to them too. As Aquinas points out, they're simply ignoring this truth because of material interests and personal status

> Can. 212 1,
> Priests and Bishops are also bound by this obedience, in fact more so since they are responsible for passing on to the faithful genuine Catholic teaching. In other words, a Bishop or Priest who dissents from Church teachings is not to be obeyed in that matter, rather all must obey the Magisterium at all times, as Vatican II states.

All along the Canons have applied to every priest, bishop, and cardinal around the world, which includes the pope. The hierarchy is quick to throw out the many comparisons of relative guilt. Why are you picking on us, we're only human? We're no worse than other religions; the public schools are infested with pedophiles, etc. etc. Sacred Scripture along with their own Catechism spells out why they need to be held more accountable than others. Can. 2121: "in fact more so since they are responsible for passing on to the faithful genuine Catholic teaching."

> Can. 1369 A person is to be punished with a just penalty, who, at a public event or assembly, or in a published writing, or by otherwise using the means of social communication, utters blasphemy, or gravely harms public morals, or rails at or excites hatred of or contempt for religion or the Church.

By their adamant refusal to justly punish any bishop for their part in the Clergy Abuse Scandal, the hierarchy has gravely harmed public morals, excited hatred of and contempt for the Church along with making it a laughing stock of the world. The hierarchy by their omissions (remaining silent) and their commission (Hiding and shuffling offending priests) promoted evil. The church did nothing about the rape, sodomization and molestation of children until they were forced into action and then only did a grudgingly pittance.

> Can. 1389 § 1 A person who abuses ecclesiastical power or an office, is to be punished according to the gravity of the act or the omission, not excluding by deprivation of the office, unless a penalty for that abuse is already established by law or precept.
>
> § 2 A person who, through culpable negligence, unlawfully and with harm to another, performs or omits and act of ecclesiastical power or ministry or office, is to be punished with a just penalty.

Hard evidence of hierarchal culpable negligence has come out across the globe for the past two decades. Ecclesiastical power has been misused all over the globe and in no place more than the Vatican in their concerted effort to thwart justice. Turning their back on Canon Law completes the blatant refutation of the Magisterium, which is nothing more than heresy.

Is it a sin to call a pope, cardinal bishop or priest a heretic? No, Sacred Scripture, the Catechism and Canon Law call them heretics. The three are there for the world to read; no interpretation necessary because the language is clear. Each one supports the other back to the words of Jesus Christ. No bishop, cardinal or pope can deny or refute them without committing a larger heresy. The hierarchy would have the laity believe that they are above it all, but their own laws tell us different. Most members of the human race don't need church law to reaffirm what they already know which is: The rape, sodomization and molestation of children is morally repugnant and intrinsically evil. Those who have both covered up these acts and protected the perpetrators are equally guilty.

> Can. 748 §1 All are bound to seek the truth in matters which concern God and his Church; when they have found it, then by divine law they have the right to embrace and keep it.

The truth is here from the mouth of Jesus, church law and church history. All three tell us the first two have been totally ignored to the detriment of children and the church. The heresies speak for themselves. Aquinas tells us they are "a species of infidelity in men who, having professed the faith of Christ, corrupt its dogmas." Aquinas is only mirroring the words of Jesus who said.

Matt.15: 7-9 You hypocrites! Isaiah was right when he prophesied about you: 'These people honor me with their lips, but their hearts are far from me. They worship me in vain; their teachings are but rules taught by men."

We can't deny the teachings of Jesus, but we can certainly deny the authority of those who have ignored and trampled upon his teachings.

The Roman Catholic Hierarchy, Homosexuality, Hypocrisy and Heresy

Can a person unschooled in Roman Catholic theology take a noted 20th century theologian and 21st century Pope's letter deriding homosexuality and turn it into a stinging rebuke of today's hierarchy simply by changing key words and adding direct quotes from Jesus as found in the Gospels? If so, can the hierarchy honestly accept one version and deny the other? Only at the expense of their own integrity and by denying the words preached by Jesus Christ in three of the four Synoptic Gospels! The ramifications of this revised document are enormous because they speak to homosexuality, hypocrisy and heresy.

On October 1, of 1986, Cardinal Joseph Ratzinger, later Pope Benedict XVI, promulgated a letter of instruction to the bishops of the world in his official capacity as Prefect of the Congregation of Catholic Faith, *"Letter To The Bishops Of The Catholic Church On The Pastoral Care Of Homosexual Persons[1]"* In that letter, he called homosexuality, "Objectively Disordered."

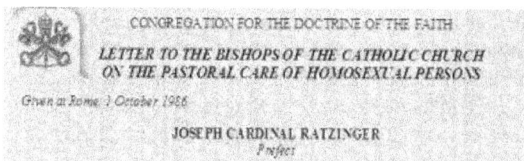

CONGREGATION FOR THE DOCTRINE OF THE FAITH

LETTER TO THE BISHOPS OF THE CATHOLIC CHURCH ON THE PASTORAL CARE OF HOMOSEXUAL PERSONS

Given at Rome, 1 October 1986

JOSEPH CARDINAL RATZINGER
Prefect

What follows is a parody of that letter, which maintains Benedict's structure, logic and reasoning. However unlike Benedict's version this version uses Sacred Scripture quoted directly from Jesus himself. Benedict XVI could not and can never use the words of Jesus to admonish homosexuality because these words were never spoken by Him in the Gospels. The revised letter uses several direct quotes from Jesus because they exist and have been recorded by the three out of four evangelists. The direct quotes from Jesus make a stronger case for the hierarchy of the Roman Catholic Church being "Objectively Disordered," sacrilegious, heretical and hypocritical than all of Ratzinger's arguments against homosexuality. Admonitions against child abuse have a strong biblical linkage going all the way back to Exodus and continuing on from Jesus to Paul and throughout the Church's own Catechism and Canon Law. Using the noted theologian Cardinal Ratzinger's logic, this extended linkage makes the admonitions for and penalties against child abuse ironclad. The Prefect of the Congregation of the Faith's has been hoisted upon his own petard. Read the revised text and judge for yourself.

LETTER TO THE POPE, BISHOPS, and LAITY OF THE CATHOLIC CHURCH ON THE OBJECTIVE DISORDERS OF THE HIERARCHY

1. The issue of clergy abuse and the moral evaluation of acts of sexual abuse by priests have increasingly become a matter of public debate, especially in Catholic circles. Since this debate often advances arguments and makes assertions inconsistent with the teachings of the Catholic Church, it is quite rightly a cause for concern to all engaged in the welfare of the church. There are many in the Church who have judged it to be of such a sufficiently grave nature to address the faithful, Bishops, Cardinals of the Catholic Church, and the Pope with this Letter on the Objective Disorder of the Hierarchy in the matter of dealing with sexually abusing, priests, nuns, bishops and cardinals.

2. Naturally, an exhaustive treatment of this complex issue cannot be attempted here because it has been going on for centuries, but we will focus our condemnation within the distinctive context of the Catholic moral perspective. It is a perspective which finds support in the most basic of human needs, protecting the most vulnerable, children and adhering to the laws of God, Scripture, Canon Law, the Catechism and of course, civil law regardless of whether or not the hierarchy sees themselves as subject to it.

Most important however, is that the Catholic moral viewpoint is founded on human reason illuminated by faith and is consciously motivated by the desire to do the will of God our Father. The Church is thus in a position to learn not only from Civil Law, but also to transcend its horizons because under God's auspices, her more global vision should seek greater justice to the rich reality of the human person in their spiritual and physical dimensions, created by God and heir, by grace, to eternal life.

It is within this context, then, that it can clearly be seen that the phenomenon of Clergy Abuse, complex as it is, and with its many consequences for society and ecclesial life, is an extremely proper focus for both the Church's concerned laity and unstained hierarchy, if any exist. It thus requires of her ministers to attentively: support the victims of clergy abuse, study the problem, actively work to remove the offenders, and eject all members of the hierarchy whose failure to remove offending priests resulted in yet more atrocities.

3. Explicit punishments, for the crime of abusing children, have been provided by the church for centuries with the first recorded Canons posted at the Council of Elvira in the year 306 C.E. The punishment for child abuse then was banning the errant cleric from receiving communion for life including the moment of death. Those Canons stressed the true horrific nature of the crime and a just punishment for the cleric involved. There was no attempt to understand and debate whether the abuse of children was a sin or a crime. At the same time the Congregation took no note of the distinction commonly drawn between pedophilic and ephebophilic actions. These actions were considered depraved and the Church looked upon their essential and indispensable finality, as being evil and "intrinsically disordered", in no case to be either ignored or condoned.

In the centuries which followed, however, an overly benign interpretation was given to the act of child abuse, some going so far as to call it a neutral act, Father's misstep, the or even child's fault,. Although the particular inclination of the sexually abusing priest is not a sin, it is a more or less strong tendency ordered toward an intrinsic moral evil; and thus the inclination itself must be seen as an objective disorder.

Therefore special concern and hierarchal attention should be directed toward those in the clerical life who have this condition; lest they be led to believe that the living out this orientation in churches, convents and rectories around the globe is a morally acceptable option. It is not!

4. An essential dimension of authentic pastoral care is the identification of causes of confusion regarding the Church's teaching. One is a new exegesis of Sacred Scripture which claims variously that Scripture has nothing to say on the subject of child abuse, or that it somehow tacitly approves of it, or that all of its moral injunctions are so culture-bound that they are no longer applicable to contemporary life. Cardinal Napier of Africa verbalized what many other cardinals believe, "child abuse is not a crime." These views are gravely erroneous, objectively disordered and call for particular attention here.

5. It is quite true that the Holy Scripture owes to the different epochs in which it was written. The Church today addresses the Gospel to a world which differs in many ways from ancient days. But the world in which the New Testament was written was already quite diverse from the situation in which the Sacred Scriptures of the Hebrew People had been written or compiled.

What should be noticed is that, in the presence of such remarkable diversity, there is nevertheless a clear consistency within the Scriptures themselves on the moral issue of harming children. The Church's own doctrine regarding this issue is thus based, not on isolated phrases for facile theological argument, but on the solid foundation of a constant Biblical testimony. The community of faith today, in unbroken continuity with the Jewish and Christian communities within which the ancient Scriptures were written, continues to be nourished by those same Scriptures and by the Spirit of Truth who's Word they are. It is likewise essential to recognize that the Scriptures are not properly understood when they are interpreted in a way which contradicts the admonitions against harming children. To be correct, the interpretation of Scripture must be in substantial accord with that Tradition.

The Vatican Council II in Dei Verbum 10, put it this way: "It is clear, therefore, that in the supremely wise arrangement of God, sacred Tradition, Sacred Scripture, and the Magisterium of the Church are so connected and associated that one of them cannot stand without the others. Working together, each in its own way under the action of the one Holy Spirit, they all contribute effectively to the salvation of souls". In that spirit we wish to outline briefly the Biblical teaching here.

6. Providing a basic plan for understanding this entire discussion of clergy abuse is the theology of God's exhortation to protect children. From the Old Testament, the second book, Exodus 22: 22-24, we have: "Ye shall not afflict any widow, or fatherless child. If thou afflict them in any wise, and they cry at all unto me, I will surely hear their cry; And my wrath shall wax hot." God, in his infinite wisdom knows the propensity that men have to ravage the helpless and therefore warns against harming women and fatherless children, common fare of predator priests. As far back as Exodus, the Bible states these acts merit God's wrath. Ezekiel 23:39, "For when they had slain their children to their idols, then they came the same day into my sanctuary to profane it; and, lo, thus have they done in the midst of mine house" This passage speaks to priests murdering the souls of children in sacristies and rectories and then having the audacity to commit the grievous sacrilege of consecrating the host while saying Mass immediately after their debauchery.

The Magisterium, teaches us that there is a hierarchy of importance in Sacred Scripture with spoken word of Jesus in the Gospels receiving the greatest weight. Therefore, a direct quote from Jesus supersedes a narrative form such as the Virgin Birth, also Paul's letters, the Catechism and Canon Law etc. Thusly, the highest priority, as it should be, is the Word of God given us directly through the teachings quoted from Jesus. In three out of the four Synoptic Gospels, Jesus spoke the same words. Therefore, there can be no doubt that it was the wish of Jesus and the Gospel's divinely inspired authors that children not be sexually abused by any person and certainly not his priests.

Matthew 18:6 "But who so shall offend one of these **little ones** which believe in me, it were better for him that a millstone were hanged about his neck, and that he were drowned in the depth of the sea."

Mark 9:42 "And whosoever shall offend one of these **little ones** that believe in me, it is better for him that a millstone were hanged about his neck, and he were cast into the sea."

Luke 17:2 "It were better for him that a millstone were hanged about his neck, and he cast into the sea, than that he should offend one of these **little ones**."

Matthew tells us of two additional admonitions by Jesus not to hurt children leaving no doubt that the teachings of the Lord prohibit the abuse of children. To violate these teachings is a blatant act of heresy. To let them continue is both sacrilegious and heretical.

Matthew 18:10 "Take heed that ye despise not one of these **little ones**; for I say unto you, That in heaven their angels do always behold the face of my Father which is in heaven."

Matthew 18:14 "Even so it is not the will of your Father which is in heaven, that one of these **little ones** should perish."

29

Ratzinger's admonition against homosexuality does not carry the weight of this authority. Against the background of this exposition of theocratic law, an eschatological perspective is developed by St. Paul when, in I Cor 5:1-2 and I Cor 5:11-13, he proposes a similar doctrine. He exhorts Christians to drive the wicked out! The hierarchy of today's church patently refuses to follow Sacred Scripture, thereby committing a vile act of heresy in willfully choosing to ignore the teachings of first Jesus and then Paul.

Corinthians 1, 5: 11-13, But rather I wrote to you not to associate with anyone who bears the name of brother if he is guilty of immorality or greed. For what have I to do with judging outsiders? Is it not those inside the church whom you are to judge? God judges those outside, "Drive out the wicked person from among you."

Corinthians 1, 5: 1-2, "It is actually reported that there is immortality among you, and of a kind that is not found even among pagans; for a man is living with his father's wife. And you are arrogant! Ought you not rather to mourn? **Let this be removed from you**!"

In the above, still building on the moral traditions of his forebears, but in the new context of the confrontation between Christianity and the pagan society of his day, Paul uses immoral behavior as an example of the blindness which has overcome the hierarchy. Put in the modern context of today: Spiritual incest is a priest, Father, having sex with his children, parishioners. Instead of the original harmony between Creator and creatures, the acute distortion of idolatry has led to all kinds of moral excess. Paul is at a loss to find a clearer example of this disharmony than incest. One can only imagine what his response to the sexual abuse of children by priests would be. Finally, Paul in full continuity with the Biblical position, singles out those who spread wrong doctrine and in Corinthians 1, 5: 6-8, calls for their dismissal stating. "Do you not know that a little leaven leavens the whole lump? Cleanse out the old leaven that you may be a new lump, as you really are unleavened."

In a singularly incredible act of unprecedented hypocrisy, Ratzinger had the unmitigated gall to cite Paul's, Roman's I: 18-32, as proof of his righteous admonition of homosexuality. There is no better description of the clergy abuse scandal and the hierarchy's handling of it in the entire bible! Here are verses 28-32: "Furthermore, just as they did not think it worthwhile to retain the knowledge of God, so God gave them over to a depraved mind, so that they do what ought not to be done. They have become filled with every kind of wickedness, evil, greed and depravity. They are full of envy, murder, strife, deceit and malice. They are gossips, slanderers, God-haters, insolent, arrogant and boastful; they invent ways of doing evil; they disobey their parents; they have no understanding, no fidelity, no love, no mercy. Although they know God's righteous decree that those who do such things deserve death, ***they not only continue to do these very things but also approve of those who practice them.***" (author's emphasis)

Paul's passage is not an admonition of a loving homosexual couple. It is a tirade against those who lust after power and excess! Paul's passage is more in line with the theme of

John Thavis' book "Vatican Diaries" which examines the inner workings of the Curia. Ratzinger should be ashamed of himself for having the audacity to use this passage as a proof in his argument against homosexuality. Then again, Cardinal Ratzinger's vision could have been clouded by what he saw day in and day out in the Vatican. He merely projected onto loving homosexual couples his only knowledge of homosexuality; that which he observed in the Vatican.

7. The Church must be obedient to the Lord who founded her and gave to her the sacramental life. For a cleric to choose a child for their sexual activity is to annul the rich symbolism and meaning, not to mention the goals, of the Creator's sexual design as well as the vows foresworn to the Creator. Child abuse is not a voluntary union. It is an abuse of power on a most egregious scale. This does not mean that priests are not often generous and giving of themselves; but when they engage in sexual activity with children, they confirm within themselves a disordered sexual inclination which is essentially self-indulgent.

As in every moral disorder, sexual abuse of children prevents one's own fulfillment and happiness by acting contrary to the creative wisdom of God. The Church, in rejecting erroneous ways of her priests, nuns, bishops, and cardinals limits the personal freedoms, rights and dignity, which the most vulnerable members of the Catholic Church should take for granted.

8. Thus, the Church's reaction to its sexually abusing clerics today is diametrically opposed to the Scriptural perspectives and inconsistent with her own Sacred Scripture and Traditions. Though today's world is in many ways quite new, the Christian community senses with profound sadness the complete and utter failure of a hierarchy to deal with the current epidemic of clergy abuse.

Nevertheless, increasing numbers of people today, within and without of the Church, are bringing enormous pressure to bear on the hierarchy to stop treating clergy abuse as though it were not the disordered, sacrilegious and criminal activity it really is. Those from both within and without the Church who argue in this fashion are often ignored by the hierarchy, who have close ties with those with similar views outside it. These latter groups are guided by a vision opposed to the truth about the human person, which is fully disclosed in the mystery of Christ. They reflect, even if not entirely consciously, a materialistic ideology which denies the transcendent nature of the human person as well as sacred vocation of the priesthood.

The Church's hierarchy must ensure that predator priests under their auspices are not allowed to thrive in an environment so profoundly opposed to the teachings of the Church. But the risk is great and there are many in the hierarchy who seek to create confusion in an effort to protect offending clerics. There chief tools being power, real and implied, money, and obfuscation. Their heresy is as monstrous as the crimes of the abusers they protect.

9. The movement within the hierarchy, which takes the form of pressure from the Vatican, attempts to give the impression that it represents all who are Catholics. As a matter of fact, its membership is by and large restricted to those who either ignore the teaching of the Church or seek somehow to undermine them. It brings together under the aegis of hierarchal paternalism clerics who have no intention of abandoning their aberrant behavior. One tactic used is to protest that any and all criticism of or reservations about the hierarchy, their shuffling of priests and maltreatment of survivors are simply diverse forms of unjust discrimination against the Church commonly known as "Church Bashing."

There is an effort by some of the hierarchy to manipulate the Church by gaining the often well-intentioned support of her members with a view to maintaining civil laws such as the Statute of Limitations, which enables sexually abusing priests to escape the justice they so richly deserve. They bring pressure about with threats of closings and bankruptcy never once admitting it was their fault in the first place. The blame is put on the victim who filed suit because the church failed to take action. This is done in order to conform to the pressure groups' concept that predator priest is completely harmless, if not entirely good! Even when the practice of sexually abusing children may seriously threaten the life and well-being of the church its advocates, the hierarchy, remain undeterred and refuse to consider the magnitude of the debilitating risks involved to the church they purport to love.

Sincerely,

Vinnie Nauheimer

PS: Ratzinger's letter goes on, but my comparison ends here in order to make the point without becoming overbearing. The hypocrisy is staggering especially when one considers the high percentage of homosexuals in the priesthood. However, homosexuality is not the issue here. The issue is the long, tried and true admonitions against child abuse and an aberrant hierarchy that has willfully chosen ignore them. Nothing in the Gospels tells us that Jesus wished to control the sexual behavior of two consenting adults. That came later from a church determined to control its members even unto their bedrooms. However, there is a great deal said about abusing children. It started in the Old Testament, Jesus spoke about it, the Evangelists memorialized it, Paul addressed it and prohibitions flow throughout the history of the Church Law from the early church up to current times against abusing children.

A hierarchy that ignores the words of the Savior to serve its own selfish needs is guilty of sacrilege, heresy, hypocrisy and moral relativism. They cannot with these sins upon their souls represent Christ on Earth because Jesus himself told us we cannot serve two masters. (Another teaching conveniently overlooked) In an effort to hide their own shortcomings, the hierarchy rail against divorce, contraception and homosexuality as if they knew something about morality. It is time for that to end.

Reference

1.http://www.vatican.va/roman_curia/congregations/cfaith/documents/rc_con_cfaith_doc_19861001_homosexual-persons_en.html

Wash Your Dirty Hands!

Suppose Cardinal Dolan's recent folksy metaphor about washing hands bespeaks the incredible hypocrisy that is endemic among the hierarchy of the Roman Catholic Church? Washing hands used as a metaphor has two meanings. The first is to clean yourself up and the second is to remove yourself from a situation vis a vis Pontius Pilate. Consider Dolan's decision in Milwaukee to pay sexually abusing priests to leave the priesthood. Instead of doing the right thing, he emulated Pilate and washed his hands of the guilty priests. Thinking like that is intrinsically disordered! It is a more or less a strong tendency geared toward an intrinsic moral evil; and thus the inclination itself must be seen as an objective disorder. Can turning sexually abusing priests loose on the public be anything but?

During the past eleven years, we have all witnessed hundreds of documented cases of bishops and cardinals shuffling sexually abusing priests between parishes, dioceses, and even countries. The end result in each case was the destruction of more young lives. Who is the bigger villain, the predator who follows his perverse inclinations or the hierarchy, who controlling the chains of the predators, allow them free reign to rape and plunder the most vulnerable of the church's members? Yet no one in the hierarchy has ever publicly admonished these offending priests either by forbidding them access to the church, decrying the desecration of the act of consecration, or even for setting and serving Christ's table with scent of children fresh on their hands. Grievous omissions like this bespeak an intrinsically disordered hierarchy and sense of outrage! It denotes a strong tendency ordered toward an intrinsic moral evil; and thus the inclination itself must be seen as an objective disorder. Can turning sexually abusing priests loose to prey on unsuspecting families of good Catholics be anything but?

Recently, protesters were turned away from St. Patrick's Cathedral for attempting to enter the cathedral with hands soiled by mere ashes. Since when are physically dirty hands a sufficient reason for keeping Catholics out of their church? Can anyone ever recall a priest being turned away from a church for having dirty hands because he used to debauch young children? Priests have been turned away from churches for protesting sexual abuse, but never for committing it. Has Dolan ever publicly told a pedophile priest to wash his hands before saying mass? Has he ever told a sexually abusing priest to wash his hands before consecrating a host? Where was his outcry against the heinous sacrilegious crime of violating altar servers in the sacristy prior to saying mass? Refusing to publicly ask sexually abusing priests to wash their hands prior to saying Mass is intrinsically disordered, but not as disordered as refusing to bar them from entering a church.

Though the thought has probably entered the mind of more than one parishioner upon finding out that they had an abusing priest in their parish, it has rarely if ever been publicly discussed. Take the following as one of many documented examples: "**Fr. Charles Engelhardt**, 64, an Oblate of St. Francis de Sales, is accused of orally sodomizing and molesting a 10-year-old altar boy in 1998 in the sacristy at St. Jerome Parish in Northeast Philadelphia." The burning question is, "Where were those hands before they consecrated the host and placed it on my lips?" Why hasn't the question been asked publicly? The answers are obvious: 1. Because it is too reviling, disgusting, and nauseating a thought to contemplate for even a second and 2. It would lead to questions of faith that no one, especially the hierarchal theologians, want the laity to contemplate. Questions like, "How could a sick perverted priest really perform transubstantiation?" Groups that the question has obviously never bothered are the bishops, the cardinals, and the Curia of the Roman Catholic Church. They simply don't and didn't care. Sacrilege as vile as mentioned above was fostered and condoned by bishops who refused to take action and played pass the pedophile. Behavior like that is intrinsically disordered! It proves a strong tendency ordered toward an intrinsic moral evil; and thus the inclination itself and the hierarchy which fostered it must be seen as objectively disordered.

Cardinal Dolan speaks of rules that must be obeyed like washing your hands before sitting at the Lord's Table, but he belongs to the hierarchy of the Catholic Church who, as a group, are notoriously infamous for their dirty hands. As a group, they have defied and defiled Civil Law, the Catechism, Canon Law, the Scriptures and the admonitions of Jesus Christ himself when it comes to dealing with sexually abusing priests, bishops, and nuns. The Cardinal didn't lock the doors on his mentor Cardinal Rigali, who proclaimed there are no active priests with allegations of sexual abuse against them in the Philadelphia Archdiocese. No, au contraire! He invited him with open arms to speak at St. Patrick's on Holy Thursday. It turns out the Philadelphia Grand Jury found 37 credibly accused priests still in ministry. Yet, because Rigali is a cardinal, and because he was Dolan's mentor, St. Patrick's doors were thrown wide open to him. Talk about hypocrisy and an innate objective disorder!

Most Catholics would rather sit in a church with fellow Catholics of all persuasions than sit in a church with one priest saying mass who was guilty of sexually abusing children. However the hierarchy doesn't see it that way. No matter how big the stench, no matter how filthy the hands, no matter how foul the sacrilege, they have jumped through unprecedented hoops to keep the doors open for the offending priest. No great effort was ever expended to prevent a priest from either saying or attending Mass and that is more proof of the objective disorder of the hierarchy.

Sadder still is the need that people feel to be part of an institution corrupted from within by a hierarchy that has long since forgotten the teachings of Jesus and the Scriptures. As Groucho Marx once said, "I would never join a club that would have me as a member!" Rephrased and applicable to this situation, it should be, "Why would I want to belong to a church that is run by such an objectively disordered group as the hierarchy of the Roman Catholic Church."

Jesus said, "When one or more of you gather in my name, I will be there." Be guided.

The Conclave

Old dinosaurs plodding through ancient doors;
Self-importance bouncing off marble floors;
Aging bones make it difficult to kneel;
No indications of missing a meal.

Museum pieces both living and dead;
Stackable dolls painted bright blood red.
Long in tooth; extremely short on truth,
When it comes to vile sins against youth.

Carnivores pretend to be herbivores
Bloody hands betray the biggest whores.
All want to be Tyrannosaurus Rex
Wearing the white hat with muscles to flex.

Sistine Chapel with its beautiful walls;
Contrasts markedly with old dried up balls.
Hypocrisy wearing bright scarlet red
Shameful color of the devil's own bed

The secret conclave where they set their tones;
Their mausoleum filled with ancient bones.
When nothing changes, all becomes a farce;
Old men blowing smoke up each other's arse!

The storm is gathering; angry, dark clouds.
Soon the dinosaurs will be wearing shrouds.
Remnants of a once proud church on display.
Dinosaur bones for which tourists will pay!

2001 Prophetic Painting Predicted Conclave Controversy

Long before accusing cardinals of complicity in the clergy abuse scandal became common fare, artist, writer, and survivor advocate Vinnie Nauheimer painted "Cardinal Sins" implicating cardinals and the hierarchy in the cover up of Clergy Abuse. This one of a set of paintings in a collection called "Stations of the Abused"

This oil painting on canvas depicts a cardinal with three heads, which represent hear, see and speak no evil. The doves holding the vestments up represent the Holy Spirit who has made the abuse public and the two children represent all the children who have suffered at the hands of the clergy.

This painting drives home the culpability of the College of Cardinals. They are guilty by either acts of commission for their part in the clergy abuse cover-up or for acts of omission by keeping silent about the egregious sins they, to their disgrace, kept silent about.

The hierarchy has frequently demonstrated their lack of long term memory and this painting serves to remind them that they need a new pope committed to righting this terrible wrong.

The End of Days or the End of Catholic Daze?

What if all the prophecies about Benedict XVI being the next to last pope are true, but not for the universal reason everyone suspects? Suppose fulfillment of the prophecies doesn't mean the end of the world, but instead means the end of a centuries old corrupt Vatican reign? The recent sordid revelations bursting forth from the Vatican will hasten the end of days for the hierarchy and the end of daze for millions of Catholics.

Prophecies from Malachy to Fatima and every one in between, including the rarely mentioned prophecy of a Japanese nun from Akita, Japan, Sister Sasagawa have predicted the end of days. However, Sister Sasagawa quoting the Blessed Virgin has a prophecy that has hit the bulls eye, with no interpretation needed, that describes current Vatican events. She said she was told, "The work of the devil will infiltrate even the Church in such a way that one will see cardinals opposing cardinals, bishops against other bishops." It wouldn't stretch anybody's mind (except maybe a bishop's) to believe that the Blessed Mother was prophesying the scenario currently surrounding Benedict's resignation.

My personal favorite prophecy is from her son, Jesus: Luke 12:1-3

He began to say unto his disciples first of all, "Beware ye of the leaven of the Pharisees (Hierarchy), which is hypocrisy. For there is nothing covered, that shall not be revealed; neither hid, that shall not be known. Therefore whatsoever ye have spoken in darkness shall be heard in the light; and that which ye have spoken in the ear in closets shall be proclaimed upon the housetops."

Is there anything more compelling than the fulfillment of Jesus' own prophecy? Is there anyone out there that doesn't or can't see the hand of the Holy Spirit moving to cleanse his church? (Present hierarchy excluded) How many times was Jesus pressed for miracles? How many Doubting Thomas' are there? How much more proof is needed? Survivors of sexual abuse, mere men and women, took on a two thousand year old church with more money and power than most global corporations and they brought the church to its knees. Could that have happened without divine assistance?

Roger Cardinal Mahony spent hundreds of millions of dollars on lawyers, PR firms and hush money. One might say he did everything humanly possible to prevent the diocesan records from being made public, but in the end all his money and power were spent in vain. Over 12,000 pages of documents outlining what many consider criminal behavior, which is the antithesis of what Jesus preached on earth, were released. In Philadelphia a monsignor sits in prison because his cardinal boss died before he could be indicted. In Kansas City a bishop was convicted of failing to notify authorities about a priest he knew was taking lurid pictures of little children! "Words that have been spoken in darkness shall be heard in the light!"

The prophecy of Jesus is reverberating through the Vatican. "That which ye have spoken in the ear in closets shall be proclaimed upon the housetops." The closeted words are now global headlines! The dam is showing strain and the once impenetrable wall of red cloaks is cracking. Vati-leaks, Swiss guards killed, the butler done it, money laundering, mob connections, power plays, Cardinal Mahony silenced, the pope' resignation and now we read there is a homosexual contingent in the Vatican. Well bowl me over with a feather boa! Homosexuals in the Vatican! That's about as surprising as finding sand in your shoes after a day on the beach. The difference is; is what has been known for a long time has been very publicly shouted from the housetops!

The gates are opened with more to come as sharks, smelling blood in a sea of red, jockey for the pole position in the race for the white hat. In addition to outing the homosexual contingent this past week, other notable cracks have come from: Cardinal Zen who has said that the Vatican should have taken a tougher stand on the Chinese government. While he, in the past, has spoken out against the government of China, he has never before broken ranks and spoke out against the Vatican's lack of action. Then there is Cardinal Keith O'Brien, who heads the Church of Scotland. He laid down a very public anti-Vatican bombshell when he said that priests should be given the option of getting married. This is in direct opposition to Benedict who in April of last year slammed priests who favored removing the requirement of celibacy and in 2010 sent a letter to seminarians world-wide extolling the virtues of celibacy. More interesting is the lack of a public Vatican reprimand for O'Brien. Rome is too busy countering the "homosexual contingent" to even bother with Cardinal O'Brien. O'Brien is a man who knows how to time his contradictions to papal policy. End of Daze?

The glue of secrecy appears to be drying up and with it the adherence to the "Don't say anything in opposition oath." Maybe there are a few non-delusional, selfless cardinals left in the church; Men who realize its "do or die time," time to take a stand and give the church the cleansing and overhaul it needs to make it a spiritual rather than a power based entity. If they don't, their dwindling church will shrink to the level of a historical monument. The Vatican claim of having over one billion Catholics worldwide is both laughable and pathetic. The statement should read, "Over one billion baptized" The idea that there are over a billion practicing Catholics in the world is as ludicrous as saying there is no evil residing in the Vatican. Under the last two pontiffs, the number of practicing Catholics in Europe and the United States has dropped dramatically. More important to the Vatican, is the coinciding drop in revenue. Tentacles will have to be lopped off and no cardinal wants it to be their arm of the Vatican. Red hats are seeing red and are prepared to do what they have to do to survive.

If the above isn't proof enough of the coming end, consider the youth. The largest numbers of non-practicing Catholics come from the under thirty group. The Vatican knows they have no way of replacing the Cradle to Grave Catholics as they age out along with the priests who serve them. In Ireland, former priest exporter extraordinaire to the world, the Church ran a multi-million dollar, multi media campaign last year. This very expensive effort garnered a mere twelve vocations. Without fresh blood or a miracle, the days of a Vatican led church are certainly numbered.

It is a safe bet that the Vatican financial people have already projected the numbers and know within a couple of years when the end of days will occur. Business as usual will only hasten both the end of daze and their end of days. Stay tuned and remember Mary's words to the good sister, "the work of the devil will infiltrate even the Church in such a way that one will see cardinals opposing cardinals, bishops against other bishops." Stay tuned!

Send in the Clones

Suppose you had a guaranteed lifetime job, long flowing red robes, more bling than you could wear, servants, secretaries (handsome ones at that), hundreds of millions of people believing that you are the spiritual descendants of the apostles and were an intermediary between them and God! Would you give that up to become more Christ like? Not a chance! Therein lies the cardinal lack of motivation to elect anyone other than a clone to fill Benedict's Prada shoes.

Baptized in the River of Denial, delusional, self-absorbed, uttering snippets to the press about the pressing issues of the poor and third world countries, the cardinals gather, feast sumptuously and strategize about who will be the next Vicar of Christ on Earth and what they will wear for the new pope's, if not their own, inauguration. It's the Vatican's version of America's Red Carpet Club. Yet, these same men, the cardinals, are the first to condemn the evils of materialism while totally oblivious to the fact that they are the polar opposites of their founder.

So why would anyone in their right mind harbor the slightest inkling that things will change?

Jesus said his church would last forever is one answer!

Who is to say that this is his church anymore? It was written in Thomas' Gospel that the church lives in those who keep Jesus in their heart. Did Jesus drive around in a golden chariot? Did he spend lavishly on hats and shoes? Did either he or his apostles wear fourteen to twenty foot silk capes known as Cappa Magnum? Or, did Jesus chastise the rich and their lavish life styles saying it was harder for them to get into heaven than to get a camel through the eye of a needle? What's that you say, "Bishops and cardinals have no money of their own; it is church money freely given?" Eating lavishly at the trough filled by the labor of others is the bigger disgrace!

Well what about the Holy Spirit! Surely he will reinvigorate and bless the conclave?

No, the Holy Spirit is too busy keeping the spark of justice alive in the thousands of abuse survivors. The Spirit has imbued survivors and their supporters with the tremendous strength and unwavering courage needed to take on a universally corrupt institution with global tentacles. Only the Holy Spirit could have sustained the survivors of clergy sexual abuse while they bore and still bear the brunt and full measure of a mega monolithic church attempting to crush them. Please pause here to remember those who didn't survive, those whose spirits were willing to come forward, but whose minds were not able to withstand the intense pain brought on by the onslaught of a ruthless church, its high powered lawyers, and their high pressure tactics. No, the Holy Spirit is too busy tending to the suffering and giving them the courage to speak about the unspeakable atrocities committed on their bodies. The Spirit doesn't have the time for those who have co-opted Christ's church.

You speak of hierarchy as though they are incorrigible. Do you truly believe that?

Those that are not criminals themselves have opted to keep silent about the ones who are. There is nothing else to say. If they haven't committed crimes of commission, they have committed crimes of omission. As Jesus said, "Bad trees don't produce good fruit!" Which cardinal who has himself committed a crime is going to vote to have himself removed? Which cardinal who sat by silently will now publicly rebuke his red-hatted brothers? Bring in the clones!

Look at the headlines currently surrounding any number of cardinals. They include but are not limited to money laundering, fronting for the mob, perjury, failure to report sex crimes to civil authorities, failure to remove sexually abusing priests, interfering with judicial processes and those are only the ones we know about. Would the Jesus in the Gospels have men like Bernard Law, Roger Mahony, Edward Egan, Donald Wuerl, Francis George, George Pell, Sean Brady as apostles? Jesus would more than likely have fitted them for millstones for turning children away from Him as three of the four Synoptic Gospels tell us.

What incentive is there to change the way business is done in the Vatican? None!

Send in the clones; it's business as usual!

And the Oscar goes to…"The Sting LA Style"

Accepting the Oscar for "The Sting LA Style" are Roger Cardinal Mahony and Archbishop Jose Gomez for their stellar performances in a remake of "The Sting." Produced, directed and orchestrated by the Vatican, it is the story of two bishops who feign fighting with each other in order to collect vast sums of money from an unsuspecting laity. Gomez plays the part of a white knight who rides in, releases documents (which was his legal obligation), derides his predecessor, and saves the Los Angeles diocese from the last vestiges of child sex abuse. Mahony, for his part, takes umbrage at being silenced by his protégé and being blamed for his dastardly deeds. Could we expect anything less from the diocese that contains Hollywood? Certainly not!

Anyone believing the sincerity of the this "made for public consumption" feud should reach into their Tinker Bell pouches and throw some pixie dust on themselves so they can remain in La La Land. Are we really supposed to believe that Gomez was unaware of the extent of Mahony's malfeasance? No more than that insulting excuse that Mahony made when he proffered, "nothing in my training prepared me for priests raping children." If true, we ought to put both their faces on the Naiveté Awards! Mahony for not knowing that the rape, sodomization and molestation of children was a heinous, immoral, and criminal act. Gomez, who obviously doesn't read, deserves his award in honor of his empty protestations that he knew nothing of how bad things were under Mahony. Really, did this man live under a rock for the past 10 years? As Mahony said, "Gomez never complained about me before." These pernicious lines were written by the Vatican spin masters to add drama to the feud and Mahony followed the script perfectly giving a convincing performance penned to create the illusion of a genuine feud. "Please Don't Throw Me into the Briar Patch, Archbishop Gomez!" wink, wink.

Why the wink, wink? Money, money, and more money!

Mahony has spent untold millions maybe even a billion dollars on PR Firms, lawyers and buying the silence of survivors. As early as 2002, he hired one of the most expensive PR Firms in LA, Weber Shandwick, which was rumored to bill at $500 per hour. Mahony then hired J. Michael Hennigan, of Hennigan Bennett and Dorman, a crème de la crème lawyer, who in turn fired Weber Shandwick and hired Sitrick and Co., a Century City-based firm whose forte was crisis management. Can you see the dollars flowing out of the LA Diocesan coffers? The outflow begun in 2002 has continued for over ten years. It is not hard to imagine the coffers of the PR and Legal firms unnecessarily swelling at the laity's expense.

Since then, there have been suits, countersuits, appeals and more appeals especially when it came to the Herculean legal effort put forth, over the past six years, aimed at preventing abuse files from being made public. The outflow of money had to be enormous, but because there are no check and balances, no transparency, the sheep in LA's pews will never know exactly how much money Mahony spent keeping up his image, countering suits, filing appeals, and that doesn't count the six-hundred-fifty-million payout to survivors. The irony is magnificent. Hundreds of millions of dollars spent to protect an image that was ultimately sullied by his protégé. Truly Machiavellian!

The Sting LA Style is on now because those monies have to be replaced! Mahony and Gomez publicly pretend to dislike each other like Newman and Redford did in the Sting, but the goal is not to fleece a mobster, their goal is to take more money from the laity. Los Angeles is the largest diocese in the richest country in the world and both Gomez and Mahony are company men. Only those who still believe in the Easter Bunny would be naïve enough to believe that the Vatican would give this prize diocese to anyone but a company man. This script was written as a contingency plan when Gomez was given the nod, of the five million Catholics in the diocese; forty percent of LA Catholics are Latino. Coincidence?

Did the Vatican's plan work? Did Gomez become the knight in shining armor for forbidding Mahony to speak in public? Yes! Did this unprecedented move (according to the press) make national headlines, yes! It has been national news and editorial fodder for over a week. Did the pew people all over the country bob their heads in agreement while saying, "It's about time!" Yes! Is Mahony the bad guy? Yes! Is Mahony feigning hurt feelings, absolutely! Is Gomez being perceived as the good guy, yes! Has Mahony's lifestyle materially changed, no! He swore a blood oath to the pope and this charade is a small price to pay for all he has been given.

Several papers have pronounced a bishop silencing another bishop as unprecedented. Not so, this same scenario was recently played out in Ireland where Diarmuid Martin, Archbishop of Dublin, made a big public display of demanding the resignations of three bishops, who like Mahony, had been instrumental in the cover-up of the sexual abuse of minors. After a suitable and very public fight, the bishops agreed to tender their resignations to Pope Benedict XVI who promptly refused to accept them. Martin went down as an Irish hero for battling the Vatican and the three bishops went back to work, business as usual.

There is a very little known rite created by, oddly enough, Benedict XIV who wrote the rules for the degradation of a bishop. **The Rite of Degradation** starts out as follows: "If the degradandus [*he who is about to be degraded*] be an archbishop, the degrading prelate removes his pallium, saying: "We deprive thee of the rights and privileges of the episcopal dignity, symbolized in this pallium, since thou hast abused them." If Benedict XVI had the chutzpah to use this rite, it would indeed be unprecedented!

However, I digress and therefore back to the point of this exposition: The fine acting performance of Roger Cardinal Mahony and his protégé Archbishop Jose Gomez. The purpose of which, is to put Gomez in the position of white knight so that he can ask for and receive more money from the good people of the Los Angeles diocese. Money, which most likely will cover the legal bills accumulated by his predecessor and those which may arise from criminal charges, if any, filed when the recently released documents have been examined.

Despite the protestations of the church to the contrary, the church can only use laity money. The Roman Catholic Church makes and sells nothing of material value. Therefore, they can only exist by virtue of what they either take or that which is given to them. The hundreds of millions of dollars spent defending the indefensible can be traced back to the laity's pocket one way or another.

According to the LA Times, Gomez has already been in touch with the New York Company, Guidance in Giving Inc. He is using professionals, like his predecessor, to study whether or not the pew Catholics of Los Angeles are ripe enough for another round of financial plucking. That folks is what this charade between Gomez and Mahony is all about.

It's all about the money!

An Open Letter to Pope Benedict XVI

What if you had the ability to undo egregious wrongs that affected hundreds of thousands of people worldwide would you, could you do it? What if there was only a sixteen day window for you to act? Would you find the time? Pope Benedict XVI, you have just sixteen days to perform this wondrous task. You've heard all about the crimes. You've heard the pleas of survivors; they have haunted you since before you took the office of pope. They will haunt your legacy for eternity too if you pay no heed to this request. I'm begging you on behalf of survivors of clergy abuse and their families all around the world, set them free, hear the pleas, hear their suffering, take to heart their pain and publicize the global clergy abuse files regardless of the rank of the offending priest. Only you can alleviate the endless suffering of victims and their families by giving their suffering validity and naming their tormentors!

Whether you wanted it or not, God gave you the opportunity to change the church and put an end to the worldwide sexual abuse of children by priests and bishops. God has given you two opportunities, one as head of the Congregation for the Doctrine of the Faith, and the second as Pope Benedict XVI to clean up this evil mess festering within His church. In both instances, you have not been up to the task. Now with just days left before the voluntary end of your papacy, you have yet a third chance. We implore you, to summon the courage before God and man to do what you swore to do in assuming your position as a priest, protect the flock.

A man of your intelligence knows beyond a shadow of a doubt about how the sexual abuse of children corrupts, has corrupted and has thrown the Catholic Church and your papacy into a tailspin. Now is the time to resurrect the church as a parting gift to the victims, the future of the church and to Jesus Christ who founded this church. It is your last chance to rectify the wrongs.

Throw open the doors and shine the light on the vermin that have been eating away at the foundations of Christianity for longer than we know. Let the light cleanse the church and heal the survivors. Open and make public all the records on clerical sexual abuse from around the world.

In 2002 your predecessor said, "There is no room in the church for priests who abuse children." In 2008 before the Youth of the world, you said, "Victims should receive compassion and care, and those responsible for these evils must be brought to justice." Your words as those of your predecessor ring hollow. You have never brought any of those responsible for these evils to justice. They still reside in your church like roaches behind the walls. You know it, we know it and the world knows.

Now is the time to act! At the end of the month after a new pope is elected it will be too late. He will say and do the same things that all the replacement bishops have said:

"That was my predecessor's fault, I never knew things were that bad, and besides, it's all in the past.

Pope Benedict XVI, things are that bad for hundreds of thousands of victims worldwide. Having your body and soul ripped asunder to feed a priest's lust does not end with the deed. It stays with you for life. You have the power to ease that pain. God Almighty is looking down at you and has given you yet a third opportunity to right the wrongs. Will you, like Peter, deny him and all the victims in this world yet a third time?

I pray not.

Sincerely,

Vinnie Nauheimer

Mahony's Legacy

Let's hear it for Cardinal Mahony!
Never was one so full of baloney;
Cunning hypocrite of the first order;
Priest, whose hypocrisy knows no border.

Panderer to the pedophile priest
Let loose the sick, hungry, ravaging beast
Who gorged upon the innocent flesh
Of our children; their pure souls to enmesh.

Roger the dodger spent untold dollars
Keeping, out of jail, rapists with collars!
Spending for lawyers to tighten the screws
On tortured child victims from the pews!

Protecting at all costs secret files;
Protecting his black heart with big smiles;
Protecting his image in the aisles;

From a paper trail running for miles.
Mahony has no more a sense of God
Than an old, dead, smelly, decaying cod
The cathedral to the great Mahony
Will be the fact that he was a phony.

A sepulcher that has been painted white;
A crystal chandelier without a light
Upon his name, church and God; he cast blight
His legacy, "Of his sins we shall write."

Roman Catholic Cardinal

Yo Joe, What's with this Gomez shit? Why's he muzzling me?

YO MO, DON'T TAKE IT PERSONAL. IT'S JUST BUSINESS!

Or Roman Catholic Criminal?

The Prophecy Comes to Pass

Beware ye of the leaven of the Pharisees, which is hypocrisy. For there is nothing covered, that shall not be revealed; neither hid, that shall not be known. Therefore whatsoever ye have spoken in darkness shall be heard in the light; and that which ye have spoken in the ear in closets shall be proclaimed upon the housetops. Luke 12: 1-3

ALL THE CARDINAL'S MONEY AND ALL THE CARDINAL'S LAWYERS

I didn't know the lasting effects abuse had on children!

I was Naive!

AND ALL THE CARDINAL'S PUBLIC RELATIONS COULDN'T SUPPRESS THE TRUTH!

Election Results Confirm Roman Catholic Hierarchy Voted Out!

The Catholic Hierarchy lost more in this past election than Mitt Romney ever could. The sin of hypocrisy has caught up with and trampled the power of what once was a powerful voice in American politics: the hierarchy of the American Roman Catholic Church. The bishops played their final hand in American politics and came up woefully short, aces and eights: the dead mans hand. Catholic bishops were undeniably roundly, soundly, and publicly rebuked in a fashion that was equal to the effort they expended to influence the election. Whether the hierarchy accepts it or not, they will now be consigned to pages of the volume: <u>No Longer Politically Relevant.</u>

Can bishops be politically significant to national politics when they can't influence their own parishioners? They can't. Bishops along with their pundits loudly proclaimed their ability to hold sway over the Catholic population of between sixty to seventy million Catholics in the United States, but as this election proved to the world, they couldn't deliver a pizza without a GPS.

Only a few years ago, Bishop Chaput, Archbishop of Denver, was able to rally Colorado Catholics as a block to defeat a revision of the Statute of Limitations Bill that would have made it easier for victims of Clergy Abuse to recover damages from their abusers and the church that protected them. This year Colorado was one of only two states that passed a bill legalizing marijuana.

Not since the days of the Legion of Decency have the bishops been so vocal. In those days they utilized all the media in their efforts to prevent scandalous movies like Baby Doll or Lolita from being viewed by Catholics under the pain of sin. Below are some of the numerous exhortations voiced against Obama by bishops of the Roman Catholic Church.

Bishop Jenky compares abortion rights supporters to the Jewish crowd in Jerusalem that pledged loyalty to the Roman Empire and demanded that Pontius Pilate crucify Jesus. Jenky wrote, "For those who hope for salvation, no political loyalty can ever take precedence over loyalty to the Lord Jesus Christ and to his Gospel of Life,"

Bishops of Pennsylvania released a letter to voters declaring that policies on contraception, abortion and gay rights backed by the White House and Democrats meant the nation was "losing its soul by little steps."

Bishop Nicholas DiMarzio of Brooklyn wrote: "It is inconceivable to me how Catholics could support such policies. Indeed, Roman Catholics who support abortion rights and vote for a candidate because of those policies, place him/herself outside of the life of the Church. In so doing, they also place themselves in moral danger."

Clearly, the bishop's admonitions were pretty much ignored except for the eleven percent of Catholics who attend mass on a weekly basis. Personally speaking, it is inconceivable how bishops and cardinals could support those within their ranks who abused children, broke their sacred covenant with God and a host of civil laws. This, "do as I say and not as I do" attitude is the real reason Catholics don't listen to bishops anymore. Catholics are tired of the hypocrisy.

What do the numbers mean?

The sixty to seventy million Catholics number, which bishops and cardinals bandy about to strike fear in the hearts of politicians is a meaningless number. Though there may be sixty some- odd million people who were baptized Catholics living in the United States there are far fewer, who are practicing Catholics. In order to get to a voting block number, let's remove about ten million who are below voting age bringing the total down to fifty million. Now consider that according to CARA, the research arm of the prestigious Catholic Georgetown University, 32% of all adult Catholics rarely go to Mass and 24% of them go a couple of times a year. That means that 56% of the adult voting age Catholics in the United States are non-practicing Catholics. That leaves a base of twenty-two million church goers that might listen to bishops. This is not speculation; the truth lies in plain sight for anyone who cares to read the results of the recent presidential election.

How did this Happen?

Hypocrisy would be the leading cause behind the erosion of hierarchal political clout. In light of the criminal activities, lying, cheating, bullying and obfuscation surrounding the Clergy Abuse Scandal, the admonitions of the bishops listed above are at the least laughable, at their worst, despicable. As Bishop Di Marzio said in his column, "It stretches the imagination!" It sure does. It blows the mind that supposed followers of Christ could dismiss with impunity the crimes, cover-ups, hypocrisy and lies committed by their own against children.

Over and over again, in the public eye, from the pope on down the hierarchy has been caught being dishonest, unethical, unwilling to abide by their own canons as well as civil laws when it involved the sexual abuse of children by priests and bishops.

Losing their Credibility through Large and Small Steps

The bishops of Pennsylvania had the process right, but as usual, they were unable to see how it applies to them. Since 2002 the hierarchy of the Roman Catholic Church has been caught denying, promoting and minimizing horrific, heinous sexual crimes committed on children by their priests and bishops. Their arrogance blinded them to the fact that their credibility was dwindling faster than a used car salesman with a "Saturday Only" special.

Below is an excerpt of a letter written to the then Vicar of Priest Personnel for NY Archdiocese: Msgr. Edward O'Donnell. This priest traveled up to Croton on Hudson to defend a notorious pedophile priest with a twenty year history of abuse and excoriate the family who filed a suit against the priest and church.

Parents who once attended church regularly now find excuses. ***They cannot answer their children when the children speak the truth without looking and sounding like you!*** How sad is that? The following is a Croton Catholic father speaking about his daughter who left the church over this scandal. [1]

The Journal News June 20, 2002

"It was difficult watching his daughter leave the church," McClean said, but he did not try to persuade her to stay. "We support her in her decision and we understand it. She's made her own decision based on her conscience and we support her in that," he said.

Croton on Hudson had the dubious distinction of having two back to back pastors removed for child abuse.

Ogden Nash once parodied a Shakespeare quote. "Oh what tangled webs we weave when we first believe children to be naïve" The arrogance, hypocrisy and criminal activity of the Roman Catholic Hierarchy has come home to roost. Children raised in the church during the last decade of the twentieth century and the first decade of the twenty-first have no interest in Catholicism. They don't get married in the Catholic Church and those children are now having children who are not being raised Catholic.

Not counting the adults the Catholic lost because of the Clergy Abuse Scandal, there are at least three generations of young people who have no regard or desire to listen to what the hierarchy of the Catholic Church has to say. The chain of cradle to grave Catholics has been broken. In addition, the bishops have taught young adults one lesson very well; the hierarchy of the Catholic Church has zero credibility.

The Pew Forum on Religion and Public Life tells us that about one fifth of the current population of the United States has no religious affiliation. The largest age group in the non-affiliated class is 18-23. Wouldn't it be interesting to find out how many of that twenty percent came from once Catholic homes?

Hand in hand with the above is the fate of the Catholic Church in Ireland. Irish newspapers tell us that Ireland, with 95% of its population Catholic cannot get vocations. An expensive, national, vocations ad campaign netted just 12 men willing to enter the priesthood. The diocese of Dublin, home to the Archbishop of Dublin accounted for one quarter of the total leaving just 8 from the rest of Ireland. The Irish Sun wrote the following in their August 5, 2012 edition

Faith worse than debt: Priesthood ad fails to collar any of 400k jobless "The Diocese of Elphin ran ads in newspapers and newsletters in counties Sligo, Roscommon, Westmeath and Galway looking for new recruits. But despite over 400,000 people on the dole, not **ONE** person applied for the job."

If the Catholic Church has lost its sway in one of the most Catholic countries in the world, what hope can bishops and cardinals have of persuading the politicians in the United States that they are relevant?

Conclusion

The Roman Catholic Church along with its cardinals and bishops are a mere shadow of their former selves. Without the culturally forced baptisms, mandatory mass attendance, and Catholic schools, the power both real and (mostly) perceived of the hierarchy will continue to dwindle. The stalwarts of the Catholic Church, the pre-Vatican II generation are dying off rapidly. The Vatican II generation, the baby boomers, are graying and are split between those who continue to cling like Voice of the Faithful and those who have left. In a few years when these two generations have passed, the Catholic Church will take its place in antiquity.

Middle aged white men running around in red dresses, is as anachronistic as their claim to speak for God. When historians write about the demise of the Catholic Church, they will write about the final crippling blow that was dealt to them by the Clergy Abuse Scandal. They will tell of the arrogance, hypocrisy and criminality of the hierarchy that came to light at the beginning of the twenty-first century. Historians will study with amazement the fact the only group who believed the lies, cover-ups and misrepresentations of hierarchy regarding the sexual abuse of minors were the same bishops, cardinals and popes making the excuses. They will ask, "Did the hierarchy really expect the pew Catholic to believe all their lies?" and the answer will be a resounding yes. Then they will ask, "Did the pew Catholics believe the nonsense that spewed forth from the Roman Catholic hierarchy?" The answer will be a resounding no and the number of people who left the church in the first two decades of the twenty-first century will stand as witness to that fact.

The presidential election is over and the hierarchy of the Roman Catholic Church in the United States was soundly defeated by all their constituencies with the exception of the dwindling number who attend Mass every week.

The sins of the fathers have come home to roost!

Finn Should be Finn ished!

Once again with great solemnity, a bishop, Finn of Kansas City, has stood at the pulpit and read from the voluminous sacred text written in the "Vatican Book of Excuses." The church, like most suffering from an addiction, has thousands of excuses for pandering to despicable human beings wearing collars who ravage children for nothing more than their own pleasure. The trigger for opening the Book of Excuses is getting caught: allowing the indefensible (the sexual abuse of children) to continue.

Bishop Finn has gotten caught allowing the indefensible to continue. A grand jury has turned in the indictment and so we shine the current spotlight on him. Just because you put a silk tutu on a slug does not mean you have a prima ballerina. The same is true of bishops. Just because you put gold vestments on a man, anoint him with oil and recite a few well chosen words doesn't mean you have either a holy man or a man who works for the best interests of Christianity. All Catholics have been taught to believe that bishops are special men who are spiritual descendants of the apostles. However, our experience tells us that what we've been taught to believe can't possibly be reconciled with the actions we've seen. Jesus was anything but a hypocrite. After those who would abuse children, his harshest words in the Gospels were for hypocrites. He says this about hypocrites:

Matt: 15:7-9: You hypocrites! Well did Isaiah prophecy of you, when he said: This people honors me with their lips, But their heart is far from me;

Matt: 23: 25-28: Woe to you, you hypocrites! For you are like whitewashed graves, which appear beautiful on the outside, but are full of death and corruption. In the same way, you outwardly appear righteous, but inside you are full of hypocrisy and wickedness...

Is there anything in Bishop Finn's actions concerning Fr. Ratigan that would give him the appearance of being a hypocrite? Perhaps the following?

1. In 2002 before the world, Pope John Paul II declared: *there can be no place in the priesthood for anyone who would abuse a child.*

2. From the 2005 Preamble of the Dallas Charter for the protection of children agreed to by the bishops of the United States and revised in 2011: *"We make our own the words of His Holiness, Pope John Paul II: that the sexual abuse of young people is "by every standard wrong and rightly considered a crime by society; it is also an appalling sin in the eyes of God"* (Address to the Cardinals of the United States and Conference Officers, April 23, 2002)."

3. The Kansas City Star article dated October 6, 2011 stated: "A $10 million settlement was reached in 2008 that included 19 nonmonetary commitments, such as establishing

victims' advocacy programs, *immediately reporting any abuse or suspicion of abuse to law enforcement authorities*, and defrocking several priests who had been accused of abuse."

4. In 2008 while in Australia at the World Youth Day, Pope Benedict XVI uttered these words: "These misdeeds, which constitute so grave a betrayal of trust, deserve unequivocal condemnation... "I ask all of you to support and assist your bishops, and to work together with them in combating this evil. Victims should receive compassion and care, *and those responsible for these evils must be brought to justice*."

In addition to the charge of breaking civil law, we have a bishop of the Roman Catholic Church who has seemingly disobeyed the direct commands of two popes. Acted contrary to the pledge of the United States Conference of Catholic Bishop's, Dallas Charter and his own pledge to survivors as part of a legal settlement to immediately report any abuse or suspicions of abuse to law enforcement officials. What can be said about a man that behaves in this manner? Are these suitable credentials for any man we would want to call bishop? Behavior like this makes a laughing stock out of the word bishop both within the church and without the church. Is this a follower of Jesus or one of the hypocrites that Jesus warned us about?

Bishops take a vow of obedience to the Pope; they swear fealty to Christ and his teachings, and are supposed to be men of their word. Timothy tells us in, 1 Timothy 3: 1-5, that these are the attributes of a good bishop:

"This is a true saying, If a man desire the office of a bishop, he desireth a good work. A bishop then must be blameless, the husband of one wife, vigilant, sober, of good behaviour, given to hospitality, apt to teach; Not given to wine, no striker, not greedy of filthy lucre; but patient, not a brawler, not covetous; One that ruleth well his own house, having his children in subjection with all gravity; (For if a man know not how to rule his own house, how shall he take care of the church of God?)"

If a man cannot put an immediate end to the sick, vile and degenerate behavior of priests like Ratigan, how can we expect him to take care of the church of God? We can't! If we can't hold a bishop blameless, how can we expect him to take care of the church of God? We can't! If a bishop refuses to listen to the words of two successive Vicars of Christ on earth, can we account him blameless? No! If a bishop can't adhere to the Dallas Charter promulgated by fellow bishops, and if he can't abide by his own legal promise to the courts, how in God's name can we expect him to take care of God's church? The answer is too obvious!

As bad as the above transgressions may be, there is one worse: a total absence of humanity! For a long time, many have tried without success to understand how and why any man worthy of the name bishop would not do their utmost to protect the most vulnerable of our treasures, children, from sexual predation. There has to be a name for the cold-hearted, amoral, lack of humanity that will not put an immediate stop to the violation of children upon discovering it. Until a better name is found, we will have to use the only name we know that sums up the worldwide group of men who have the dubious distinction of continuously turning their backs on the rape, sodomization, molestation and violation of children: the hierarchy of the Roman Catholic Church.

N.C.A.A. Acts Swiftly to Punish Roman Catholic Hierarchy

Satire By Veritas Vinnie (AKA Vinnie Nauheimer)

Dateline: Rome

Following the just penalties recently imposed on Penn State by the National Collegiate Athletic Association, Catholics around the world wildly applauded the sanctions placed upon the Vatican by the National Catholic Atonement Association (Also called N.C.A.A). Following the lead of the collegiate sports association, the Atonement Association announced its penalties against the College of Cardinals for their unmitigated failure to stem the rampant sexual abuse of children committed by priests, nuns and lay staff.

The first order of business was to remove Papal Bull from the Vatican. For too long Papal Bull has been standing between Catholics and their God. Papal Bull has been force fed to Catholics in the same manner that priests have forced themselves upon children. For those not familiar Papal Bull, here are but a few examples: "The sexual abuse of minors is strictly an American problem." JPII said this about clergy abuse: *"by every standard wrong and rightly considered a crime by society; it is also an appalling sin in the eyes of God"* *Yet he made Cardinal Law Archpriest in charge of the Basilica dedicated to the Blessed Mother.* Benedict XVI said, *"*Victims should receive compassion and care, *and those responsible for these evils must be brought to justice."* To date, not one cardinal or bishop guilty of enabling sexually abusing priests and bishops has been laicized let alone faced criminal charges. In addition to removing Papal Bull, all images and likenesses of the chief bull thrower, Benedict XVI, will be removed from all Roman Catholic Churches and properties regardless of whether they are on public or private display.

The Atonement Association further stated that it would be penalizing the College of Cardinals with what they are calling corrective and punitive measures. These measures are designed to cut off the unlimited funds the College of Cardinals has used to defend priests and bishops guilty of both sexually abusing priests and covering up said abuse. The N.C.A.A. cited the 11+ million dollars spent by the Archdiocese of Philadelphia to defend Msgr. Lynn, plus the unknown costs it will incur to appeal his conviction, the hundreds of millions of dollars spent by the Los Angeles Archdiocese under Cardinal Mahony on legal fees and the billions of dollars spent worldwide to date. For the next four years, funds collected by parishes from parishioners can only be used by and for the parish in which they are collected.

The N.C.A.A. made scathing remarks on the egregious, criminal and inhumane actions of the hierarchy of the Catholic Church in covering up the decades long sexual abuse of Catholic children. The association hotly debated whether or not to impose the so-called Death Penalty clause, which would shut down every Catholic Church where an act of sexually abusing a child had taken place, but decided against it. Closing that many churches, it deemed, would be a fatal blow to the church. Ultimately they decided that this would be unfair to Catholics who only wanted to practice their faith even though their continued contributions, silence and failure to demand the heads of the hierarchy had allowed the problem to fester.

Additional penalties will allow whistleblower priests to become free agents and move to any religion of their choice without having to forego either their pensions or their medical benefits. The N.C.A.A. has determined that fear was the number one cause of the failure by respectable priests to call the public's attention to the widespread abuse of children, which was well known throughout the priesthood.

Lastly, the N.C.A.A. has imposed a six-year recruitment moratorium prohibiting parishes from recruiting priests from seminaries that have historically produced the greatest number of sexually abusing priests. The hierarchy of the RCC up until this point has adamantly opposed identifying the seminaries, which have produced the greatest number of sexually abusing priests, citing the need for confidentiality.

A spokesperson for the Vatican has vehemently decried these just, long overdue, and well-deserved penalties imposed by the N.C.A.A. citing the fact that "They answer to a higher authority!"

A Unifying Theory of Roman Catholic Clergy Abuse

Scientists look at a unifying theory as one that covers all aspects of a given phenomena. In short, it is a catchall that can explain most of the perplexing aspects as well as the simplest of a given problem. For almost twelve years I have searched for an explanation that would shed light on what has become known as the Roman Catholic Clerical Sexual Abuse Scandal. Questions needed to be both posed and answered. Like physics, the sexual abuse of children and its related permissiveness raises extraordinary questions that require answers. What follows are valid arguments until proven otherwise.

How could men, who purport to believe in the teachings of Jesus Christ, permit such heinous crimes to be committed against defenseless children? Once finding out about these crimes how can men purporting to believe in the teachings of Christ allow these crimes to continue unabated? How could these same followers of Christ viciously attack the abused, their parents and anyone else who chose to make public the crimes of rape, sodomization and molestation of children? How could this go on for centuries with no repercussions and lastly, how does the hierarchy of the Roman Catholic Church keep nuns, priests, bishops and cardinals from speaking out on the subject?

What follows is a unified theory that attempts to provide an overall umbrella for understanding the clergy abuse scandal. The facts speak for themselves, the historical references are cited and the truth is laid bare.

Dehumanization

Starving, gassing, burning, hacking, bombing and mutilating on a large scale are all well documented crimes against humanity. In each case humanity reflects on how inhuman man can be to his fellow man, decries and tries to destroy the offending dictators or regimes and puts up a memorial in the hope it doesn't happen again. The travesties generally last no longer than the time span of the despot's rule: I.e. Hitler, Pol Pot Idi Amin etc. There is however, one very notable exception. That exception is the rape, sodomization and molestation of children by the clergy of the Roman Catholic Church. There is ample documentation showing this carnage has been carried out unabated for centuries!

The focal point of this essay is not the pedophile priest, for we know what he is. He is a sick twisted deviant who relishes despoiling innocence. He is the predator. An animal that exists for his next meal: despoiling an innocent child. Like the jackal, he preys on the weak and vulnerable in order to feed his sick insatiable appetite. This examination will focus on the following: How the pederast became an integral part of the clergy, why their handlers, the bishops, allow these jackals free reign to prey on children, and the causes for the utter silence of the priesthood at large on the subject of the sexual abuse of children by priests.

59

What do you call a man who knowingly allows a malevolent individual to prey on children? What term can be coined for a man who upon finding out that a perverted priest has violated a child, moves said priest to new hunting grounds? How do you address someone who knowingly sends a serial child molester into a parish with an elementary school? What term can accurately describe a man who sends a child raping priest out of his country to prey upon the children of poor indigent people; whose only hope in life is an afterlife in heaven? Sadly, there is one answer to all of these questions, you call him bishop!

Any man worthy of the name man, with merely a meager amount of humanity, would run and hide in deep shame at the thought of allowing innocent children to be sexually abused, but not a bishop. Any father, who understands what it means to have, hold, raise and love a child, would cringe at the thought of putting any child in the path of a sexual predator, but not a bishop. If a man's son or daughter runs afoul of a sexual predator, he cries and berates himself for years burdened with the guilt of thinking he has failed his child, but not a bishop. If the child commits suicide as a direct effect of the abuse, that man takes his burden to the grave, but not a bishop! A bishop will defend his logic for allowing children to be raped by a priest from a pulpit, in front of cameras and even under oath in written depositions. Normal human beings just don't do that!

Normal people are simply not capable of casually allowing children as young as four years old to be raped, sodomized or molested. This is not a character trait found in the general public! Why, then, does it exist in the hierarchy of the Catholic Church? Societies as well as cultures around the world have stringent laws against sexually abusing children. Interpol has the prevention of sexual abuse of children as one of its main goals. The U.N. through its UNICEF organization has put together "The Convention on the Rights of the Child," which states a child has the right to grow up unmolested. It has been signed by most of the civilized countries of the world with one major exception, the Vatican.

There is no love in and even less humanity in any person who moves sexually abusing priests among parishes as easily as he would move a chess piece across a board. Men such as this can't possibly stake a claim to humanity or to the teachings of Jesus. Therefore, the imperative question is, "What caused these men: priests, bishops and cardinals, to shed their humanity and act in ways that defy human dignity?"

Cultural Inbreeding

The answer, for all who care to look, lies in the history of Catholic Church. Much has been written about the term culture. Culture is something that defines an individual or groups of individuals. It includes things like, beliefs, foods, language, dances, music, etc. Cultures also have traditions some of which can date back hundreds or even thousands of years. Rites of passage into manhood have long been a cultural tradition.

Circumcision is a good example. It goes back millennia. So it is safe to assume that if the same thing continuously occurs within the same group over hundreds or even thousands of years, it is deeply embedded in that culture. So let it be known that history tells us that the sexual abuse of children is a longstanding part of the culture of the clergy in the Roman Catholic Church.

The following are historical examples of this malevolent cultural practice recorded over a sixteen-hundred year period.

The Fourth Century: From the Council of Elvira 306: There were a host of Canons, internal church laws, which came out of this Ecumenical Council. Here are just two of many that speak to the subject of sexual abuse.[1]

18. Bishops, presbyters, and deacons, once they have taken their place in the ministry, shall not be given communion even at the time of death if they are guilty of sexual immorality. Such scandal is a serious offense.

71. Those who sexually abuse boys may not commune even when death approaches.

Laws are not written to protect children from things that don't occur and if the church enforced these laws today, the number of clerics receiving communion the world over would drop significantly.

The Eleventh Century: St. Peter Damian's Letter 31, the Book of Gomorrah (Liber Gomorrhianus), Randy Engel says it is "the most extensive treatment and condemnation by any Church Father of clerical pederasty and homosexual practices. [2] His manly discourse on the vice of sodomy in general and clerical homosexuality and pederasty in particular, is written in a plain and forthright style that makes it quite readable and easy to understand." [2]

Pierre J. Prayer translated Peter Damian's work and in his introduction, he makes this comment: "One of his consistent themes was an attack on the sexual immorality of the clergy and the laxness of the superiors who refused to take a strong hand against it." [3]

We can take away two things from this book. 1. The problem of sexual immorality had to be so widespread that Damian deemed it necessary to write this treatise in a time when writing was a tedious job done with quill and ink on very expensive paper. 2. If the Church Fathers had disagreed with Peter Damian, his treatise the on sexual immorality of the clergy would have never survived and he would never have attained sainthood.

The Seventeenth Century: From Karen Liebreich's book Fallen Order: "One of Fr. Calasanz's recruits in particular, Father Stephano Cherubini, was to prove a disaster. Cherubini was dogged throughout his career by allegations of inappropriate behaviour with pupils, but his powerful family ties and connections with the Inquisition made

Calasanz wary of expelling him. Instead, he invented that staple of the Catholic church in subsequent centuries when faced with paedophile priests - he promoted him, writing to the priest he charged with clearing this up: "I want you to know that your reverence's sole aim is to cover up this great shame in order that it does not come to the notice of our superiors"[4]

The Twenty-First Century: From the Boston Globe referring to Cardinal Law: "He knew about allegations that John J. Geoghan, the now-convicted child molester, had been attacking little boys and returned him to parish work nevertheless. Law knew that the Rev. Peter J. Frost was an admitted sex addict and child abuser and still held open the prospect of future ministry for him." [5]

Author's note: There are numerous books such as Sons of Perdition by Jay Nelson or Sex, Priests, and Secret Codes: The Catholic Church's 2,000 Year Paper Trail of Sexual Abuse by Doyle, Sipe, and Wal dedicated to chronicling clerical sexual abuse both over its long and sordid history as well as during specific periods.

We can therefore deduce the following about the culture of the church regarding clerical sexual abuse: Any member of the hierarchy who even attempts to claim ignorance of clerical sexual abuse or its history in the church is either a liar or an ignoramus.

Celibacy and complete Chastity are unattainable myths. If the combined force, intelligence and fear of God commanded by the church over a millennium cannot teach priests to adhere to their vows, the vow is impossible to keep. It is said that is repeatedly doing the same thing over and over again for centuries and expecting a different outcome is insanity. Celibacy and chastity belong under this definition.

Clerical child abuse has been going on uninterrupted in the RCC for a millennium and a half. These are not new crimes; just old ones getting new publicity. For the last thousand years, the tradition has been to gloss over and cover up the existence of violations of both celibacy and the sexual abuse of children. The hierarchy of the Catholic Church has passed the tradition of protecting priests at all costs down through the ages to where it has become a cultural policy.

The Depths of Depravity: Dehumanizing Actions

The culture of the RCC has been to totally ignore their victim's pain and suffering. There is not a shred of historical information that proves otherwise. The RCC has steadfastly refused to promote the healing and wellbeing of children who have fallen victim to predator priests. Even to this day, the church fights tooth and nail in their attempts to ignore their victims. Are these the acts of an organization with humanitarian goals or one that has been dehumanized? Certainly they do not follow the precepts of Jesus.

The too obvious questions are: "What kind of men would allow heinous crimes against the bodies and souls of children to go unpunished?" What kind of men would then leave these children to suffer in silence? Never once has a bishop said that he considered the children when transferring sexually abusing priests to a new parish. Heartless is a kind moniker. Inhumane is a better one. The less obvious and more important question is why would men allow these same crimes against humanity to persist over centuries? To really understand that question, you have to first understand the depths of depravity reached by priests committing these crimes before you can truly appreciate the inhuman actions of person that lets them continue unabated.

The detachment molesting priests are capable of borders on sociopathic; meaning there is no remorse for even the most monstrous of crimes. The following stories are true and the reader must remember these are not the worst. Propriety and respect for the reader prohibit going into graphic detail regarding the sordid crimes priests have committed upon the bodies of children. However, for those seeking verification, a quick search of the Internet reveals over three quarters of a million entries on the subject of clergy abuse. The query "survivor stories of clergy abuse" produces almost ninety thousand entries.

The Archdiocese of St. Paul and Minneapolis was accused of helping an Ecuadorian priest flee the United States in November of 2008 after he allegedly molested a 4-year-old girl in Minneapolis.[6]

A woman goes to her parish priest for counseling. She tells the priest that she wants to be a good Catholic, but is having a hard time because she was sexually assaulted by a priest as a young girl. This priest gains her confidence and uses her needs to get to her twin boys and sexually abuses both of them. One of the boys, as a result of the abuse, attempts suicide. As he lay in his hospital bed hovering between life and death with his mom at his side, who comes to her offering prayers and consolation? None other than her counselor, her parish priest, and her son's abuser, the same man who's sexual abuse drove the boy to attempt suicide in the first place!

Behavior like that defies any connection with either a conscience or humanity, yet it happened. Worse still is the abusing priest who has the unbridled audacity to say the funeral mass for one of his victims that succeeded in committing suicide. This behavior strongly mirrors that of the arsonist who delights in watching his flames devour a building.

Just as twisted as the above but on a different level is the priest who while buttoning the cassock of the young altar boy fondles the boy's genitals. Ten minutes later, he is using those same fingers to lift and consecrate a host. In yet another few minutes, he is using those same fingers to place the host on the tongues of adoring parishioners seeking communion with Jesus. He moves blithely from one despicable act to the next with no remorse, no conscience or one so suppressed as not to exist. He has no fear, not even the wrath of God. His abominable sacrilege and desecration of children and the host continues Sunday after Sunday.

How can anyone claiming ties to humanity perpetuate these acts by moving offending priests from parish to parish? Yet, bishops, cardinals and popes have done it as routinely as saying mass. First they ignored the complaints. Then, when the complaints grew too loud, they simply moved the priest to another unsuspecting parish, with unsuspecting parents and vulnerable children. With a fifteen hundred year history of sexually abusing children, the RCC can hardly expect us to believe they "Didn't know!" Bishops knew children were being raped, sodomized and molested, but simply did not care. Behavior such as this is both heartless and inhuman. For centuries, bishops have knowingly tossed children to predator priests as easily as throwing peanuts to an elephant. Consider the following: In Canada, there are over 50,000 aboriginal children missing. They either died or were murdered in residential schools across the country.

"An international tribunal found the government and several churches guilty of the crime of genocide. Ever since June, 1998, when an international tribunal in Vancouver found your government, the RCMP, and the Catholic, United, Anglican, and Presbyterian churches guilty of acts of Genocide against native people, the world has waited to see if your government and the churches in question would respond to the charges brought against you by survivors of the residential schools. Your government and these churches have shown by your silence that you do not dispute the charges of mass murder and Genocide being made against you.[7]"

The story from Ireland is just as bad.

In Ireland, several commissions on Clergy Sexual Abuse have filed their reports over the past few years and each report from the Ferns Report to the most recent Dublin Report unequivocally condemns the Roman Catholic Church for their dismal failure in dealing with priests who abuse. The reports deal with the thousands of Irish children abused while the bishops of the church in Ireland did nothing to put a halt to it.

Why is it that bishops have no fear? There are a couple of possibilities: either they know there is no God, think they are gods or they believe they will suffer no consequences because they were appointed by god. The first one is difficult to prove, but there is a plethora of evidence for the latter two. Defying criminal law, while hiding behind a false interpretation of "separation of church and state," bishops believe they are the only ones who can censure the criminal acts of a priest. Believing they are appointed by God, they act horrified when anyone has the effrontery to cast aspersions on their character and they have history on their side because of the thousands of cases where bishops knowingly shuffled pedophiles, to date not one has been jailed. Not one bishop has paid the consequences for the most egregious crimes against humanity dating back a thousand years.

Somewhere during first thousand years, after the Council of Elvira, the hierarchy realized there could be no such thing as a celibate priest and the stringent rules were relaxed. Concurrent with this knowledge, men in the hierarchy have lost touch with both their humanity and the teachings of Jesus.

The Culture of Power and Hubris

Cultural clerical inbreeding has wed the "god complex" with hubris. A person who is said to have a "god complex" does not believe he is God, but acts so arrogantly that he might as well believe he is a god or that he was appointed to act by a god" and hubris applies to any outrageous act or exhibition of pride or disregard for basic moral laws."

Hubris or the outrageous acts and total disregard for moral laws displayed by today's hierarchy are readily explained by the above. Now compare the definitions above to the passage below. It was written to the members of an organization known as the Conference of the Major Superiors of Men by their then Executive Director. These words, written shortly after Boston's sex scandal broke were truly prophetic. The organization's name alone should give the reader a preview of how high they hold themselves in their own esteem. The CMSM represents all the religious orders of priests. Behold the words of those who believe themselves the divinely appointed betters of the human race.

"The days of the pass or station house adjustment for Father or Brother by the Irish cop or prosecutor are over. Either we will learn to become more comfortable in the gaze of the rude and scoffing multitude (depending on our attitude) or we will be dragged kicking and screaming into a new future for religion and religious life"[8](italics are the author's emphasis)

The thought processes that allow priests to refer to the laity as the "rude and scoffing multitude" are the same ones that allow and even encourage priests to use children as sex objects. "Less than" is the operative concept; it allows the children to be treated as though they are mere baubles to be used, abused and discarded. This is the dehumanized effect: those who believe they are "better than" humanity are the ones who, in reality, lose their humanity. They suffer "the disconnect" of being separated from humanity by their vows so they had to conjure up a rationale to compensate for that disconnect. Nowhere is this false ideology more clearly stated than in Vehementer Nos an encyclical promulgated by Pious X in 1905.

"It follows that the Church is essentially an unequal society, that is, a society comprising two categories of persons, the Pastors and the flock, those who occupy a rank in the different degrees of the hierarchy and the multitude of the faithful. So distinct are these categories that with the pastoral body only rests the necessary right and authority for promoting the end of the society and directing all its members towards that end; the one duty of the multitude is to allow themselves to be led, and, like a docile flock, to follow the Pastors."[9]

Being chosen by God to lead sinners into the light goes a long way to rationalizing their separation from and superiority over humanity. But it only goes so far because it never satisfies the true itch.
.

In Genesis 2, God says, referring to Adam, "It is not good that the man should be alone." In Matt. 19:5 Jesus said, "Have you not read that he who made them from the beginning made them male and female, and said, "For this reason a man shall leave his father and mother and be joined to his wife, and the two shall become one flesh?" Leave it to the Catholic Church to countermand both the Father and the Son just as they have done in Matthew 18 where Jesus uses his harshest language to describe the fate of child abusers. Then again in Matt: 23: 9 where Jesus says: "And call no man your father on earth, for you have one Father, who is in heaven." Isn't it about time someone read this passage to the "Holy Father"? Hubris?

Much has been written about the need human beings have for intimacy. Studies have found that human babies needed physical and emotional contact in order to thrive. The operative word here is thrive. More than that, recent studies prove the need for intimacy continues into adulthood and those who are not afforded intimacy generally turn to addictions of all sorts. God instilled in man and woman the need for intimacy. The only organization that has refused to recognize this concept is the Roman Catholic Church. The Eastern Orthodox Church came to grips with it a long time ago.

The lack of intimacy created by the unfounded and unproven beliefs of the Roman Catholic Church about celibacy has created a unique brand of both hetero and homosexuality. The clerics that rule the church have created an institution of men and women, who because of their vows, can only indulge in unfulfilling sex. Whether with one another, one night stands, prostitutes, sexual abuse of children, adults, or pornography; they are all classic symptoms of those who lack intimacy in their lives. Contrary to what the church would have us believe, being married to the church doesn't fill that void. God put two sexes on the earth so man and woman would fulfill each other. Louise Hagget's Bingo Report [10] sites loneliness as the primary reason for breaking vows and what is loneliness but the lack of intimacy.

A prominent psychiatrist who worked for the church had this to say:
In fact, statements by Dr. Jay Feierman support a link between sexual repression and pedophilia. As a psychiatrist who has met with hundreds of pedophilic priests at a Catholic treatment center in New Mexico, Feierman is in a position to recognize the connection.
Feierman says celibacy is not "a natural state for humans to be in." Pointing to the celibacy requirement as a cause of clergy abuse of children, he explains: "If you tell a man that he's not allowed to have particular friends, he's not allowed to be affectionate,

he's not allowed to be in love, he's not allowed to be a sexual being, you shouldn't be surprised at anything that happens."[11]

"You shouldn't be surprised at anything that happens" and the RCC isn't, because it is the oldest continuous enclave for hetero and homosexual men seeking all forms of self gratifying sex. There is no other institution in the world with a longer, well documented, continuous history of the sexual abuse of children than the RCC. Their own records stand in testimony to this fact.

In either hetero or homosexual relationships where there is intimacy or the expectation of it, there is a commitment. A homosexual couple raising a child would be just as outraged at having their son or daughter defiled by a priest as would a heterosexual couple. Why, because they have what priests lack, a commitment, intimacy and love. By their very nature, human intimacy and a priest's commitment to his vows are mutually exclusive. Therefore attempts to seek intimacy through sexual gratification always fall short leaving the sex unfulfilling and the priest unfulfilled.

This failure, on a grand scale, to adhere to celibacy mandated that a rationale be concocted to excuse breaking the vow. Celibacy itself became one of the chief rationales; the excuse used for allowing exceptions. "Oh, you a good priest and it is so hard to keep your vows; say your confession and try not to do it again." The biggest coup in history for the hierarchy was the laity swallowing it hook, line and sinker. How many Catholics have said, "A priest is entitled to break a vow once in a while, after all they are only human." Cardinal George gave us the best known public example of this type of exemption in this quote:

Cardinal George said, "There is a difference between a moral monster like Geoghan," who preys in serial fashion, and an individual who, "perhaps under the influence of alcohol," engages in inappropriate behavior with "a 16- or 17-year-old young woman who returns his affections."[12]

Even this rationale couldn't soothe the conscience of the clerics. And so a grand philosophy had to be constructed; one that would forever blind or bind the conscience of priests and bishops. Enter the scion of the marriage between the God Complex and Hubris: the Dehumanizing Effect. This stated that all who received Holy Orders were called directly by God. The act of being selected directly by God made priests better than the rest. The myth of celibacy was the linchpin that proved priests were the betters of man. Ipso facto, the rude and scoffing multitude could be used and abused without penalty. (If anyone really thought God was calling these perverts to serve in the priesthood, they would all be running for the exit doors.) The irony is that this myth of being better than the rest is precisely why the hierarchy has been rendered soulless.

For centuries the hierarchy has had an ingrained attitude that there is nothing wrong with habitual dalliances by members of their priesthood with men, women and children. This thought process became a clerical tradition and the tradition became church policy.

67

It readily explains the process by which the hierarchy lost any semblance of humanity when dealing with children being raped, sodomized or molested by their priests. It took a proclamation by the pope in the sixteenth century to declare that Native Americans had a soul. Hitler referred to his idea of sub-humans as mud people. American slave owners declared slaves property. Religious orders call them, "the rude and scoffing multitude." Whoever the abuser, they all see their victims as: "less than," which makes any crime against them palatable.

Do priests really consider themselves to be divinely selected? Proof of the god complex theory comes to us from the surveys done to gather information for Louise Haggett's Bingo Report.[13] According to the survey, a full third of priests surveyed said they either agreed or strongly agreed with this statement: "I believe in priestly divinity" an additional 10% said they neither agreed nor disagreed with the statement.

A Different Hypothesis:

The late, great, erudite New York Senator and Catholic, Daniel Patrick Moynihan wrote an essay titled: Defining Deviance Down.[14] His premise was that society keeps lowering the bar by which they define deviant behavior. If he were alive, he would certainly understand how his work applies to the RCC especially this paragraph.

"In this pattern, a growth in deviancy makes possible a transfer of resources, including prestige, to those who control the deviant population. This control would be jeopardized if any serious effort were made to reduce the deviancy in question. This leads to assorted strategies for re-defining the behavior in question as not all that deviant, really."[15]

Moynihan's observations lead to a completely new perspective on the permissiveness of the Roman Catholic Church. The permissiveness pervasive in the church now has a purpose behind it: The bishop's control would be seriously jeopardized if any attempt were made to eliminate sexual deviants from the ranks of the priesthood. The greater the deviance allowed in the priesthood, (a virtual feudal system) the greater control and power the hierarchy exerts over its priests. This would certainly explain the unprecedented inhumanity exhibited by bishops towards children. Sexual abuse was redefined from a crime to a sin. Ephebophilia was split off from pedophilia to make sex crimes with post-pubescent boys a few degrees more palatable since a teenager is not a prepubescent boy or girl. (Defining deviance down as if there were a distinction in abuse) That distinction with post-pubescent boys was made to place the blame squarely on homosexual community within the priesthood totally ignoring the sexual abuse of teenaged girls by priests. The bishop's had a very clear choice, their power or children's lives. The bishops opted to keep their power by tightening their power over this group.

The hierarchy has an incredibly strong hold on its priests. Marketing 101 has the 4P's: Product, Price, Packaging and Promotion. The hierarchy of the RCC has its four P's for absolute power: Placement, Promotion, Penance and Pension. All four are controlled exclusively by either the bishop or the order's superior. The 4P's are strong enough strings to make most priests dance. It is the difference between being stationed in the inner city or a country club parish. The four P's are real power and very real control. Anyone of these strings when pulled by a superior can affect behavior. When all four are controlled by the same person, it is a recipe for total control. The four P's of hierarchal power explain a great deal of the global priestly silence, but they can't explain it all away. Enter Moynihan's theory of defining deviance down in order to maintain control.

Combine the 4P's of power with the concept of deviant control and you seal lips forever. Take an abusing priest of either homo or heterosexual nature. How much stronger is that priest's allegiance when the priest knows his bishop or cardinal will protect him? Defend him by every means available? Will keep him out of jail, out of site and then ship him to a new parish, a.k.a. hunting grounds, where he can once again ply his immoral trade?

The Code of Silence Testifies to These Truths

Edmond Burke said," All that is necessary for the triumph of evil is for good men to do nothing." This could be the motto of the Roman Catholic Church. One of the most astonishing and disturbing facts of the Clergy Abuse Scandal is the singular solidarity of both priests and bishops in refusing to speak out against their brothers who have abused children. This silence is a condemnation of the entire church and its leadership. Out of forty thousand priests in the United States, only a handful have ever publicly spoken out against clergy abuse. Only a handful have ever aided victims in their quest for justice. The only internationally known priest advocate for survivors is Fr. Tom Doyle. The silence of the priesthood is not only about the abuse, it also applies to the outrageous crimes committed by the hierarchy in their handling of clergy abuse cases. The bishops have brought down great scandal upon themselves, their priests and the church yet the majority of "good" priests remain silent.

The question begs itself, why this deafening silence from men of God? Crimes as heinous as the rape, sodomization and molestation of children should inspire outrage, yet there was and is only silence. The cover-ups by the hierarchy should have resulted in calls for removal, yet there was and is only silence. The monumental scandal and shame brought down upon the church should have brought screams of anguish from every pulpit, yet there was and is only silence. Has every priest, like their bishops, lost every spark of humanity, been so dehumanized as to be indifferent? Are we to believe that in the thousands of rectories across the United States not one good priest is upset about this? What compels men of God to maintain their wholesale silence?

As striking as the silence of the priests is regarding clerical sexual abuse, it is just as striking on the subject of homosexuality. The RCC is one of the most vocal anti-homosexual religions in the world. The tirades let loose from the pope on down to the pulpit on the evils of homosexuality are legendary. They are strong, inciting, inflammatory and resolute in their condemnation. Yet at the same time, the website Religious Tolerance [16] offers, from a wide variety of sources, various projections (anywhere from 15% to 75%) on the number of homosexual men in the priesthood. Their conclusion is that about a third of the priests in the United States are homosexual. Is that anything new? I refer the reader to the church's own history mentioned earlier.

How must these priests of the homosexual persuasion suffer listening to the constant tirades streaming down from a hierarchy whose own ranks are replete with homosexuals? How does the hierarchy tie the tongues of good men and why do good men allow their tongues to be tied? Fear and shame are the names of the game.

These Facts Underscore the Truth

Scientists, in order to test a theory, keep looking for the one thing which will disprove their theory. If none of the known facts refute the theory, it is considered a truth until such time as proof is offered to the contrary. So let it be with the following statements:

The RCC has known about priestly sexual abuse within its ranks and has actively covered it up for over one thousand years.

The RCC is the only organization in the Western World that has had men living with men on a continuous basis for fifteen hundred years.

The RCC has had some of the world's most brilliant minds working on their behalf during the last fifteen hundred years as priestly philosophers, scientists and writers, yet none of them have figured out how to make celibacy work.

The priesthood of the RCC has had active heterosexuals, homosexuals and child abusers in the clergy for over a thousand years. At varying times in their history, the size and scandal of one or more of the above groups has reached epidemic proportions.

At various times in church history, there has been a public rebellion against the clerical decadence that became pervasive. We are currently in one of these periods.

The RCC knows more than any other organization in history about trying to keep men celibate during the last millennium. Yet they still fail. God's design is too strong for church doctrine. Judging by the fact that celibacy and chastity are still vows, it is obvious that there exists another reason to keep unholy vows. Knowing full well these vows can't be kept by normal people, why does the RCC keep them as well as the sordid sexual perversions they have produced. The new hypothesis is the RCC has kept chastity and celibacy as vows for no other reason than to exert control over the members of the priesthood as in the manner stated by Moynihan in Defining Decadence Down. [17]

This is the foundation of mutual protection as evidenced in Crimens Solicitationis,18 (the crime of soliciting) which turns all reported sexual abuse into a "Secret of the Holy Office," the pope and essential gags everyone who has knowledge of the crime under the penalty of excommunication. How far will members of the hierarchy go to protect sexually abusing priests? Up until now, Cardinal Law had been the poster boy, but he has been replaced by Cardinal Roger Mahony who has been fighting for a dozen years to keep the names of predator priests a secret. We've already discussed the moral turpitude of a man who knowingly protects child abusers. This is a sterling example of the lengths the cardinal has gone to prevent the names of abusive priests from being made public. It is an excerpt from a motion filed by the archdiocese of Los Angeles to squirm out of a commitment it made to survivors when they settled the sexual abuse claims against it

The relationship between a Roman Catholic priest and his employer, the Archdiocese in this case, is a uniquely close, all-encompassing one, in which the employer is also the direct spiritual superior of the employee, and between them there can be no secrets."[19]

Therefore, as per the words of the cardinal himself, all bishops and cardinals have tacit knowledge of all the actions of sexually abusive priests in their employ. Once again, the often repeated words of the hierarchy, "I didn't know!" ring hollower by the moment.

The child abusers only account for a minority of priests. What about the rest of the priests, does deviance bind them to the bishop in the same manner? Yes, but the deviance is not child abuse, it is the deviation from their vows. The bishops know who is philandering with whom and their sexual preferences, which places the majority in the same boat as the minority. Once you compromise yourself each and every deviance has to be accepted. The bishops have to protect everyone including those with the most egregious sexual appetites. The price for this protection is the priest's absolute silence regardless of the shame attached. Appointing a confessor further guarantees the silence under the seal of confession.

The Real Threat of Homosexual Priests to the Church

This also explains why homosexual priests stay in an organization that openly condemns them? What buys their silence? The same 4P's plus the deviant control and the fear of being exposed as a homosexual? How does a good hardworking homosexual priest feel living and working among parishioners who have been conditioned to believe that homosexuality is either an abomination or an aberration? How painful is it for them to read that a bishop has refused communion to supporters of homosexuals with no more cause than an identifying ribbon? How painful is it to know that the opportunistic sex homosexual priests are forced to partake in, because of celibacy, carries greater risks such as a higher incidence of Aids than the general population? This is high price to pay for an attempt at intimacy.

Has anyone wondered why the church is so adamantly opposed to legitimizing homosexual unions through marriage? One very real possibility is that homosexual marriages present a genuine threat to the priesthood and therefore the church itself. Over the past twenty years, homosexuality has integrated into the mainstream. It is shunned by a few, tolerated by some and accepted by most of the general population. Since Vatican II, many heterosexual priests have left the priesthood to get married. They left for the intimacy that was designed into their beings and fulfilled their natural needs.

When homosexual priests realize that they too can live a shameless life with a lifetime partner, a commitment, and intimacy among the general public, the priesthood will lose its appeal as a safe haven for homosexuals. This bears repeating: the priesthood will lose its appeal as a safe haven for homosexual men. When homosexual priests start to leave the priesthood for committed relationships outside the priesthood, they will leave the church in critical condition. Along with that, the number of homosexual men needing refuge in the priesthood will drop too.

Behavior no longer considered deviant, equates with no more power. The RCC is pulling out all the stops to prevent the legalization of homosexual marriages because its future depends on it. If it doesn't succeed, it is doomed to atrophy. Their recent bid to attract Anglican priests upset by the ordination of homosexuals is nothing more than attempt to shore up their dwindling clerical numbers. Without homosexual priests, the church will deteriorate at an even faster pace spurred on by an extremely critical shortage of priests.

Portends for the Future

Someone once said, "Hope springs eternal." In the case of the RCC, we have to have serious doubts. Despite fifteen hundred years of evidence to the contrary, celibacy and chastity are still required as means of assuring control of the priesthood. The inhumanity that it has created has been catastrophic. The following is your assurance that nothing will change in the near future.

The pope was head of the Congregation for the Doctrine of Faith for some twenty odd years and during those years maintained the culture's status quo. He says he was horrified by the stories he read as head of the CDF. As pope, he has assured the maintenance of the status quo by appointing Archbishop Levada to his former post. Jesus predicted this well when he said, "Woe to you, scribes and Pharisees, hypocrites! for you traverse sea and land to make a single proselyte, and when he becomes a proselyte, you make him twice as much a child of hell as yourselves."

Since past behavior is pretty much indicative of future behavior, we need to look at Levada's record regarding sexual abuse to determine if he is a party to the culture that has dominated and perverted the Catholic Church over the past thousand years. Let's start and end with the case of Bishop Ziemann which defines the depths to which

Cardinal Levada will sink. Ziemann combines the elitist culture with the lack of humanity we've been discussing. Bishop Ziemann was arrested while receiving oral sex from a priest in his own car. To make matters worse, Ziemann forced this priest wear a pager so that he could be summoned for sex at the Ziemann's whim. According to the priest's testimony, Bishop Ziemann had twice given him Venereal Disease infections. When Ziemann left the diocese of Santa Rosa, he left it sixteen million dollars in the red. Consider the following from the San Francisco Weekly.

"He has been protected by and remains intimately connected with three influential fellow hierarchs, including San Francisco Archbishop William J. Levada. It was Levada who presided over Ziemann's skipping away from Santa Rosa with criminal impunity after church officials refused to fully cooperate with authorities. Ziemann's mentor and chief patron is Los Angeles Cardinal Roger M. Mahony, whose problems with pedophile priests rival the scandal-plagued Boston archdiocese's. The other member of the troika is Manuel Moreno, who until his surprise resignation this month for health reasons, was bishop of Tucson, Ariz., and in whose diocese Ziemann was given refuge at the Holy Trinity Monastery... Moreno has a long and tawdry record in covering up for pedophile priests...

At a time when someone else might have tossed him to the wolves, Levada lauded Ziemann to the bitter end in Santa Rosa. The day Ziemann resigned, shortly after a lurid audiotape surfaced exposing the bishop's illicit relationship with the priest, Levada extolled his friend as someone who had done much to help the diocese. It didn't seem to matter that, right up until the revelation of the bishop's tape-recorded apology to Father Jorge Hume Salas for forcing him to engage in sex, Ziemann's personal attorney proclaimed him to be "a very holy man" and the bishop steadfastly denied any misconduct."[20]

Bishop Ziemann subsequently passed away retaining all his faculties.

Why did Benedict XVI pick Lavada to replace him as head of the CDF? His unwavering loyalty, no matter how disgraceful, to a brother bishop and the church seems like the most logical answer. Silence is the golden rule. Levada has publicly proven the depths to which he is willing to sink in order to protect a fellow bishop from criminal prosecution. His is a sterling quality, a la Bernie Law, which is obviously deeply appreciated by the Pope. When handling future accusations of sexual abuse against priests and bishops, Levada has already shown how low he can be expected to drop the deviance bar. With Levada at the helm of the CDF, the culturally imbedded concept that bishops have the right and obligation to cover-up for abusers will carry on into the future.

Not being satisfied with Levada and Law, the pope has recently given Bishop Raymond Burke a slot at the Vatican. This is a man who handed out excommunications like pedophiles hand out candy. Like the queen of hearts in Alice and Wonderland, he ran around yelling, "To hell with your souls!" Burke is noted for his ability to silence victims as noted here.

But some members of Raymond Burke's former flock paint a far different portrait of the erstwhile bishop of La Crosse. If cases of clergy sex abuse were few and far between, they say, it was because Burke was a master at keeping a lid on them. Several victims who claim they were abused by priests in La Crosse tell Riverfront Times they were stonewalled by Burke, who declined to report their allegations to local authorities. And while some of his fellow church officials nationwide were reaching hefty settlements with victims, Raymond Burke was unyielding in his refusal to negotiate with victims' rights groups. He declined to make public the names of priests who were known to have been abusive, and he denied requests to set up a victims' fund. Most strikingly, Riverfront Times has learned, while bishop in La Crosse Burke allowed at least three priests to remain clerics in good standing long after allegations of their sexual misconduct had been proven -- to the church, to the courts and, finally, to Burke himself.[21]

Burke has recently been appointed by the pope to an office that will handle the worst cases of the clergy sexual abuse as the prefect of the Supreme Tribunal of the Apostolic Signatura. Once again, we have the pope planning for the future and insuring the status quo. What chance is there of change with men like these in positions of power?

Conclusion
The unified theory of clergy abuse shows how supposedly good men are so hypocritical in their nature, that they can one day preach justice and morality before a packed cathedral and the next day transfer a serial child rapist to another parish as easily a donning a vestment. It also explains the "less than" treatment of victims caused by the loss of humanity and exposes the sick culture that has put these values in place..

This is not only the pinnacle of hypocrisy, but it is so much more than that. It is about a totally corrupted culture that not only trains men to behave in this manner, but which has become the only quality that will ensure their promotion.

And what of the Catholic laity? Ashamed, embarrassed, angry, distraught, hurt, victims of a culture that uses fear and human sexuality to maintain control; what is to become of them? They have been trained well to pay, pray, and obey. Those that wake up to hypocrisy will leave discontented, others will pray for change, some will try to affect it, and the rest will pray and pay regardless of how outrageous the acts of the hierarchy become because more than anything else in the world, they want to go to heaven. It is thus fitting to close with a line from Defining Deviance Down. "A society that loses its sense of outrage is doomed to extinction."[22] So is the Catholic Church!

Reference

1. From: The Council of Elvira, ca. 306, retrieved November 26, 2009
http://faculty.cua.edu/pennington/Canon%20Law/ElviraCanons.htm

2. Engel, Randy. St. Peter Damian's Book of Gomorrah:A Moral Blueprint for Our Times - Part I Nov. 26, 2009 Retrieved from: http://www.ourladyswarriors.org/articles/damian1.htm

3. Damian, Peter. The book of Gomorah an Eleventh Century Treatise Against Clerical Homosexual Practices. Translated by Pierre J. Payer. November 26, 2009 Retrieved from:
http://books.google.com/books?id=hr4VAAAAMAAJ&pg=PA11&lpg=PA11&dq=eleventh+century+clerical+abuse&source=web&ots=kBcxq4YpkG&sig=PwlMgSfUtRxys6KqhwrSJNf4GSE&hl=en&sa=X&oi=book_result&resnum=1&ct=result#PPA12,M1

4. Liebreich, Karen. Fallen Order – November 27, 2009 Retrieved from:
http://www.liebreich.com/LDC/HTML/Books/FallenOrder.html

5. Farragher, Thomas. Admission of awareness damning for Law. Nov. 26, 2009.
http://www.boston.com/globe/spotlight/abuse/stories3/121402_admission.htm

6. Estrada, Herón. Archdiocese helped priest flee, suit says. Nov. 26, 2009
http://www.startribune.com/local/stpaul/28150429.html?elr=KArks:DCiUnP::DE8c7PiUiD3aPc:_Yyc:aUU

7. Annett, Kevin. Open letter, Nov. 26, 2009 Retrieved from: http://signatoryindian.tripod.com/id80.html

8. Keating, Ted, From the Executive Director. July/August Bulletin, 2002 Retrieved from:
http://www.cmsm.org/index.shtml Author's note, site is no longer open to public.

9. Pious X. Vehementer Nos. (encyclical on the French law of separation) 1905, retrieved from
http://jlngalls.com/holy_father/pius_x/encyclicals/documents/hf_p-x_enc_11021906_vehementer-nos_en.html   Nov. 26, 2009

10. Hagget, L. The Bingo Report, Mandatory Celibacy and the Clergy. CSRI Books (October 20, 2005)

11. Sommer, J. Clerical Celibacy and Pedophilic Priests. Nov. 27, 2009
http://www.humanismbyjoe.com/clerical_celibacy_and_pedophilic.htm

12. Wilgoren, J. Scandals in the Church: The Lay Members; In Chicago, Group Urges A Suspension of Donations. NYTimes, Published: Saturday, April 27, 2002,
http://query.nytimes.com/gst/fullpage.html?res=940DEEDA103EF934A15757C0A9649C8B63&partner=rssnyt&emc=rss

13. Ibid, 9

14. Moynihan, D. P. Defining Deviancy Down. American Scholar (Winter 1993) Retrieved from:
http://www2.sunysuffolk.edu/formans/DefiningDeviancy.htm

15. Ibid,

16. Homosexual orientation among Roman Catholic priests. Nov. 27, 2009. Retrieved from:
http://www.religioustolerance.org/hom_rcc.htm

17. Ibid, 14

18. Wikipedia, Crimens Sollicictations. Retrieved from
http://en.wikipedia.org/wiki/Crimen_sollicitationis_%28document%29 Nov. 26, 2009

19. City of Angels Blog, October 1, 2008 Retrieved from:
http://cityofangels13.blogspot.com/2008/10/objection-to-transfer-of-personnel.html

20. Russell, R. Bishop Bad Boy. San Francisco Weekly, March 19, 2003 Retrieved from: www.bishop-accountability.org/news/2003_03_19_Russell_BishopBad.htm

21. Gay, M. Immaculate Deception. Riverfront Times, August 25, 2004, Retrieved from:
http://www.bishop-accountability.org/news3/2004_08_25_Gay_ImmaculateDeception_Raymond_Bornbach_etc.htm

22. Ibid, 14

"But Lord, I'm supposed to be the next Pope!"

A short story

Sitting in his plush recliner, the rotund cardinal had just finished a fine hand-rolled, mildly scented cigar. He was fascinated with watching the bright red ember on its tip slowly die. A true cigar aficionado knows you never put out a cigar, you let it exhaust itself. As was his want, he watched the white smoke emanating from the cigar while dreaming of the day the white smoke would be for him a signal that the white hat was his to wear for the rest of his life. The cardinal watched the cigar with an unusual interest this night. He reached for his pewter stein emblazoned with his coat of arms holding the last chilled remnants of his favorite imported beer. He relished using the last swig of the night as a mouthwash rolling it over and under his tongue while swishing it between his teeth. There was something about commingling the tastes of the beer and cigar that delighted him.

As he reached for the stein with his left hand he felt an intense pain; as if a white hot poker had suddenly been thrust under his arm. The pain radiated down his arm, up to his shoulder, under his ample chin and across his chest all at the same time. He froze believing if he moved but an inch, his chest would explode. In that instant, his eyes zeroed in on his cigar. A tiny puff of white smoke signaled the last ember from the lighted end had just expires and with it, he realized, could be his chance for the white hat.

Suddenly everything became very hazy, out of proportion, but then slowly things began to come back into focus. He felt like he was waking up from a hangover, wondering where he was and trying to think how much he had to drink. Slowly, he remembered watching TV and puffing on his cigar with beer in hand. Then panic set in as the memory of the sharp pain in his chest resurfaced. Did I die, are they working on me, is this an out of body experience, surely god knows I'm to be the next pope? As these thoughts raced through his mind, his surroundings began taking on solid form.

The cardinal found himself sitting at a table across from a nun whose most remarkable feature was her eyes. They held him transfixed. Staring into them he felt the full range of emotions they elicited. They were at once peaceful, volatile, knowing, understanding, fiery, firm and deep. He thought to himself, this must be what it is like to view the universe and then dismissed the idea. She remained silent while he stared into her eyes watching and waiting as his discomfort grew.

When he could take no more, the Cardinal demanded, "Who are you sister? Where am I and what am I doing here? She simply replied, "Look inside yourself for those answers.

Look Sister, I'm a cardinal and a sure bet to be next pope. Now tell me what is going on here. Looking around the room he said tersely, "Where the hell is the door? How did I get in if there's no door? What kind of game are you playing here?" "The door to hell is closer than you think," she said with a smile.

Let me guess the cardinal bellowed, "I've been kidnapped by the Leadership Conference of Religious Women? The LCRW is behind this is that it?

What could nuns possibly gain from kidnapping you the woman asked calmly?

A lot because they know I'm destined to be the next pope and when that happens, they'll have to go back to being obedient servants of the Church adhering to church doctrine or leave! Now let me out of here!

Fire flashed from behind the nun's eyes and the cardinal felt an unnatural power behind those strange eyes.

Tell me cardinal the lady asked in a soft voice. Have you ever read the Gospels?

Don't be ridiculous of course I have.

No, I mean have you ever really read them?

Why do you ask?

Because if you had read and understood them, you would know that the lives of nuns working with the poor, sick, hungry and the unwanted castoffs of society more closely resemble the ministry of Jesus than that of any bishop sitting around comfortably in a leather recliner smoking cigars and drinking beer.

Listen Sister, I don't need any criticism from you about my lifestyle. In this whole world, there are only three hundred cardinals controlling over a billion Catholics. You have no idea how hard I worked to get what I've got. You've no idea what it takes to run a parish, diocese or an entire archdiocese. I'm entitled to what I've got, I've earned it. You've taken the vow of obedience and I'm ordering you to fulfill your vow and let me out of here. Now!

I'll say one thing for you; you certainly are bossy for someone who doesn't know where they are or how they got here.

How do you think I got where I am? Not by being an indecisive wimp! I'm no namby-pamby nun dealing with school kids. I deal with real problems. I did what I was told and now I do the telling. I'll tell you what, you play ball with me and I'll make you the head of the LCRW. That post will be open soon and you can have it; just tell me who put me here and how to get out!

"You'll be going soon enough," she said. At the same moment her sentence ended the cardinal felt a distinct pull and everything became scrambled again as if he were watching a cable channel that wasn't in his package. The picture was skewed, zigzagged and out of proportion. When the cardinal's vision came back into focus, the nun was gone and he found himself in front of a Girl Scout. There was something vaguely familiar about her, but he didn't think about it long enough to recognize it.

Where did the nun go? What's going on here? He demanded of the girl.

It looks like you were hit with the paddles again, she said in the quiet voice of a twelve-year-old.

What do you mean paddles? Who hit me? What are you talking about?

They say the spirit is still attached to the body for a while after death and sometimes it can be pulled back into the body if the doctors are successful in restarting the heart.

"And you're telling me that's what's happening to me?" The cardinal asked giving the young girl an incredulous look.

Would you believe me if I said yes?

Look you little brat, this is not a game. I don't know what you are, who you are or what you and that nun are up to, but I'm not going to put up with it any longer, he shouted. Suddenly he saw the fire in her eyes. It was the same fire as the nun's. Feeling himself losing control and leery of doing so until he had more information, the cardinal shifted tactics. Changing his countenance he wore his biggest broadest smile and beamed it at the young Girl Scout. Tell me young lady, what is your name?

Mary, she replied.

Nice name, Mary, for a pretty young girl like yourself. Tell me Mary do you obey your parents when they tell you to do something?

"Most of the time," she replied.

Now there's a truthful and honest young lady. I like that in young girls. Tell me, are you Catholic?

No, not anymore.

Why do you say, not anymore?

Have you ever read the Gospels?

I'm a cardinal, what is a little girl going to tell me about the Gospels?

Only that Jesus loved children and I know He wouldn't let some stupid priest say we can't use the church hall for Girl Scout meetings anymore!

Little girls shouldn't be calling priests stupid young lady! There are things you are too young to understand like the importance of church doctrine and adhering to it. There are more important things in Catholicism than little girls running around in green uniforms.

That's not what Jesus would say and by the way, if I'm too young to understand your doctrine, how come I'm not too young to understand the doctrines you accuse the Girl Scouts of accepting?

We'll have to discuss that in more detail some other time, right now I've got to get out of here.

There's more said the girl matter-of-factly; I was raped by Fr. Becker!

The cardinal's face went ashen for just a second. Then he roared, "Jesus Christ Almighty!" That's what this is all about! The nuns, the Girl Scouts and now clergy abuse, I must be dreaming this nightmare he said pinching himself in the hopes of waking up. "Did SNAP put you up to this?" he bellowed. Then his mind started to swirl. Have I been kidnapped by SNAP, the nuns or the Scouts? Is this another nightmare induced by mixing Jameson's and beer; is this a bad version of the Christmas Carol? His mind was racing trying to put facts together. What was that she said about the body's connection to the spirit? Just as he was trying to put his finger on it, his vision instantly became a scrambled screen again. When it cleared he was hovering over a body in what looked like an operating room. As he looked closer, he saw the body lying on a table was his own. There he was with his chest bared, surrounded by doctors and one was yelling "clear!" as he placed two paddles his chest.

He watched from above as his body jumped and twitched; simultaneously he felt another tug. Suddenly, he was back at the table, another tug and he was back looking down at his body from above. He heard the word clear again and feeling like a ping pong ball was back at a disjointed table with a new figure sitting there. This person had outline of a man and as his vision cleared, he took note that the face was the same as every depiction of Jesus Christ he had ever seen.

The cardinal looked at the man seated across from him in awe. Then he noticed something about the eyes, but he dismissed it. "Jesus is that you?" he asked.

Yes, in a bodily form that you would easily recognize was the reply

"Thank God!" uttered the cardinal. I mean, well you know what I mean anyhow thank you he said ever so reverently. Now listen he said, as if he was confiding in his closest friend, I'm not exactly sure of what's going on here. But if it is what I think it is, I need your help. If this is a dream you have to wake me up and if its not, well you have to put me back in my body on earth.

"Why is that so important?" replied Jesus.

Because I'm next in line to be the pope! I will initiate the changes that will bring our church back to its former glory. The church on earth is falling apart, the laity doesn't listen, the nuns are rebelling and it needs a strong hand, my hand, to reinforce the doctrines that will bring them all back into the fold. I've been working behind the scenes to get these things done for you, but you probably knew that and that's why we're having this conversation. If I leave now, there's no telling when you'll get another chance to make things right in your church.

It is my understanding that you are a firm believer in the doctrine of moral authority. Is that true?

Yes, Lord. When we get everyone following doctrine again, you will see how your church on earth will grow.

Where do you get your authority for these doctrines of faith and morals that you cling to?

From you Lord. It is from your divine inspiration that the pope and the bishops speak. We speak with your authority on all matters of faith and morals.

I see, and what about those bishops on earth that are sinners, criminals and have no more morals than a hungry hyena. Do they speak for me too?

Of course Lord, you are only too familiar with the foibles of mankind. Where are you going to get men who are not sinners?

So if a bishop is a philanderer, child molester, thief, hypocrite, murderer or given to any other such unsavory devices; he still speaks for me in matters of faith and morals? Is that what you're telling me?

If you want to propagate the faith, it can't be any other way. The hierarchy, right or wrong must be listened to because your guidance is always, as you promised, with us.

And what are the faithful supposed to think?

That's the point; they'll think whatever we tell them to think because you provide, through the Doctrine of Divine Inspiration, our power and regardless of how they feel about the actions of the hierarchy, they will never abandon you!

So you use my authority to enforce your own ends?

Not our ends Lord, it is for your greater glory!

And the millions that have left the church over the past decade; did they leave because of hierarchal hypocrisy?

No Lord, the fault lies not with the hierarchy, it is the laity; they left because they refuse to accept your doctrine. It is too rigorous for them. I will rebuild your church starting with the devout faithful and build it from there. Just give me the chance.

I haven't heard this kind of asinine rationalization since Leo X tried to justify to me his extorting money for indulgences. The rational was that since he had the authority to forgive sins he could forgive sins in return for money; money that he used to further the materialistic designs of a corrupt church. Is there anything you know about me that would lead you to believe that I would trade forgiveness for mere pieces of shiny metal?

Barely audible, the cardinal answered, "No, but on earth, we need those, as you call them, shiny pieces of metal to continue the work of your church.

Leo craved the shiny metal; you and your kind worship at the altar of dead presidents! Cardinal, have you ever read the gospels?

 "That question again!" the cardinal said unable to hide the irritation in his voice. Of course I've read the Gospels, why do you ask?

I was rather hoping that you answered no thus allowing me the opportunity to attribute your arrogance to your ignorance.

Tiny beads of sweat started to form on the cardinal's head and his voice had a distinct tremble to it like that of a child responding to a scolding by a displeased parent. Maybe I missed a passage or two. Which parts are you referring to?

I was referring to Luke 19:22: when I said, "Out of thine own **mouth** will I judge thee, thou wicked servant. Thou knowest that I was an austere man, taking up that I laid not down, and reaping that I did not sow."

Or if you have trouble understanding Luke, how about Matt. 15:8-11: "This people draweth nigh unto me with their mouth, and honoureth me with their lips; but their heart is far from me. But in vain they do worship me, teaching for doctrines the commandments of men. And he called the multitude, and said unto them, Hear, and understand: Not that which goes into the mouth that defiles a man; but that which cometh out of the mouth defiles a man."

An evil tree cannot bear good fruit and I cannot abide in an evil heart. How dare you assume that I would ever condone evil or give divine inspiration to either a hypocrite or criminal!

Seeing the fire in the Lords eyes, the cardinal remembered where he had seen that fire before. It was in the eyes of the nun and the Girl Scout and realizing it caused the cardinal to shake like a leaf in a windstorm.

Did I ever say in the Gospels that my kingdom was earthbound?

"Not that I recall," said the cardinal.

But didn't you just say that you would restore my church to it former glory on earth?

You wear red to symbolize that you would shed your blood for the pope, would you shed your blood for me?

"Of course!" said the cardinal.

Would you shed the blood of others for me?

"Of course!" said the cardinal.

In all of the Gospels, I never once shed blood! Likewise, is there anything in the Gospels that would lead you to believe I'd pay money to a child raping, soul murdering, criminal, and son of perdition just because I wanted nothing more to do with him? Did I not chase the moneychangers from the temple?

Yes Lord!

What do you think I would do to priests raping children in my church?
"It would be better for them to have a millstone hung from their neck?"

Exactly!

The cardinal momentarily smiled knowing he had finally gotten one right and then said, "But Lord, they are bankrupting our church!"

And the Lord responded, "Consider the ravens: for they neither sow nor reap; which neither have storehouse nor barn; and God feedeth them: how much more are ye

83

better than the fowls?" Don't you know my kingdom has no walls; my kingdom has no bounds, no edifices, and is not limited by material either fine or coarse? My kingdom lies within the heart and soul of both man and woman and costs not.

The cardinal was about to respond when he felt another strong tug and once again things became scrambled. The Lord, the table and the room became fuzzy. At the same time in the hospital, a white uniformed nurse made the sign of the cross, reverently bent over, said a prayer, kissed the cardinal's ring affectionately and pulled a sheet as white as her uniform over his head. Then she smiled and in an almost prayerful voice said, "I guess you'll be having breakfast with the lord this morning!

The Litany of the Laity: "But, that's not my Church!"

Mary, having heard the cries of the suffering children and the prayers of a laity in the throes of turmoil, intercedes on their behalf with Jesus. He too is exceedingly dismayed by what his church has become, the hierarchy's adamant refusal to change, the poor disenfranchised faithful, and decides to take action. He summons the Furies, whose job it is to punish those who break sacred trusts by sending them to, Judecca, which is a section of Dante's Ninth Circle of hell reserved for those who, by betraying their God, their vows, and humanity, have committed crimes with great historical and societal consequences. The Furies are relentless in their pursuit of these defilers of faith and never stop pursuing either them or those who support them.

When the Furies are in his midst, Jesus charges them to seek out the laity and spell out the crimes of the hierarchy to them. Knowing full well the capacity of Catholics to rebuff the verbalization of hierarchal crimes as "Church Bashing," and remembering, Doubting Thomas, Jesus admonishes the Furies to only mention crimes that have made headline news over the past ten years concentrating on the ones that have most recently been publicized, are Internet searchable and have been confirmed by the press thereby leaving little doubt in the laity's mind as to the true nature of their hierarchy. In keeping with their task, the Furies have gathered the laity and are reciting the litany of hierarchal crimes against children, law, society and God. The laity responds with its own litany.

The Furies: A couple of weeks ago in Cardinal Dolan's old diocese, Milwaukee, according to Judge Susan V. Kelley, the depositions of bishops Weakland and Sklba contained material so "scandalous", that she would not release them to the public, apparently afraid of the impact they will have on the church's reputation and ability to function as a business.

Parishioners: But, that's not my church!

The Furies: Then whose church is it?

The Furies: The Catholic Church working with dictatorial government authorities took babies from political dissidents and gave them to couples they deemed to be acceptable parents.

Parishioners: But, that's not my church!

The Furies: Then whose church is it?

The Furies: The Catholic Church sold babies for a profit in Spain, Ireland, and Australia.

Parishioners: But, that's not my church!

The Furies: Then whose church is it?

The Furies: The Catholic Church working for the Canadian Government has been recognized as an active participant of the genocide of Native North American Children. Parishioners: But, that's not my church!

The Furies: Then whose church is it?

The Furies: The Catholic Church through its Vatican Bank has been accused of laundering money.

Parishioners: But, that's not my church!

The Furies: Then whose church is it?

The Furies: Earlier this year, the largest Catholic publishing company in Germany, Weltbild, owned by German Bishops, with 1.7 billion Euros in sales, was forced to disclose it has been publishing pornographic novels for years. The biggest source of revenue is from what the bishops called Erotic novels; others have labeled such titles as, "Sluts Boarding School and Lawyer's Whore," porn!

Parishioners: But, that's not my church!

The Furies: Then whose church is it?

The Furies: In Ireland, the Catholic Church forced young women into servitude for years just because they were pregnant, they're parents couldn't afford to raise them or because they were too good looking.

Parishioners: But, that's not my church!

The Furies: Then whose church is it?

The Furies: Over the past several years, the behavior of hierarchy of the Catholic Church in failing to deal with clergy sexual abuse has been condemned by Grand Juries across the United States and three separate commissions in Ireland.

Parishioners: But, that's not my church!

The Furies: Then whose church is it?

The Furies: The Catholic Church is a global purveyor of the crime of sexual abuse against children with credible cases of clerical sexual abuse reported in over forty countries around the world. It has also sent known pedophiles from one country to another to protect them.

Parishioners: But, that's not my church!

The Furies: Then whose church is it?

The Furies: The Catholic Church has seminaries where local bishops have sexually abused young seminarians.

Parishioners: But, that's not my church!

The Furies: Then whose church is it?

The Furies: The Austrian seminary of Sankt Pölten was found to have over 40,000 pornographic photos on their computer system including bestiality and child pornography.

Parishioners: But, that's not my church!

The Furies: Then whose church is it?

The Furies: Currently in Kansas City, a bishop is on trial for failure to report a priest who was found with child pornography on his computer.

Parishioners: But, that's not my church!

The Furies: Then whose church is it?

The Furies: Currently in Philadelphia, lurid details of sexual abuse and their cover-up by a cardinal are released on a daily basis as the trial of Msgr. Lynn progresses.

Parishioners: But, that's not my church!

The Furies: Then whose church is it?

The Furies: Recently a Canadian, a bishop was arrested for bringing child pornography into the country on his computer.

Parishioners: But, that's not my church!

The Furies: Then whose church is it?

The Furies: In Palm Beach, Fl., two successive bishops J. Keith Symons and Anthony J. O'Connell were allowed to retire after admitting to sexual abuse, one of them with seminarians.

Parishioners: But, that's not my church!

The Furies: Then whose church is it?
The Furies: Last year, Roger Vangheluwe, a Belgium bishop admitted to abusing his two nephews, the Pope Benedict XVI allowed him to retire.

Parishioners: But, that's not my church!
The Furies: Then whose church is it?

The Furies: The Pope Benedict XVI made this statement at the World Youth Day in Australia, "I ask all of you to support and assist your bishops, and to work together with them in combating this evil. Victims should receive compassion and care, and those responsible for these evils must be brought to justice."

Parishioners: Now that's my church!

The Furies: But, that's not your church!

The Furies: The Catholic Church has excommunicated bishops over matters of doctrine, but has yet to laicize a single bishop for their personal sexual abuse or for covering up the sexual abuse of priests in their charge no matter how heinous the act.

Parishioners: But, that's not my church!

The Furies: If this is not your church, whose church is it?

Parishioners: But, that's not my church! My church is my parish community. We know each other, we love each other, help each other and we believe in and live the Gospels.

The Furies: Why have you let the hierarchy bring such shame down upon you? According to Matthew, Jesus said: "Call no man your father upon the earth: for one is your Father, which is in heaven."

The Laity: We believe in one, Holy, Catholic, and Apostolic Church

The Furies: Why have you permitted the hierarchy to squander the spiritual riches of your church?

The Laity: We were taught to pray, pay and obey!

The Furies: Why have you permitted the hierarchy to squander the good will of the church?

The Laity: We believe in one, Holy, Catholic, and Apostolic Church

The Furies: Why have you allowed the hierarchy to force untold thousands to flee the church?

The Laity: We were taught to pray, pay and obey!
The Furies: Why have you permitted the hierarchy to, close your schools, your churches and rip your parishes asunder?

The Laity: We believe in one, Holy, Catholic, and Apostolic Church

Furies: Did you bear witness to hierarchal behavior with your silence?
Laity: Yes, not for the hierarchy, but for the sake of my parish community!

Furies: Have you tacitly approved of hierarchal behavior by putting your vote in the collection plate every Sunday?

Laity: Yes, not for the hierarchy, but for the sake of my parish community!

Furies: Have you asked you fellow parishioners to withhold money until changes are made?

Laity: No, not for the hierarchy, but for the sake of my parish community!

Furies: Have you been vocal about the scandal and shame the hierarchy has brought down upon you and your church?

Laity: No, not for the hierarchy, but for the sake of my parish community!

Furies: Have you listened to your conscience in matters of hierarchal criminal behavior?

Laity: No, not for the hierarchy, but for the sake of my parish community!

Furies: Are you saying that your parish community is not part of the greater church?

Laity: O my Father, if it be possible, let this cup pass from me.

The Furies: Why do you allow the hierarchy to continue to betray you and all that Jesus has taught? Have you not read Matthew 23:13-29?

Laity: O my Father, if it be possible, let this cup pass from me.

The Furies: Matt 7: 15-20 Jesus said: "Beware of false prophets, who come to you in sheep's clothing but inwardly are ravenous wolves. You will know them by their fruits. Are grapes gathered from thorns, or figs from thistles? So, every sound tree bears good fruit, but the bad tree bears evil fruit. A sound tree cannot bear evil fruit, nor can a bad tree bear good fruit. Every tree that does not bear good fruit is cut down and thrown into the fire. Thus you will know them by their fruits.

Laity: O my Father, if it be possible, let this cup pass from me.
 Furies: Cut down the bad tree and throw it into the fire!

The Furies: St. Paul in his Epistle Corinthians 1, 5: 1-2, tells you "It is actually reported that there is immortality among you, and of a kind that is not found even among pagans; for a man is living with his father's wife. And you are arrogant! Ought you not rather to mourn? Let this be removed from you."
Laity: O my Father, if it be possible, let this cup pass from me.

Furies: Let this evil be removed from you!

The Furies: Corinthians 1, 5: 6-8, Do you not know that a little leaven leavens the whole lump? Cleanse out the old leaven that you may be a new lump, as you really are unleavened.

Laity: O my Father, if it be possible, let this cup pass from me.

Furies: Cleanse out the old leaven, start anew!

The Furies Corinthians 1, 5: 11-13, But rather I wrote to you not to associate with anyone who bears the name of brother if he is guilty of immorality or greed, or is an idolater, reviler, drunkard, or robber-not even to eat with such a one. For what have I to do with judging outsiders? Is it not those inside the church whom you are to judge? God judges those outside, "Drive out the wicked person from among you."

Laity: O my Father, if it be possible, let this cup pass from me.

Furies: Drive out the wicked hierarchy from you! Corinthians 1, 15: 33, Do not be deceived: "Bad company ruins good morals.

Laity: O my Father, if it be possible, let this cup pass from me.

Furies: Listen to Paul, bad company ruins good morals!

The Furies: Canon 748 states: "All are bound to seek the truth in the matters which concern God and Church; when they have found it, then by DIVINE LAW they are bound, and they have the right to embrace and keep it."

The truth is your hierarchy is killing your church, depriving you of your religion, making a mockery of your religion and setting it on the path of destruction. They do this for no other reason than to maintain control, maintain their riches, their power, and feudal hold they on you the faithful. Let them be removed from you!

The Laity: Lord give us the strength to right these wrongs.

.

The Furies: Take your strength courage from He who died upon the cross.

The Pope's Lament

Why can't nuns be silent, just go away?
Why can't nuns remember: obey and pray?
Damn, this isn't a democracy.
Bring back the good old theocracy.
Only then can I exercise my rule
And never be made to look the fool.

Why won't they let me have my way?
Why can't the nuns obey and pray?

I am the pope, pontiff given the nod,
Preferred by cardinals, chosen by God.
There are sacred issues I don't debate
Nuns changing church laws I don't tolerate
Doctrine says I can rule as I see fit
There's nothing to question, I'm not a twit.

Why have the faithful gone away?
Why can't the nuns obey and pray?

Gone is the era when my word was law
No decent Catholic would point out a flaw.
Gone is the era when nuns feared my glance,
Piercing their hearts like the point of a lance.
Gone is the era when they kissed my ring.
Now I get blamed for every damned thing!

Don't they know it's me they betray?
Why can't the nuns obey and pray?

Nuns haven't any rights to make demands
About consecrating their lovely hands.
Against the rules! And while on a roll,
Stop spouting nunsense about birth control?
What happened to sacrifice, offering up pain?
Let the children starve in there isn't grain.

It is the pope who holds the sway
Why can't the nuns obey and pray?

Only a male priest can transsubstaniate
Who cares if a few boys they masturbate?
I can't understand nuns going wild
Who has more value, my priests or a child?
Outrage! Nuns demanding my priests behave!
How many souls can one child save?

I am the pope and cannot stray.
Why can't the nuns obey and pray?

Who do these outspoken nuns think they are?
They'll think twice when all their convents I bar!
See if they speak when their assets I grab.
I'll pick at them like a lingering scab.
When I come roaring back; I'll make them wince
Because this is my church and I'm their prince.

I'm the pope and I'll get my way;
Once more nuns will obey and pray!

In and around 2004, Sister Maureen, very bravely, was writing letters to the editor and having them published decrying the actions of the bishops under the moniker of Sister Immaculata Dunn. There was an all out effort to find out who this nun was on the part of the hierarchy which included hiring private detectives and leaning on religious superiors to no avail. Sister Maureen was and still is both a visionary and leader in the battle against clergy abuse while becoming a permanent thorn in the side of the hierarchy.

This was written to honor her word as a champion of survivors,

Nun Sense

Sister Mary Immaculata Dunn
Was putting heartless bishops on the run
Proving the pen mightier than the sword
Sister upset the red-hatted horde.

When she scolded about survivors rights
Bishops always froze like deer in headlights
Who is this woman they wanted to know
Meanwhile her rep, continued to grow.

Sister's signature was a nom de plume.
Bishops, cardinals, monsignors did fume
If they could catch this woman one of their own
They'd flay her open down to the bone.

For clergy abuse she took them to task
"How could a nun belittle us?" they'd ask.
As they read her lines of unvarnished truth
They knew this nun had the stature of Ruth

Anonymous, it was one of her ways
Fighting clergy abuse back in the days
Sister Mary Immaculata Dunn
Had cardinals and bishops on the run.

Cardinal Dolan's Gamble

The subtleties of Cardinal Dolan's mind are unmatched. New York's newest comedic cardinal has outdone himself in devising a strategy to bring the house down at Last Supper services on Holy Thursday. Cardinal Dolan, never accused of being shy, has come up with an incredibly unique way to imprint the message of the Last Supper on the minds of New York's Catholic elite who attend services on Thursday at St. Patrick's. All we can do is marvel at Dolan's sharp and rapier like wit. After asking God to allow Judas to speak on the subject of betraying Christ and being turned down, Dolan came up with the perfect living substitute. He invited Cardinal Justin Rigali in his stead!

Let's hear it for the newly minted cardinal for having the audacity to pull off a stunt like this! Who better to speak about the betrayal of Jesus Christ than the disgraced former head of the Archdiocese of Philadelphia? Who knows more about turning his back on the teachings of Jesus Christ than Cardinal Rigali whose former diocese is now steeped in disgrace and scandal? Disgusting graphic reports hit the papers on a daily basis as testimony is given describing the seamy underbelly of the church and sexually disturbed priests having lurid sex with minors. Excellent qualifications for someone to speak to the betrayal of Jesus. What will this pitiful, contemptuous former Vatican secretary to the pope have to say about his equivalent of thirty pieces of silver?

Speculation is running wild about the light that Rigali can shed on what makes a man turn his back on Jesus Christ while throwing children to the wolves in a manner that is the polar opposite of being a Good Shepard. Is it me Lord? That was the question Judas asked. Are there anymore offending priests still working in Philadelphia was the question. NO, was Rigali's answer and yet several months later, when forced to, he announce not one, not two or three priests, but two dozen priests were to be suspended. Like Judas saying is it me, Rigali knew of his guilt.

One can only commend Dolan on finding such a suitable replacement to speak on Judas' behalf. Of course, we could say it was divinely inspired, but we don't want to take anything away from Dolan. However, it is our sincerest wish that Dolan does not have the rug pulled out from under him by Rigali. If Rigali can turn his back on his God, what assurances can Dolan have? What happens if at the last moment Rigali decides that he doesn't want to explain his reasons for betraying Christ? What happens if he gets up and tries to play the role of a Good Shepard? What if he tries to tell New York Catholics how they should behave? How they should be more Christ like? Will Dolan's reputation be able to withstand the shock? New Yorkers appreciate good theatre, but what bombs in Philly generally doesn't float in New York. So it will be with Rigali.

Dolan is gambling on a Judas. Will Rigali speak to his betrayal of Christ, children and Catholics around the world or will he play Dolan for the fool by playing the Good Shepard? Stay tuned!

Eau de Pope; Scents, Sense and Nonsense

St. Peter, "What is that smell?"

"Its pope Benedict XVI, Jesus," said St. Peter.

But he's not supposed to die for another couple of minutes.

I know Jesus, but his cologne always gets there five minutes before he does!

As philosophers remind us, in every piece of humor is some truth. What possible truths could be associated with an 84-year-old pontiff having a custom-blended scent for him to wear? Maybe the toilet water in the Vatican is backing up or maybe the stench of the rotting empire is too much to bear. Then again, maybe this is what happened:

The Story of how Sexual Abuse Became Policy

In the beginning there was clerical sexual abuse and then came all the hierarchal excuses for it. The excuses were nonsense and without merit. And darkness fell over the church, the victims and their families. And the victims, their families and the laity spoke among themselves telling each other, "This is a crock of shit and it stinks to high heaven."

So the families went to the monsignor and said, "Clergy abuse is a bunch of crap and we can't stand the stench!" And the monsignor went to the bishop and said to them, "Clerical abuse is like a container of excrement and a very strong one at that. The laity can't stand it! The strong smell is driving people to leave the church."

And the bishops pondered the excrement in sacred convocation and went to the Cardinals saying to them, "Clergy sexual abuse is a crock of fertilizer and the smell isn't as bad as the laity would have us believe.

And the Cardinals discussed the problem among themselves and they said to one another, "Fertilizer is a good thing because it contains that which allows plant growth, provides food and nutrition."

And the Cardinals went to the pope and said, "Clergy abuse will promote growth and provide nutrition. It will grow the church and benefit both the clergy and their flocks." And the Pope looked upon the plan, saw that it was good, blessed it and the plan became policy.

This is how clergy abuse became policy and why the pope needs Toilette Water not Holy Water to keep the odor of corruption from his aging nostrils.

When the Jurist Loses Prudence, Goliath Hammers David

It is obvious to the most casual observer that jurist prudence was snapped by the decision to allow lawyers for the Catholic Church carte blanche to pilfer, pour over and ponder twenty three years of personal files in the hands of the survivor's group known as SNAP. One has to ask just how blind justice is when an organization steeped in the sexual abuse of children, the Roman Catholic Church, is allowed to compel the leading advocate group for survivors of clergy abuse to turn over confidential records unrelated to the case in question.

The Roman Catholic Church is an internationally recognized promoter of child abuse having multiple documented allegations of sexual abuse in over thirty countries around the world including its home base, Italy and its home city, Rome. The Roman Catholic Church was been found guilty of acts of genocide against Native American Children in Canada by an International Tribunal in 1998.1 In Ireland, they enslaved and abused children for years in workhouses.2 The European commission has accused the Vatican of money laundering.3 The NY Times recently reported that priests and nuns in Spain and Argentina were guilty of trafficking in babies and selling them for profit.4 That report generated a similar complaint out of Australia.5 Every grand jury convened in the United States to investigate clergy abuse and their equivalent in Ireland roundly criticized the church for their always abominable and in some cases, criminal behavior. In Germany, the largest Catholic publishing company, Weltbild, with 1.7 billion Euros in sales has been publishing pornographic novels for years. The biggest source of revenue is from what the owners of the publishing house, the bishops, call Erotic novels; others have called titles such as Sluts Boarding School and Lawyer's Whore, porn.6

Based on the truths above, giving the lawyers for the Roman Catholic Church unfettered access to SNAP files is the moral equivalent of giving the Mafia unlimited access to FBI files. It is simply unconscionable! Did the church take advantage of the hole created by an imprudent jurist? You bet they did. They opened a six-lane highway and lined it with dumpsters prepared to take away everything they could get away with. The proof is in the transcripts from Mr. Clohessy's deposition. The church went back twenty-three years though the incident in question only happened recently. In six hours of deposition given by Mr. Clohessy, most of the questions had nothing to do with the case of Rev. Michael Tierney who is accused by four people of sexual abuse. The NY Times tells us, "most of the questions were not about the case but about the network — its budget, board of directors, staff members, donors and operating procedures." Surely the jurist could have limited the scope of the deposition as has been done so many times to so many victims trying to depose church leaders.

This is an unparalleled attack on SNAP and as Bill Donohue, the church's mouthpiece, tells us; it was a centrally planned attack supported by the fact they recently filed a similar fishing expedition suit in St. Louis. Hopefully the jurist deciding this case will see through the charade and act with more prudence by refusing to allow Kansas City to set precedence.

The target of the Holy Roman Empire is David Clohessy and the organization known as SNAP. Total income for SNAP in 2010 was $352,903; probably less that than the value of almost any church property in any US city. Some twenty years ago when the clergy abuse scandal could no longer be contained due the enormity of the abuse, several groups formed to aid survivors in their quest for justice. The hierarchy of the Roman Catholic Church was not then or now interested in justice. They adamantly oppose anyone who would dare bring scandal upon the church by complaining that their child had been victimized in a criminal act by a priest or bishop. Having no other recourse, victims sought the arbiter of last resort, the courts. The church steeped in their hypocrisy, conceit and self adoration deemed themselves above the law and used every legal and underhanded trick in their voluminous playbook to thwart survivors and their families who had the audacity to complain. Thus the survivor groups of the day sprung into existence. SNAP went on to be largest survivor group and became the de facto spokesmen for survivors of clergy abuse. In that position, many survivors of clergy abuse have turned to the SNAP for help. Help in dealing with their abuse, help for finding resources to deal with the inherent problems of sexual abuse and of course, help in seeking justice for the crimes committed upon their bodies and souls. It is the latter that has enraged the hierarchy for it has cost them in terms of credibility and more dear to them than their integrity, their money.

And now we are the crux of the matter, money: the hierarchy of the Roman Catholic Church worships at the altar of dead presidents. The clergy abuse scandal has cost them dearly and they are targeting the organization which the largest number of survivors seeking help turn to when they wish to go public. The church holds SNAP responsible for their losses. How sad that after ten years in the spotlight, hundreds of millions of dollars spent fighting the truth, and countless survivors trampled, some so badly they committed suicide, that the hierarchy has still refused to look in the mirror. They are the source of their own problems and have yet to come to grips with it. However, the laity is beginning to recognize the source of the church's problems, which is causing the bishops more angst and money. Thus in the fashion of a cornered animal, they are lashing out.

Regardless of the outcome in either Kansas City or St. Louis, survivors will continue to come forward and expose sexually abusing priests. If David Clohessy and SNAP are martyred, another will take their place and another after that. Like the early apostles of the church, the word will spread regardless of how heavy handed the tactics of the Roman Empire become. The hierarchy of the Roman Catholic Church is corrupt and suffers from the same moral decay as the original Roman Empire. Lions and tigers and gladiators couldn't stop the word from spreading two thousand years ago and it is not going to prevent the truth from seeing the light of day now.

Let those that have ears hear and those that have voices speak out against this travesty.

References:

1. Annett, Kevin. Open letter, Nov. 26, 2009 Retrieved from: http://signatoryindian.tripod.com/id80.html

2. http://www.icl-fi.org/english/spi/oldsite/Magdalen.html

3. http://rt.com/news/vatican-bank-money-laundering/

4. http://www.childrensprotection.info/2011/10/catholic-church-global-baby-trafficking.html

5. Ibid

6. http://firedoglake.com/2011/11/06/sunday-late-night-the-german-bishops-porn-publisher/

Meet Timothy Cardinal Dolan, New York's Newest Comedian

Speaking at a diocesan convocation on public policy last week, freshly minted cardinal Timothy Dolan made his New York debut as a comedian. The critics all agree that the funniest line of the night was, "If you want an authoritative voice, go to the bishops. They're the ones that speak for the truths of the faith." The line was uttered with such solemnity that one almost forgot it was a comedy sketch. It immediately brought the house down and left them rolling in the aisles from belly laughter. Which bishop should we go to for the truth, Timothy Dolan? Should we go to Bishop Keith Symons or Bishop Anthony J O'Connell both of who resigned because they themselves were sexual abusers? How about Bishop Raymond Lahey who was caught bringing child pornography into Canada on his computer? What about Bishop Patrick Ziemann who was caught, in his car, getting oral sex from a priest forced to wear a pager so he could be summoned when the bishop had an urge. Perhaps we should consult Bishop Roger Vangheluwe who sexually abused two of his nephews. Okay, enough with the bishops, this could turn into a litany.

Maybe Dolan meant that we go to a higher level of authoritative voice, like that of a cardinal. Edward Cardinal Egan appointed a known abuser in 2002 to St. Benedict's, a parish with an elementary school; the priest was subsequently defrocked. According to the Bronx Press Review, a parishioner called Cardinal Egan insane; did Egan speak for truth? In Chicago we have Cardinal George whose faux pas' are legendary. The most recent involved Fr. McCormack, a known abuser from his days in the seminary, but Cardinal George refused to remove him. This despite Cardinal George being a signatory to the Charter for Protection of Children produced in Dallas in 2002. I'm sure he speaks for the truth. Cardinal Mahoney of Los Angeles is another stellar truth teller who spent untold dollars fighting survivors with his adamant refusal to release records of sexually abusing priests. Who would look to anyone but him for the truth? Maybe we should ask for the truth from Philadelphia's recently deceased Cardinal Anthony J. Bevilacqua who ordered aides to shred a 1994 memo that identified 35 Archdiocese of Philadelphia priests suspected of sexually abusing children? Now there was an authoritative voice that speaks the truths of the faith!

Certainly, we can look to the infallible pope for the truth. The fact that none of the above were ever fired speaks volumes about the amount of truth the pope is willing to part with.

So let's repeat that line. "If you want an authoritative voice, go to the bishops. They're the ones that speak for the truths of the faith." With lines like that, Dolan proved himself a first rate comic, but good comedians need more than one good line to make a performance, and Dolan met the call. The NY Times reported on March 4, this line from the same performance, "I don't recall a right to marriage." In his jocular fashion Cardinal Dolan went on to say that every day someone finds another right. Well he ought to know, the Roman Catholic Church leads the way in finding new rights. They have the right to hide sexually abusing priests, they have the right to destroy evidence, they have the right to shuffle sexually abusing priests from parish to parish, diocese to diocese and in some cases country to country; talk about inventing rights! But more than that, let's talk about inventing the right to the wholesale destruction of the lives of children without the expectation of consequence.

On a roll, the newly minted prince of Catholic comedy was greeted with peals of laughter when, straight faced, he told the audience, "It's not about contraception and it's not about women's health, it's about an unwarranted, unprecedented intrusion into a church's ability..." The audience didn't know which part of that statement was funnier, the "it's not about women" or it's "all about government intrusion into church affairs." Of course, his hilarious line about, "Fat, balding, Irish bishops," was in reference to the unwarranted, unprecedented intrusion into Irish governance by the Vatican when it issued a memo to Irish bishops saying that they didn't have to obey Irish law! Therefore, the fat, balding Irish bishops didn't turn in criminal priests who were raping, sodomizing and molesting Irish children therefore allowing the abuse to continue. The discovery of this memo warranted an unprecedented public reprimand of the Vatican by Enda Kenny Prime Minister of Ireland. To emphasize the point, Dolan said, "I hate to tell you that the days of the fat, balding, Irish bishops are over,"

For the sake of our children let's hope he's right!

Pope Clings to Obscenity, Law, Aimed at Mary, Mother of Jesus.

Catholics have a long history of becoming quite vocal when perceived obscenities are produced directed at either Jesus or his mother Mary. Why is it they are deathly silent about the longest, largest, most vile obscenity ever directed at Mary, mother of God? In 1987 photographer Andres Serrano's photograph depicting a crucifix submerged in a bottle of urine caused an uproar that permeated the entire Christian community. In 1999, the painting Holy Virgin Mary by Chris Offili raised another firestorm because this depiction of Mary had pieces of elephant dung incorporated into the painting. Once again outrage from every corner of the Catholicism especially from then New York City Mayor Giuliani was vocalized. It was declared an obscenity, blasphemous and every other adjective that could be mustered to describe the horrors perceived in putting a piece of elephant dung on the same canvas as a picture of the Virgin Mary.

Moral Relativism says there are no permanent morals and allows for morality to be dictated by the times. Pope Benedict XVI said his fight against moral relativism would be a cornerstone of his papacy. So, where's the connection? What obscene abomination is Pope Benedict XVI allowing against the Blessed Virgin?

To fully understand the connection and the depth of this depraved indifference and blasphemous act against the Blessed Virgin, one first has to understand the importance of the Mary, Mother of Jesus, to the tradition and culture of Catholicism. Sacred, blessed, venerated are all words that describe the importance of Mary to members of the Roman Catholic Church. The word Marian describes the congregations that have made the adoration of Mary their life's work. It is also used to describe churches built in her honor around the world. Of all the churches built around the globe to honor the name of Mary, there is none greater than the Basilica of Mary Major or Basilica Sanctae Mariae Maioris as it is known by its official title. Built in the fifth century and dedicated to Mary, it is among oldest Catholic Churches dedicated to Mary. It is also one of only four Basilicas outside the walls of the Vatican and the place where the Pope annually says mass on the Feast of the Assumption dedicated to Mary. This is where the blasphemy against Mary begins.

The sacred name of Mary, the dedication to Mary, and all that she stands for would make the any Catholic believe that the man given the responsibility for running the Basilica created to honor her would at least be above reproach. One would also expect that that person emulate some of Mary's qualities especially her love and devotion to children starting with Jesus. After all, the Blessed Virgin's best known appearances on earth have been to children in Lourdes and Guadalupe. The Blessed Virgin's visit to Sister Agnes Sasagawa, a nun in Japan, perhaps foretold of the blasphemy against her being committed by the pope. Sister Sasagawa tells us that the Blessed Mother revealed the following to her: "the Church will be full of those who accept compromises, and the demon will press many priests and consecrated souls to leave the service of the Lord"

The appointment of Cardinal Bernard Law to the position of archpriest of her basilica speaks to compromises with the devil.

The infamous Bernie Law is the living symbol of the filth, corruption and hypocrisy that is rampant in the Roman Catholic Church. He stands as a living testimony to how the global abuse of children is permitted by the hierarchy of the Roman Catholic Church. The mere presence of Cardinal Law as archpriest of the Basilica of Mary Major (Jesus' mother) is a blatant slap in the face to every man, woman and child in the world who calls themselves Catholic. It is also an abomination to the hundreds of children from Boston who were victims of Law's gross negligence.

Pope John Paul II said, the sexual abuse of young people is "by every standard wrong and rightly considered a crime by society; it is also an appalling sin in the eyes of God" Yet he made Cardinal Law Archpriest in charge of the Basilica dedicated to the Blessed Mother.

Cardinal Egan called the abuse of children by priests an abomination. What word describes a cardinal that would allow the sexual abuse of children to continue? The word is Law!

Pope Benedict XVI said the following about the sexual abuse of children, "I ask all of you to support and assist your bishops, and to work together with them in combating this evil. Victims should receive compassion and care, and those responsible for these evils must be brought to justice." Yet he allows Cardinal Law, Archpriest of the Basilica dedicated to the mother of Christ, to remain in charge of Mary's basilica and assist him at mass in her honor on the Feast of the Assumption.

As long as Cardinal Law serves as Archpriest of the Basilica, there is dung spread across tapestry of the basilica. Yet there is no public outcry. Where is the outrage from the Marianists, from the laity, from the clergy true to the teachings of Christ? They can't stomach a depiction of Mary on canvas along with dung, but accept without a murmur the living blasphemy of Cardinal Law at the helm of the most sacred church in Catholicism dedicated to the Blessed Mother. The symbol of all that is wrong and evil within the hierarchy of the Roman Catholic Church stands as a living insult to all that Mary represents. Yet there is nothing but silence.

The newspapers tell us that members of the hierarchy from the Vatican joined Cardinal Law for a lavish birthday party celebrating his 80th birthday this past week. This confirms that Law represents something more subtle than the profanity of child abuse. He is the unspoken symbol that perpetuates the evil within the RCC. His presence as archpriest is a very public reassurance to every cleric that loyalty to the Church is the only thing that counts. Crimes, blasphemies, heresies and sins can be overlooked as long as fidelity remains intact. The message is perfectly clear: The current hierarchy of the Roman Catholic Church doesn't give a damn about either the global raping, sodomization and molestation of children nor the teachings of Christ. If they did, would they put the Bernie Law on display as a loyal servant of the church and Mary, Mother of God? Hypocrisy doesn't get richer than this!

The only question left is when will the Marianists and all those loyal to the teachings of Christ going get off their asses and do something about this insidious beacon of evil purposefully placed in the Blessed Mother's basilica as a show of strength?

Author's note: About a month after this essay ran, Cardinal Law resigned from his position as Archpriest of the basilica.

One Can Dream Can't They?

Dateline: BERLIN

In the historic Reichstag building yesterday, Pope Benedict XVI warned politicians not to emulate the Vatican and Roman Catholic Hierarchy by evoking images of church excesses like burning witches and heretics just to silence them. He further warned them against stifling the freedom of the German people by limiting the ideas, and books available to them as he recalled the church history of burning books, manuscripts and their authors while he briefly touched on the dreaded INDEX upon which book titles were put denying Catholics the right to read them under pain of mortal sin and/or excommunication. The world, he said, must be made into a free place were people can live, work and worship as they choose.

In a moment of sheer and utter honesty, the pope said, "Being both German and Pope, I know from my own experience what happens when power is corrupted" He then went on to describe how the Nazis tried the emulate the Church as a highly organized band of zealots, capable of threatening the stability of the whole world in their quest for total and absolute power across the globe.

Benedict took note that even under the Nazis, for their short existence, and for centuries Europe under the auspices of the Catholic Church, that there had always been people who stuck to their beliefs thereby doing humanity a great service. To a standing ovation, he cited the heroic work of Martin Luther who, through a network of resistance, was able to escape the tentacles of the church and cause unprecedented reform.

Benedict XVI then turned his attention to the Sexual Abuse Crisis that is currently plaguing the church. He started out by apologizing for using the term "scandalized" when referring to what priests did to victims and their families. That, he said, "is like saying Hitler was anti-Semitic, though it is accurate to a degree, it in no way shape or form describes the horrors suffered by the Jews under Nazi rule. I apologize to all victims and their families for that white-washing description of the pain and suffering they endured." As an afterthought he added, Even the pope has PR flacks writing for him. The afterthought was greeted by knowing, but icy smiles.

Benedict continued saying, "Even today, there is ultimately nothing else I could wish for but forgiving and listening hearts. The capacity to discern between good and evil, and thus to establish true law, by which to serve justice and peace,' he said, 'has been entirely lost on the hierarchy of the Roman Catholic Church." So arrogant and self-serving is the bureaucracy of the Vatican that we keep the scion of clergy abuse, Cardinal Law, on as archpriest of the St. Mary Major Basilica. The appointment and the cardinal are a testimony to the depth of our own depravity in Rome as well as being a public affront to the name of Mary, mother and protector of children.

Instead of triggering a ringing round of applause, the statement put the German parliament in a stunned state of silence. The pope continued, "Our first act of contrition and reformation will be to remove Cardinal Law and suspend his offices. Next I am asking that all sitting bishops who have knowingly transferred active pedophile priests to another parish to submit their resignations to me upon publicly releasing personnel the files of all abusing priests and their current whereabouts. Then I will begin the process of laicization against all sitting and retired bishops who have been credibly accused of abusing children beginning with Bishop Roger Vangheluwe of Bruges who has admitted abusing his own nephews.

The members of Germany's parliament having been stunned into silence then burst into wild applause which lasted for several minutes. At the urging of the Pontiff, silence once again fell over the chamber as the pope spoke again. "Upon doing the aforementioned, and thereby cleansing the church of the worst part of its evil, I will set in motion events which will lead to a Great Reformation within the Catholic Church and when I am satisfied that all of this will come to pass, I will resign and live the rest of my life doing penance for the evil that I allowed to flourish under my auspices."

I sat bolt upright clapping my hands to the strains of "What a day for a Daydream" playing on the radio alarm and my wife looking at me as though I had six heads. One can dream can't they?

Collage of Cardinals
2003

You know me as the Cardinal Vice
With the church and sweets I do entice
Painting a picture that looks real nice
I abuse children not thinking twice.

My title is Good Cardinal Lust,
I don't require a bosom bust.
Just little girls and boys full of trust
And I destroy their souls, as I must.

My name is the Cardinal Remiss
I allow priests young children to kiss
What could be wrong with a little bliss
For priests saving souls from the abyss?

My moniker is Cardinal Sin.
He smiled with a devilish grin.
I'm responsible for all that spin
Increasing the odds my church will win.

My name is Cardinal Zuchetto
I pull the strings in this libretto.
Carving out puppets like Jepetto
Feeling my grip, they sing falsetto!

My name is that of Cardinal Law.
I know which of my priests have a flaw.
Because secretly we've kept the score
Of the children we've sent to hell's door

My title is the Cardinal Point
My job, "Keeping priests out of the joint."
Their unholy acts I will anoint.
I protect and I don't disappoint.

In truth I'm Cardinal Morality
Understanding that I'm a rarity.
Run over, I'm a fatality
Of the churches corrupt sexuality.

The Pope Made a Tweet!

They hail it as a grand feat
The pope made a tweet!
Priests take children between the sheets
And the headline says: "The pope tweets!"

The Irish documented Vatican deceit
They demand answers; turn up the heat.
The headlines ever so neat
The pope made a tweet!

Priests and Bishops are indiscreet
Vatican's going down in defeat
The world watches this conceit
OH MY! The pope made a tweet!

A church in turmoil, but life is sweet
OH MY GOD! The pope made a tweet!
Who sits on St. Peter's seat?
The old man that just make a tweet!

Isn't it time to stop being elite?
Come down to the people in the street
The ones they so badly mistreated.
The cause celebra, the pope tweeted!

Abusing priests, bishops he should delete.
Then maybe there'd be something to tweet.
When virtue and holiness become obsolete
Announce the pope just made a tweet!

A Declaration of Independence from the Current Hierarchy of the Roman Catholic Church

When in the Course of human events, it becomes necessary for the people to dissolve the religious bonds which have connected them with Rome, and to assume among the gifts of the God, the separate and equal station to which the Laws of Jesus and the church entitle them, a decent respect to the opinions of mankind requires that they should declare the causes which impel them to the separation.

We hold these truths to be self-evident, that all men and women are created equal and can serve the Lord, that they are endowed by their Creator with certain unalienable Rights, that among these are Life, Liberty, the pursuit of Happiness, Justice and Unmolested Children.-That to secure these rights, Religions are instituted among Men, deriving their just powers from God and the consent of the followers, -That whenever any Form of Religion becomes destructive of these ends, it is the Right of the People to alter or to abolish the ruling hierarchy, and to institute new hierarchy, laying its foundation on such principles and organizing its powers in such form, as to them shall seem most likely to effect the practice of the Principles of their Religion and the Safety and Happiness of their Children. Prudence, indeed, will dictate that Religions long established should not be changed for light and transient causes; and accordingly all experience hath shown, that mankind are more disposed to suffer at the hands of Rome, while evils are sufferable, than to right themselves by abolishing the forms to which they are accustomed. But when a long train of sexual abuses, lies, hypocrisy, denial, and blame shifting, pursuing invariably the same Object evinces a design to reduce them under absolute Despotism, it is their right, it is their duty, to throw off such a vile hierarchy, and to provide new Guards for their future security and that of their children.-Such has been the patient sufferance of the Catholic Laity; and such is now the necessity which constrains them to alter their former hierarchal structure. The history of the present hierarchy is a history of repeated injuries, deceptions and hypocrisies all having in direct object the establishment of an absolute Tyranny over the Catholic Laity. To prove this, let Facts be submitted to a candid world.

Whereas priests and bishops of the Roman Catholic Church have been found guilty of raping, sodomizing, and molesting minors around the world.

Whereas the hierarchy of the RCC has known of these criminal acts for decades and made every effort conceivable to hide these acts from the public.

Whereas the hierarchy of the RCC has used every means at their disposal to silence and defame those who complained about these criminal acts against children.

Whereas the hierarchy of the RCC did nothing to protect children and rid themselves of the priests responsible for these criminal acts until forced to by an enraged public.

Whereas the hierarchy of the RCC by their refusal to act has brought great shame, humiliation, and scandal to the people of the Roman Catholic Church.

Whereas the hierarchy of the RCC has consistently refused to take the responsibility for their failings in causing this scandal.

Whereas the hierarchy has continuously foisted ludicrous excuses including but not limited to blaming psychologists and psychiatrists, Vatican II, the Sexual Revolution, etc. upon the laity.

Whereas the hierarchy of the RCC has put themselves above the words of Jesus Christ.

Whereas the hierarchy of the RCC has ignored the words of Scripture.

Whereas the hierarchy of the RCC has ignored the precepts of Canon Law

Whereas the hierarchy of the RCC has ignored the precepts of the Catechism.

Whereas the hierarchy of the RCC have put themselves above Civil Law.

Whereas the hierarchy of the RCC has ignored that which is the most wholesome and necessary for the good of the Eucharistic Body.

Whereas the hierarchy of the RCC has silenced and ostracized religious men and women who have criticized their sinful and criminal behavior.

Whereas the hierarchy of the RCC has established a double standard insofar as they have laicized offending priests, but have not laicized one offending bishop.

Whereas the hierarchy of the RCC has deliberately withheld information from civil authorities and hidden from view the depository of their Records regarding sexually abusing priests and bishops.

Whereas the hierarchy of the RCC, for the sole purpose of fatiguing survivors into compliance, has dragged court cases on for years with despicable measures hoping the truth would disappear.

Whereas the hierarchy of the RCC has dissolved parish councils for opposing church closings and fired consultants they have hired when the answers weren't to their liking thereby flaunting their power and ignoring the rights of the faithful.

Whereas the hierarchy of the RCC by both their omissions and commissions have caused untold numbers of Catholics to leave the church.

In every stage of these our Oppressions We have Petitioned for Redress in the most humble terms: Our repeated Petitions have been answered only by repeated injury. Princes of the church whose character is thus marked by every act which may define Tyrants, are unfit to be the rulers of the church whose principles were established by Jesus Christ.

Nor have We been wanting in attentions to our hierarchy. We have warned them many times of both their refusal and the refusal of Rome to extend protections to our children, families, and beliefs. We have reminded them of the circumstances of our anger and the abuse of our children. We have appealed to their sense of justice, religious conviction and magnanimity, and we have conjured them by the ties of our common God and Savior to disavow these transgressions, which, would inevitably interrupt our spiritual health and welfare. The local bishops too have been deaf to the voice of justice and of consanguinity. We must, therefore, as told to us by Jesus Christ separate the wheat from the chafe understanding that He spoke to us in these words.

"Be on your guard against false prophets; they come to you looking like sheep on the outside, but on the inside they are really like wild wolves. You will know them by what they do. Thorn bushes do not bear grapes, and briers do not bear figs. A healthy tree bears good fruit, but a poor tree bears bad fruit. A healthy tree cannot bear bad fruit, and a poor tree cannot bear good fruit. And any tree that does not bear good fruit is cut down and thrown into the fire. So then, you will know the false prophets by what they do" (Matthew 7.15-20)

We, therefore, the Catholics of the World, know what we have to do. Appealing to the Supreme Judge of the world for the rectitude of our intentions, do, in the Name, and by Authority of the good People of the Roman Catholic Religion, solemnly publish and declare, That the laity by God's Right ought to be Free and Independent of the tyranny, sexual abuse, and oppression foisted upon them by the current hierarchy of the Roman Catholic Church; that the Laity be Absolved from all Allegiance to Rome, and that all Religious connection between the Laity and current hierarchy of the Roman Catholic Church, is and ought to be totally dissolved; and that as Free and Independent thinking Catholics, we have full Power to keep our faith, our children safe, to ordain those who are deemed worthy regardless of sex or sexual persuasion, to elect our own bishops, to rescind that right when a bishop fails in his obligations and to do all other Acts and Things which independent Catholic thinkers should do in their effort to give honor and glory to God. And for the support of this Declaration, with a firm reliance on the protection of divine Providence, we mutually pledge to each other our Lives, our Souls and our sacred Honor.

John Jay Study Equates Hierarchy's Mentality to that of Abusing Priests

Did the United States Conference of Catholic Bishops unwittingly expose a direct link between their actions and those of sexually abusing priests with the John Jay Study? The recently released John Jay report The Causes and Context of Sexual Abuse of Minors by Catholic Priests in the United States, 1950-2010 indicates that they have. The study has received a lot of press over what wasn't said; however, we may need to pay more attention to what was said. The study, which the USCCB commissioned, clearly demonstrates the behavior of the hierarchy when dealing with abusive priests is as fundamentally flawed as that of abusive priests!

In an effort to explain how abusers can continue to abuse, the researchers delve into the techniques employed by an abuser to rationalize his heinous crime thereby allowing him to continue abusing. When reading these techniques, one fact jumps out at the reader: "These are the same tactics the hierarchy has used." If the reader happens to be a survivor, he or she says, "They did these things to me and in doing so re-victimized me!" It is astonishing that none of the researchers either recognized or pointed out how the behaviors of bishops and abusers mirror each other. This information is critical to understanding just how sick the mentality of the hierarchy was when dealing with victims. Neutralization techniques also explains how and why bishops could live with their actions after permitting the rape, sodomization, and molestation of children by putting abusing priests back on the street and how they could re-victimize those survivors who summoned the strength to complain.

The techniques of neutralization are not something made up by the researchers at John Jay. They are accepted ideas upon which many books have been written and studies done. According to Wikipedia: "Techniques of neutralization are a theoretical series of methods by which those who commit illegitimate acts temporarily neutralize certain values within themselves which would normally prohibit them from carrying out such acts, such as morality, obligation to abide by the law, and so on. In simpler terms, it is a psychological method for people to turn off 'inner protests' when they do, or are about to do, something wrong." As applied here, it allowed the bishops to cast off the mantles of both humanity and Christianity.

This is the relevant passage from the John Jay Study quoting Sykes and Matza, two well known researchers in this field:

One factor that is consistent with nearly all sexual abusers is the adoption of techniques of neutralization," which alleviate feelings of guilt and shame, thus enabling offenders to commit the acts of abuse. Sykes and Matza list five primary neutralization techniques: the denial of responsibility, denial of injury, denial of the victim, condemnation of the condemners, and appeal to higher loyalties.[1]

For ease of understanding, the five techniques of neutralization will be listed as they appear above. Below each technique are annotated clear-cut examples citing how each technique was used by the bishops of the Roman Catholic Church against survivors of clerical abuse who had the audacity to speak out. Several of these techniques are addressed within the pages of the John Jay Study have been attributed to the hierarchy. However, they were identified as errors in judgment made by the hierarchy and not their true name, Neutralization Techniques.

Any neutralization technique admitted to in the John Jay Study is in bold and italicized. Underneath these examples may appear clarifications of just how harshly the example was used in real life. This list could go on ad nauseum, but for brevity's sake, only a few examples are used under each technique to prove the point.

Denial of Responsibility

• *Diocesan leaders attempted to deflect personal liability for retaining abusers by relying on therapists' recommendations or by employing legalistic arguments about the status of priests.*[2]

Nothing is more obscene than the repeated legal machinations used by bishops in their denial of their responsibility for the criminal actions of the priests under their jurisdiction.

Cardinal Egan, Archbishop of New York, while bishop of the archdiocese of Bridgeport, CT, presented this argument to the courts: The archdiocese was not responsible because priests were independent contractors and not employees of the diocese.[3]

A similar argument was put forth that stated the sexual abuse of minors was not part of the priest's job description and therefore the diocese was not responsible for his actions. This same argument was later used by the Vatican to defend itself.[4]

• *The response of diocesan officials to civil litigation by victims was often vigorous and perceived as aggressive and intimidating.*[5]

The following is a list of the vigorous, aggressive, and intimidating devices used against victims and their families who spoke out: Blaming rape victims for their own recklessness, Hiring private investigators to track down incriminating evidence, Suing victims for slander, Suing minor victims' parents for failing to watch over them, Intimidating witnesses, Concealing evidence, Stonewalling court proceedings, and Denying knowledge of abuse — unless the victims can prove otherwise.[6]

Persisting in his efforts to make the complaint, he faced a series of responses from diocesan officials: "You must be mistaken; you're the only one; you're going to ruin this priest's life; you're lying; why now after all these years? Their first response was denial; the second, you're the only one; if they didn't work, then obfuscation. Last was the appeal to guilt: It's your fault; you seduced Father. You'll ruin his life."[7]

Denying the Victim

The hierarchy became incredibly astute at denying the victim with a plethora of well thought out strategies. As the abuse scandal grew, they honed these skills until a victim of clergy abuse who complained had about as much of a chance of being heard as a sparrow in the midst of a tornado.

Tactics were employed that insured victims and their families were run around in circles, sometimes for months or years.

• *Diocesan leaders rarely provided information to local civil authorities and sometimes made concerted efforts to prevent reports of sexual abuse by priests from reaching law enforcement, even before the statute of limitation expired.*[8]

• *Diocesan officials tried to keep their files devoid of incriminating evidence. The exercise of the episcopal prerogative to maintain "secret archives" was at odds with the advice of counsel and the guidelines of the Five Principles.*[9]

With Cardinal Mahony getting ready to retire from the Roman Catholic Los Angeles Archdiocese, his eminence is pulling some strange, ill-conceived moves again, now refusing to maintain an updated list of sexually abusive priests on the archdiocese's web site.[10]

In California, a bishop reprimanded a priest for writing a letter of apology to an 11-year-old girl he had molested. After a transfer to a rural parish and a promotion to pastor, the priest was accused of abusing three victims at his new assignment, including a 3-year-old girl. The diocese's lawyer sought to deflect responsibility from Church leaders, stating that a psychiatric evaluation of the priest, who admitted abusing 25 children, did not "render any diagnosis of pedophilia."[11]

B. Archdiocese leaders employed deliberate strategies to conceal known abuse.

In the face of crimes they knew were being committed by their priests, Church leaders could have reported them to police. They could have removed the child molesters from ministry, and stopped the sexual abuse of minors by Archdiocesan clerics. Instead, they consistently chose to conceal the abuse rather than to end it. They chose to protect themselves from scandal and liability rather than protect children from the priests' crimes.[12]

Roughly two-thirds of the top U.S. Catholic leaders have allowed priests accused of sexual abuse to keep working, a practice that spans decades and continues today, a three-month *Dallas Morning News* review shows.[13]

Appealing to a Higher Authority

The case files are filled with victims who were told that by going public they would hurt the church; to belabor the point is a waste of time.

Who better to use as an example appealing to a higher authority than that of Pope John Paul II? In 2002 he called the American bishops to Rome and made this proclamation about Clergy Abuse. He called it "Mysterium Iniquitatis" or in laymen's terms, "the mystery of evil" thereby shifting the blame from priests to the second most powerful entity in the world, Satan. Not only did he appeal to a higher authority, but he denied any fault of their own.

In the world according to Father Benedict Groeschel, the Catholic Church's sexual abuse scandal is largely the stuff of fiction. Reporters "doing the work of Satan" are driven to lie, the New York priest says, because they hate the church's moral teachings.[14]

"I told my mom that he had hugged me in a very uncomfortable way and that he had kissed me in his bedroom on his bed and that I was lying down." She said her stepfather contacted another priest, who reported the matter to Monsignor Dennis Dorney, vicar general of the Tulsa Diocese. "They advised us so many times over and over again, Don't say anything until he is gone, because it would hurt the church." "[15]

The case files are filled with victims who were told that by going public they would hurt the church; to belabor the point is a waste of time.

Minimization of Harm

• *Diocesan leaders failed to understand the importance of direct contact with victims, thereby giving the impression that they felt no personal responsibility for the harm sustained by victims.*[16]

• *The bishops did whatever they felt like doing and whatever they could to avoid tarnishing their image.*[17]

Father Rogers was never punished or held to account for his unchecked sexual predations or the devastation they caused. He was permitted to retire in 1995, his "good name" intact. The message clearly communicated by the Archdiocese's actions — to victims and abusers alike — was that it would protect the reputation of its priests at all costs. This twisted sense of priorities was not lost on Fr. Rogers. In 2002, according to a Philadelphia Inquirer article, Fr. Rogers admitted to having sexual relations with Russell but minimized its significance and questioned the importance of the disclosure. Father Rogers said that the abuse "may have happened but it was not as prolonged as he says it was ... Naturally, he was young and I was older, so I should have known better. I don't know why it has to come out now ... It will just ruin my reputation."[18]

To this day, bishops are still doing this. No greater example can be given then the John Jay Study itself; paid for by the bishops to exonerate the bishops. As noted in the first paragraph in this section, they paint a nice picture that says, "Bishops gave the impression" when in fact, they never gave a damn about the victims. Of the 300 bishops in the United States there has only been one advocate of survivors, Bishop Gumbleton, and he only became an advocate after he retired.

Of the 300 plus cardinals around the world, there is not one who can be called an advocate for victims.

Perhaps the most notable minimization of victims is the lack of the use of the word crime. Crime is omitted from the Title. Sexual abuse of minors is a crime and it was a crime prior to the Sexual Revolution. A far more accurate title would have been The Causes and Context of the Crime of Sexual Abuse of Minors by Catholic Priests in the United States, 1950-2010. Yet even this minimizes the harm done. The words "sexual abuse" are a very soft term that makes the rape, sodomization, and molestation of children more palatable because sexual abuse is a catchall. It keeps the readers guessing. Which sounds better, 1,000 children were raped by priests or 1,000 children were sexually abused by priests?

The second play on words was to reduce the impact of the word pedophile. To this extent, the ephebophile word was created. A word, that the studies authors are quick to point out, is not in the Diagnostic and Statistical Manual of Mental Disorders (DSM). So why use it? The ephebophile is someone who has rapes, sodomizes, or molests post pubescent children over thirteen, but under eighteen. The church wanted to create confusion, doubt and minimize the harm. By their standards, a priest sodomizing a fifteen year old is not as shocking as a priest sodomizing a ten-year-old. If a priest has anal sex with a fifteen-year-old, according to the church, that is a homosexual relationship and not "statutory rape" as it should be called. The hierarchy and their minions are adept linguists who are well practiced in the art of neutralization techniques and verbiage.

Condemning the Condemners

• *The response of diocesan officials to civil litigation by victims was often vigorous and perceived as aggressive and intimidating*[18].

Persisting in his efforts to make the complaint, he faced a series of responses from diocesan officials: "You must be mistaken; you're the only one; you're going to ruin this priest's life; you're lying; why now after all these years? Their first response was denial; the second, you're the only one; if they didn't work, then obfuscation. Last was the appeal to guilt: It's your fault; you seduced Father. You'll ruin his life."[19]

Roman Catholic Bishop Bernando Álvarez said "There are 13-year-old adolescents who are under age and who are perfectly in agreement with, and what's more wanting it, and if you are careless they will even provoke you," he said.[20]

A Roman Catholic bishop in Mexico has sparked outrage by suggesting eroticism on television and internet pornography were to blame for child sex abuse by priests. He also claimed sex education in schools was making it more difficult for priests to remain celibate. Bishop Felipe Arizmendi was speaking before the Pope arrived in Malta where he is meeting victims of abuse by Catholic priests.[21]

Boston's beleaguered **Cardinal** Bernard **Law** is now making his yearly fund-raising appeal to the city's 2 million Catholics. He needs $16 million for the chancery's overhead—and won't get it. His approval rating sank to a new low last week when he asserted in court papers that Gregory Ford was responsible for his own alleged abuse, through "negligence," despite being 6 when it began.[22]

Cardinal Oscar Andres Rodriguez Maradiaga, in a May interview with the Italian-Catholic publication 30 Giorni, claimed Jews influenced the media to exploit the current controversy regarding sexual abuse by Catholic priests in order to divert attention from the Israeli-Palestinian crisis.[23]

The Holy See press office director under John Paul II, Dr. Joaquin Navarro-Valls, has today criticized the media for "a raging phobia" against the Church over pedophilia while ignoring the problem in the rest of society which he says is widespread.[24]

Fr Anthony Charanghat, director, Catholic Communication Centre. "You must also understand that the global porn industry is responsible for blowing these reports out of proportion. They have been trying to demonize the Catholic clergy, since the Church has been fighting them," he added.[25]

Some still complain, although privately, that the entire crisis, the Long Lent of 2002, was manufactured by the media and motivated by anti-Catholicism. There is only some truth in that. Without the media there would have been no felt crisis. There is a generous measure of anti-Catholicism in the media, as elsewhere, but without the deeper crisis of the infidelity and negligence of bishops, the media could not have produced the public and, consequently, episcopal sense of crisis. The scandal was in the chanceries, parishes, and seminaries before it was on the front page or television news.[26]

The Superiority Complex

Although it is alluded to in a paragraph the John Jay Study it bears mention because it adds another dimension to understanding the deplorable behavior of the bishops.

• *Relative advantage—the perceived degree of relative advantage over the status quo. Rogers notes the significance of "social prestige factors" concerning this attribute. As it pertains to the sexual abuse crisis, this factor may have affected the way bishops weighed concern for victims against their expectation of institutionally damaging publicity.* [27]

If one considers their victim less than, it is easier to justify inhumane treatment of them. Slave owners consider slaves their property. It took an 16th century edict from the Vatican to declare that Native Americans had souls. Hitler considered Jew and others "Mud People" so as to justify their destruction. The superiority complex of the hierarchy is legendary and because of it, it that much easier for them ignore the crimes of their priests, deny the claims of victims and allow priests to rape, sodomize and molest at will. Nowhere is this false ideology of Divine Right more clearly stated than in Vehementer Nos an encyclical promulgated by Pius X in 1906. [28]

Consider here what a pope had to say about the superiority of the clergy.

"It follows that the Church is essentially an unequal society, that is, a society comprising two categories of persons, the Pastors and the flock, those who occupy a rank in the different degrees of the hierarchy and the multitude of the faithful. So distinct are these categories that with the pastoral body only rests the necessary right and authority for promoting the end of the society and directing all its members towards that end; the one duty of the multitude is to allow themselves to be led, and, like a docile flock, to follow the Pastors." [28]

This passage written about the sexual abuse scandal several years ago by then-director of the Conference of Major Superiors of Men (Notice the word Superiors), Fr. Ted Keating picks up on the point.

"The days of the pass or station house adjustment for Father or Brother by the Irish cop or prosecutor are over. Either we will learn to become more comfortable in the gaze of the rude and scoffing multitude (depending on our attitude) or we will be dragged kicking and screaming into a new future for religion and religious life"

There are two things to note in this statement. The first is the unequivocal admission by Fr. Keating that priests, who committed crimes, were not arrested by police. The second is Keating's use of the term *"the rude and scoffing multitude"* **when referring to the laity. It smacks of arrogance and superiority while mimicking Pious** X's statement on superiority of the clergy.

Conclusions

1. The above examples provide a concrete link between the mentality of the abusing priests and the bishops who protected them. The hierarchy of the Roman Catholic

Church has an abusive mentality when it comes to the victims of clergy abuse. To say otherwise is to spit in the face of reason.

2. The bishop's abusive mentality is well documented and follows the same line of warped reasoning that allows all perpetrators of despicable acts against children to live with themselves their actions and their crimes.

3. The twisted mentality of the hierarchy is not limited to bishops and cardinals in the United States. The tactics employed by the US bishops are the same ones used by the worldwide hierarchy. It is indicative of mentality deeply ingrained in the culture of the Catholic Hierarchy.

4. John Jay tries to create the appearance of a them (abusing priests) versus us (bishops) situation where the offending priests are the bad guys and the bishops are the good guys. This is not the case at all. The number of credibly accused bishops is on par with the percentage of abusing priests as evidenced by the list of abusers on bishopaccountability.org. The only difference is that not one bishop has ever been defrocked. Let us not forget that most of the bishops currently in power were in the seminary during time period measured by John Jay.

5. The sexuality of bishops was never called into question. Bishops are human beings and therefore have a sexuality be it hetero, homo or bi sexuality. The study treats them as asexual only looking at the sexual norms of seminarians and priests. John Jay is not the only one to avoid mentioning bishops. In his twenty-four page response to the John Jay Study, John Jay 2011 Study on Sexual Abuse: a Critical Analysis, William Donohue, an ardent Catholic conservative and lays the blame for the sexual abuse scandal clearly at the feet of homosexual priests. He never mentions the word bishop and homosexual in the same sentence. He too holds that the bishops are above it all in his dissertation.

Donohue ends his dissertation on homosexuality as the root cause of the clergy abuse scandal with the following: "There is no way that priests who are faithful to the precepts of the Church's teachings on sexual ethics could possibly live a life of sexual recklessness. Only by jettisoning the teachings—casting celibacy and chastity as anachronistic—could they do so."[29]

This will end by saying: There is no way that a pope, cardinals or bishops who are faithful to the precepts of the Church's teachings on sexual ethics could possibly have allowed criminal sexual abuse by priests to flourish. Only by jettisoning their faith, the teachings of Jesus, Holy Scripture, Canon Law and the Catechism could the bishops have done it. In other words, they had to adopt the mentality of an abuser and whole-heartedly endorse the techniques of neutralization while becoming heretics in the process to deal with victims seeking justice.

For further discussion see: According to Aquinas, There Are Heretics in the Vatican.[30]

119

Reference

1. John Jay College Research Team The Causes and Context of Sexual Abuse of Minors by Catholic Priests in the United States, 1950-2010 Retrieved May 23, 2011 from http://www.usccb.org/mr/causes-and-context-of-sexual-abuse-of-minors-by-catholic-priests-in-the-united-states-1950-2010.pdf

2. Ibid pg. 89

3. http://www.nytimes.com/2000/06/16/nyregion/egan-is-leaving-unfinished-work-on-abuse-victims-say.html?pagewanted=4 May 30, 2011

4. http://www.csmonitor.com/USA/Justice/2010/0628/Supreme-Court-allows-sex-abuse-case-to-proceed-against-the-Vatican May 30, 2011

5. John Jay College Research Team The Causes and Context of Sexual Abuse of Minors by Catholic Priests in the United States, 1950-2010 Retrieved May 23, 2011 from http://www.usccb.org/mr/causes-and-context-of-sexual-abuse-of-minors-by-catholic-priests-in-the-united-states-1950-2010.pdf

6. http://www.bostonphoenix.com/boston/news_features/top/features/documents/01780639.htm May 30, 2011

7. John Jay College Research Team The Causes and Context of Sexual Abuse of Minors by Catholic Priests in the United States, 1950-2010 Retrieved May 23, 2011 from http://www.usccb.org/mr/causes-and-context-of-sexual-abuse-of-minors-by-catholic-priests-in-the-united-states-1950-2010.pdf

8. Ibid pg. 89

9. Ibid pg. 89

10. http://blogs.laweekly.com/informer/2010/09/cardinal_roger_mahohy_predator.php May 30, 2011

11. http://www.catholicsexabuse.com/THE_PHILADELPHIA_GRAND_JURY_REPORT/Section_III__Overview_of_the_CoverUp_by_Archdiocese_Officials May 30, 2011

12. http://www.catholicsexabuse.com/THE_PHILADELPHIA_GRAND_JURY_REPORT/Section_III__Overview_of_the_CoverUp_by_Archdiocese_Officials

13. http://www.dallasnews.com/sharedcontent/dws/spe/2002/bishops/stories/041702dnrelbg.

852d3201.html May 30, 2011

14. http://www.dallasnews.com/sharedcontent/dws/spe/2002/bishops/stories/041702dnrelbg.

852d3201.html May 30, 2011

15. http://www.bishopaccountability.org/news3/2002_07_31_Branstetter_Bishop

Admits_Kenneth_Lewis_4.htm May 30, 2011

16. John Jay College Research Team The Causes and Context of Sexual Abuse of Minors by Catholic Priests in the United States, 1950-2010 Retrieved May 23, 2011 from http://www.usccb.org/mr/causes-and-context-of-sexual-abuse-of-minors-by-catholic-priests-in-the-united-states-1950-2010.pdf

17. Ibid pg. 90

18. Ibid pg. 89

19. Ibid pg 90

20. http://madmikesamerica.com/2010/04/tenerife-catholic-bishop-blames-child-abuse-on-the-children/ May 30, 2011

21. http://thecornfieldonline.com/index.php?topic=19504.0;wap2 May 30, 2011

22. http://www.highbeam.com/doc/1G1-85590510.html May 30, 2011

23. http://www.adl.org/PresRele/ASInt_13/4135_13.asp May 30, 2011

24. http://www.ncregister.com/blog/navarro-valls_on_the_abuse_crisis#ixzz1Nm08iQi4 May 30, 2011

25. http://www.mid-day.com/news/2010/mar/310310-mumbai-catholics-reaction-vatican-paedophilia-scandals.htm May 30, 2011

26. http://www.firstthings.com/article/2009/02/scandal-time-iii-43 May 30, 2011

27. JJS

28. http://www.vatican.va/holy_father/pius_x/encyclicals/documents/hf_p-x_enc_11021906_vehementer-nos_en.html May 30, 2011

29. Donohue, W. John Jay 2011 Study on Sexual Abuse: a Critical Analysis, May 30, 2011

30. Nauheimer, V. According to Aquinas' Definition, There are Heretics in the Vatican. http://reform-network.net/?p=6431

The John Jay Report Ignores History While Focusing on the Wrong Culture

There are lies, damned lies and statisticians as the old saw states. After reading the noxious claims of the recent John Jay report attributing the sexual abuse scandal of the Roman Catholic Church to the social norms of the Sixties and Seventies, we have to revise the old saw. The new one states, "There are liars, damned liars, statisticians and then the Roman Catholic Church!" Their crimes also belong to all those who aid and abet them in their attempt to cover up and trivialize the sexual abuse of children. Shame on you John Jay College; for you have sullied the good name of John Jay, a man whose life was devoted to seeking justice; and for what, thirty pieces of silver?

 Those who are not familiar with Roman Catholic Church history are doomed to believe the lies the current hierarchy has just paid to produce. The Roman Catholic Church is desperately trying to convince the world that the clergy only began abusing children during the sexual revolution of the late nineteen sixties! Ad absurdum has never been better defined. Squealer, Orwell's <u>Animal Farm</u> propagandist pig must be squealing with delight. The despicable, shameful, centuries long, and well documented history of sexual abuse in the Catholic Church, flies in the face of the John Jay Excuse.

 The first fallacy presented by John Jay is using the Sexual Revolution as an excuse for deviant sexual behavior. For the vast majority, the new sexual freedom referred to by John Jay, did not include sex with children. Hetero and Homosexual liaisons became casual and open while for heterosexual liaisons, the pill, shattered the old norms. Was there a minority element from that era that encouraged sex with children? The unfortunate answer is yes. There was a small group allied to the homosexual activist groups of the era who wanted to eliminate the "age of consent." These people were opportunists who saw the sexual revolution as a chance to legitimize their criminal acts. As gay rights groups became more mainstream, those professing to believe that having sex with children was okay, became so marginalized that they eventually formed their own splinter group called NAMBLA, the North American Man-Boy Love Association.[1] One of the earliest proponents of NAMBLA was the notorious Fr. Paul Shanley of Boston infamy who was tried and convicted of rape. Though the John Jay Excuse confirms a number of priests decided to follow the NAMBLA path and engage in sex with children, they fail to explain why. Why were so many priests experimenting with deviancy by going after children when the rest of the adult world was engaging in hetero and homo sexual sex?

 Perhaps the answer lies in the history of the Roman Catholic Church. A history, though invisible to John Jay researchers, is obvious to any interested party who can type and use the Internet. Let's start with the controversial document called Crimen Sollicitationis. This is perhaps the most damning and yet at the same time the most marginalized proof of the Vatican's knowledge of the pedophilia problem among its clergy. The fact that the importance of this document has been so trivialized is nothing

122

more than a testimony to the power of the Vatican spin machine. They have succeeded in making the world believe that the document pertains only to acts of solicitation committed in the confessional.

Title V of Crimens Sollicitationis is subtitled: "The Worst Crime" as seen from this excerpt:

Title V

The Worst Crime

73.   To have the worst crime, for the penal effects, one must do the equivalent of the following: any obscene, external act, gravely sinful, perpetrated in any way by a cleric or attempted by him with youths of either sex or with brute animals (bestiality).

74.   Against accused clerics for these crimes, if they are exempt religious, and unless there takes place at the same time the crime of solicitation, even the regular superior can proceed, according to the holy canons and their proper constitutions, either in an administrative or a judicial manner. However, they must communicate the judicial decision pronounced as well as the administrative decision in the more serious cases to the Supreme Congregation of the Holy Office.[2]

For those who state that this document only applies to the act of soliciting in the confessional, I ask only one question, "When was the last time anyone saw a four legged sheep enter a confessional?" Perhaps the John Jay crew can study that problem.

The wording of Title V is extremely important as it confirms the Vatican's own knowledge and acceptance of the fact that the sexual abuse of children, regardless of sex, is a crime. The Vatican did not use the words evil, sinful, offensive, lapse of judgment, moment of weakness or illness. They used the words "worst crime" which is the only word that can adequately describe the act of a priest preying on a child for his own sexual gratification. The John Jay Excuse must have missed this tidbit. A careful and meticulous organization like the Catholic Church is not going to call an act criminal and create a punishment for said act if they weren't aware of its existence. Laws are written to protect people from crimes that are known and the church knew about these crimes. Laws against cyber crime weren't written fifty years ago because it didn't exist then, however, Crimens was.

Crimens was sent out in 1962 under the reign of John XXIII, which unfortunately for the John Jay Excuse was prior to the sexual revolution. Fr. Tom Doyle tells us in his 2008 essay: "THE 1922 INSTRUCTION AND THE 1962 INSTRUCTION"CRIMEN SOLLICITATIONIS," PROMULGATED BY THE VATICAN" the following:

Crimen sollicitationis is essentially a set of procedural norms for processing cases of accusations against priests for soliciting sex while in the act of sacramental confession. Solicitation is an especially heinous canonical crime and one which results in severe penalties for those found guilty. This document on solicitation was preceded by one issued on June 9, 1922 by the Supreme Sacred Congregation of the Holy Office. It was signed by the prefect, Cardinal Merry del Val, and was approved by Pope Pius XI. Like the 1962 document, it was issued in strict secrecy and its content was never published in the official publication of the Holy See, the Acta Apostolicae Sedis.[3]

We now know that the problem existed back in the 1920's, Here is another quote that comes to us from the "Roaring Twenties" courtesy of the then Superior General of the Irish Christian Brothers, Patrick Hennessy: "The fondling of boys, the laying our hands upon them, is contrary to the rules of modesty and is decidedly dangerous" The good Superior General seems to have had a distinct knack for understatement while at the same time a full understanding of the abuse that was taking place within the ranks of the Irish Christian Brothers. However, if the John Jay crew knew this history, in line with their latest findings, they'd attribute it to the lack of morality that characterized the Roaring Twenties.

Had the researchers at John Jay known 17th century church history, they might have excused pedophilia because it was the "Age of Discovery!"

From Karen Liebreich's book Fallen Order: "One of his recruits in particular, Father Stephano Cherubini, was to prove a disaster. Cherubini was dogged throughout his career by allegations of inappropriate behaviour with pupils, but his powerful family ties and connections with the Inquisition made Calasanz wary of expelling him. Instead, he invented that staple of the Catholic church in subsequent centuries when faced with paedophile priests – he promoted him, writing to the priest he charged with clearing this up: "I want you to know that your reverence's sole aim is to cover up this great shame in order that it does not come to the notice of our superiors"[4]

Going back a little farther in history, we come across St. Peter Damian in the 11th century.

St. Peter Damian's Letter 31, the Book of Gomorrah (Liber Gomorrhianus), Randy Engel says it is "the most extensive treatment and condemnation by any Church Father of clerical pederasty and homosexual practices. [2] His manly discourse on the vice of sodomy in general and clerical homosexuality and pederasty in particular, is written in a plain and forthright style that makes it quite readable and easy to understand."[5]

Pierre J. Prayer translated Peter Damian's work and in his introduction, he makes this comment: "One of his consistent themes was an attack on the sexual immorality of the clergy and the laxness of the superiors who refused to take a strong hand against it."[6]

We can take away two things from this book. 1. The problem of sexual immorality had to be so widespread that Damian deemed it necessary to write this treatise in a time when writing was a tedious job done with quill and ink on very expensive paper. 2. If the Church Fathers of the time had disagreed with Peter Damian, his treatise on the sexual immorality of the clergy would have never survived and he would never have attained sainthood. Surely, the John Jay crew would attribute this outburst of pedophilia in the Middle Ages to a carryover from the centuries spent groping in the Dark Ages.

The buck stops as the church enters the fourth century because that is when the church as we know it coalesced. So from the fourth century, we give you the Council of Elvira:

From the Council of Elvira 306: There were a host of Canons that came out of this Ecumenical Council. These are but a few that speak to the subject of sexual abuse.

18.   Bishops, presbyters, and deacons, once they have taken their place in the ministry, shall not be given communion even at the time of death if they are guilty of sexual immorality. Such scandal is a serious offense.

71.   Those who sexually abuse boys may not commune even when death approaches.[7]

As mentioned above, laws are not written to address crimes that are unknown. They are written to address the crimes of the day. John Jay researchers would probably say that the sexual abuse of children in the Fourth Century was obviously a classic symptom of a civilization entering the Dark Ages.

On page 118 of the report, the John Jay crew says the following about the history of the clergy abuse scandal. "The "crisis" of sexual abuse of minors by Catholic priests is a historical problem. Data from multiple sources show that incidence of abuse behavior was highest between the mid-1960s and the mid-1980s."[8] The only words that can be construed as being accurate are "Historical Problem." What the John Jay researchers need to learn is the true meaning of the words "Historical Problem." If they did, then they would understand that the clergy abuse crisis was not an aberration caused by a change in social norms, but it is actually a function of a deeply embedded culture within the Catholic Church. Having been tolerated for such a long period of time, it cannot be otherwise.

Reference

1. http://www.allamericanblogger.com/682/the-shadow-sexual-revolution-the-push-to-legalize-pedophilia/ May 20, 2011

2. http://www.priestsofdarkness.com/crimen.pdf July 10, 2008

3. http://www.richardsipe.com/Doyle/2008/2008-10-03-Commentary%20on%201922%20and%201962%20documents.pdf May 20, 2011

4. http://www.liebreich.com/LDC/HTML/Books/FallenOrder.html May 20, 2011

5. http://www.ourladyswarriors.org/articles/damian1.htm May 20, 2011

6. http://books.google.com/books?id=hr4VAAAAMAAJ&pg=PA11&lpg=PA11&dq=eleventh+century+clerical+abuse&source=web&ots=kBcxq4YpkG&sig=PwlMgSfUtRxys6KqhwrSJNf4GSE&hl=en&sa=X&oi=book_result&resnum=1&ct=result#PPA12,M1 May 20, 2011

7. http://faculty.cua.edu/pennington/Canon%20Law/ElviraCanons.htm May 20, 2011

8. http://www.usccb.org/mr/causes-and-context-of-sexual-abuse-of-minors-by-catholic-priests-in-the-united-states-1950-2010.pdf May 20, 2011

Another Day of Infamy at the Vatican

Is the Catholic Church so starved for saints that they have to rush the process through to canonize John Paul II? There was a time when the church canonized children who gave their lives in defense of their innocence. Now, they rush to canonize a man who did nothing to stop priests and bishops who stole that innocence from children. Has the moral compass of the Roman Catholic Church swung that far around? Sadly, the obvious answer is a definitive yes.

How must the sainted children who gave up their lives protecting their virtue feel as they look down from heaven at the impending sacrilege of canonizing Pope John Paul II? Children like St. Agnes of Rome who at age 12 or 13 was ordered to make sacrifices to pagan gods and lose her virginity by rape. She declined and paid the ultimate price. Then there is St.Belina, a peasant girl gave her life in defense of her virginity when threatened with rape by her feudal lord. The most famous of all children saints is Saint Maria Goretti. A farm hand tried to rape her and she fought, yelled that it was a sin, and was stabbed fourteen times for refusing to sin. Her virginity was more important to her than her life because she protected it with her life. Does it strike anyone how terribly wrong this is? How anyone could place John Paul II in the company of these sainted children is both incomprehensible and the height of hypocrisy.

Incomprehensible is the fact that a New Hampshire legislator referred to a Catholic Bishop, John McCormack, as a "pedophile pimp" and the world knew immediately what he meant by that comment. The bishop had the unmitigated gall to pretend to be concerned about society's most vulnerable! For those who are not familiar with Bishop McCormack, he worked for the notorious Cardinal Bernard Law of Boston infamy and has been steeped in accusations regarding covering up and moving offending priests to new parishes without warning the parishioners of the danger they posed.

Benedict XVI has beatified the pope who whisked Cardinal Law out of Boston. According to some accounts, Law left Boston just hours before he was to be subpoenaed to answer for his dismal failure to protect the children of Catholic families in the Boston Archdiocese. After Law tendered his resignation, John Paul II appointed Law to a post in Rome. Not any position, but John Paul II put the disgraced Cardinal Bernard Law in charge of the Basilica di Santa Maria Maggiore, with the title of Archpriest. This was a sacrilegious act of the highest order on the part of John Paul II. Pulling the protector of sexually abusing priests out of Boston to evade civil law is one thing, but to name that same man to oversee the largest Basilica in Rome dedicated to Mary, the Mother of God, is affront to all that is holy.

Sainted children who died protecting their innocence pray for the soul of John Paul II for he does not deserve to be on the same platform with you.

The blasphemy of that appointment by John Paul II is compounded when one takes into account the special relationship that Mary, Mother of God has with children. Mary's visitations on Earth have mostly been to children. She is the Mother of God and therefore in the eyes of the church: mother to the children of the church. When one considers the vile nature of sexual abuse of children, it is not difficult to imagine the pain and agony inflicted on the mothers of victims. The Basilica di Santa Maria Maggiore was twice defiled by John Paul II. Once for placing vermin like Cardinal Law in the position of caretaker and twice for the insult because all Mary stands for is repudiated by the presence of Cardinal Law in the basilica dedicated to her holy motherhood.

One could wish that this was the only grievous error of John Paul II, but sadly, it is not. The list of his accommodations to those who have abused children is lengthy. Who can forget his incredulous statement about clergy abuse in 2002 when instead of ridding the church of priests who abused children, he called it a mystery of evil, *mysterium iniquitatis*, thereby laying the blame on the evil in the world (Satan) and failing to recognize the evil within his own church. A scapegoat was offered which was homosexual priests, however the homosexual priests accounted for neither the abuse to females nor pedophilia. More importantly, it never addressed why bishops had forsaken Scripture, Canon Law and the Catechism by covering up for abusing priests and allowing them to remain in the priesthood.

Along with the above statement, Pope John Paul II wrote, "People need to know that there is no room in the priesthood and religious life for those who would harm the young." By any standard this was an excellent condemnation. Sadly, the statement turned out to be mere words that never had the weight of the office put behind them. In fact, these words turned out to be a monstrous hypocrisy as the appointment of Cardinal Law just a few months later would prove.

Then there is the equally infamous case of Fr. Marcial Maciel and his Legionaries of Christ which predated the appointment of Cardinal Law. John Paul II consistently refused to acknowledge the mounting accusations against Fr. Maciel. Those accusations have now been verified and the body of evidence uncovered has become proof positive of the warped, insidious and demonic nature of Fr. Maciel. How ironic that once the Vatican looked for collaborating evidence of the accusations made in the 1990's, when JP II was pope, that they found it plus more than they bargained for.

Is this the stuff that saints are made of?

Nobody is denying the good that John Paul II did. The lives of most men are made up of good and bad things. In the end, we all hope that the good we've done outweighs the bad. However, one thing is conclusive: John Paul II's response to the rape, sodomization and molestation of children around the world by priests, bishops and religious was abysmal. The most vulnerable population of the church, the children, were sacrificed for the sake of the reputation of the church. This was a grievous omission that should disqualify him from the process of sainthood.

His error was compounded by appointing Cardinal Law to preside the largest basilica in Rome dedicated to the Blessed Mother. Does that make JP II an evil man? No, but maybe it speaks to what he really was: A man with all strengths and weaknesses of man.

Does it make him a saint? Not by the standards of the sainted children who gave their lives for their beliefs. In an irony that boggles the imagination, the man who did not have the courage, convictions or will to rid the church of either child abusing priests or those who protected them is to be elevated to a level equal to the sainted children who forfeited their lives rather than be violated. Compared to them, John Paul II's measure comes up short.

The Spinmeister

An opinion on <u>Straight Talk about the Catholic Church</u> by William Donohue

One of the sad truths that history teaches us is that hand in hand with a great evil comes the great spinmeister. Whether the Minister of Propaganda is drawn into the vortex of evil or is intrinsically evil himself can be debated like the chicken and the egg. The answer is irrelevant, but the fact that they feed the evil and are responsible for the perpetuation of evil will always be relevant.

The twentieth century has given us two extraordinary spinmeisters: Joseph Goebbels, Hitler's Minister of Propaganda, and Squealer the Pig in George Orwell's Classic book "Animal Farm." The first part of the twenty-first century has given us, in my opinion, another: William Donohue, the president of the Catholic League.

Mr. Donohue recently published a brilliant PR piece in the form of a paid advertisement in the NY Times. This is right out of Goebbels' playbook, "Goebbels' Principles of Propaganda" Number 6: "To be perceived, propaganda must evoke the interest of an audience and must be transmitted through an attention-getting communications medium." thus the paid advertisement in the NY Times. Subterfuge, distortions, omissions and denial were intricately woven to portray the church as the object victim in what is now considered the Global Clergy Abuse Scandal. Such a fine piece of work cannot and should not go unnoticed. Mr. Donohue is indeed a master manipulator of language.

Joseph Goebbels, Hitler's Minister of Propaganda, knew the importance of a scapegoat. Hitler is reported to have said of Goebbels that his success was due to both his mastery of language and intellect. Mr. Donohue has both these qualities as does Squealer in <u>Animal Farm</u>. Goebbels chose for his scapegoat the Jews and subsequently through the force of language and sheer intellect, led an entire nation to believe that the source of their problems were the Jews. Although Donohue mentions the clergy abuse problem among Rabbis, he was careful not to go too far for fear of being branded anti-Semitic.

Goebbels's eighteenth dictum in his principles of propaganda is as follows: "Propaganda must facilitate the displacement of aggression by specifying the targets for hatred." The scapegoat selected by Donohue is none other than the pariah of the Catholic Church, Homosexuals! Notice how the clever Donohue never uses the words homosexual priests together in the entire length of his essay! (see dictum 18 above) Notice how deftly Donohue omits the preposterous presumption that there would ever be homosexual priests in an organization that considers homosexual acts to be depraved. (http://www.catholic.com/thisrock/2004/ 0407sbs.asp) Blame without an in depth examination is the trademark of a great spin doctor. Throw it out, let it stick to the wall and then move on. Donohue defines the clergy abuse scandal as a homosexual problem. The beauty of ignoring the relevance of homosexual priests is that it avoids embarrassing questions such as: Why does a church so profoundly anti-gay ordain so many gay priests?, Why upon discovering the homosexual acts with minors, did it actively protect these priests and what do theses actions say about the sexuality of the hierarchy? Donohue believes he has found his true calling. He is single handedly shielding his church from the homosexual horde that seeks to undermine his church and those that promote them

Consider the outlandish proposition that the victims are not children! In this case Mr. Donohue makes a blanket statement that would make both Goebbels and Squealer turn green with envy. "Let's get it straight—they weren't children and they weren't raped" This statement is made with authority. It is confusing and meant to confuse, which was the hallmark of Squealer. The spinmeister speaks as if he is the first and last word on what constitutes a child; speaking from authority is a benchmark of a great spin doctor. Without saying what they were, he implies that the abused weren't children. Notice how the propaganda leaves out ages. The readers say to themselves well if they weren't children, they must have been older. Does older mean its okay? Does it make a difference if a child was ten, thirteen or fifteen when they were assaulted by their priest? Though the former may be termed a child and the latter an adolescent among those who utilize psychobabble (Spinmeisters) to make the act more palatable to their audience, does the rape, sodomization or molestation make the crime any less heinous? A good propagandist knows it does and employs the tactic every chance they get.

Goebbels seventh law part d.: states that the propaganda must be boomerang proof. Donohue does a masterful job of omitting young girls from the equation by insisting the clergy abuse scandal is all about homosexuality. By minimizing the number and nature of crimes against female minors he makes his argument about homosexuals boomerang proof. Quoting numbers such as over 80% of the abuse cases were of a homosexual nature he sets the parameters of clergy abuse. Once this is ingrained in the readers head, they will completely ignore the fact that the Vatican itself states that worldwide 30% of the cases of sexual abuse by priests is of a heterosexual nature and 10% is other. Donohue skips by this so fast that one never has the time to ponder either what the 10% other is or the fact that thirty percent plus ten percent equals forty percent so it is mathematically impossible to have over 80% of the sexual abuse be of a homosexual nature. Like Squealer and Goebbels, he knows that if he is ever called on it in the future, he can say he included the numbers, but in true fashion, he expects no one to call him on his numbers and if somebody did, he would dismiss them with the wave of a hand.

Who could possibly deny the brilliance of framing his argument as a dalliance among priests? A mere touch, a palpable touch nevertheless. "Minimization of the act" is the operative mandate. The acts of raping, sodomizing and molesting minors are considered felony crimes in most countries, Donohue never goes there. He avoids the criminal aspect like the plague for it would not do well to have anyone associate the Catholic Church with criminal activity or see the words criminal priest in a sentence. Like Squealer, Donohue utilizes his command of language to justify the unjustifiable acts of priests who abused children and the hierarchy who covered up these acts. He has the traits of a lap dog and a pit bull: blind allegiance to his church and the tenacity to never let go. Bringing in teachers and other organizations says to the public: yes, we have a few problems, but there are other groups such as the schools, other religions, etc that have problems too. "Its not only our problem" is another minimization tactic that is hard to rebuff. To his credit, Donohue cleverly avoids the global scale of Roman Catholic Clergy Abuse because it serves no purpose to let people know that there are credibly abused priests in over thirty countries around the world. Schools aren't global and don't move priests, bishops and cardinals around the world at will so Donohue localizes the issue to minimize it.

One cannot overrate the need for minimization of clergy abuse. A church that professes to be the one true church, whose priests are chosen by God, whose pope is the spiritual descendant of Christ and whose stated mission is to speak for the poor and vulnerable simply cannot either be associated with or guilty of sexual abuse. Donohue knows this and it is in this framework he tirelessly expends his energy.

In the neighborhood where I grew up, we had an expression when someone was trying to con us. It was, "Stop pulling my chain!" In the spirit of that expression, I nominate William Donohue for the "Pull It Sir Award." for his first rate propaganda. This BOOH is for you!

Causes of the Unfathomable Clerical Silence on Clergy Sex Abuse

Edmund Burke said, "All that is necessary for the triumph of evil is for good men to do nothing" Living proof of this quote comes from the clergy of the Roman Catholic Church. Raping, sodomizing and molesting children is intrinsically evil. Yet the clergy, as a whole, has remained incredibly silent about these deplorable crimes. In doing so, the evil of sexual abuse has triumphed at all levels of the Church. There is no better quote to describe the excruciating pain caused by the global silence of priests, bishops and cardinals regarding the vile sexual crimes committed against children. Or is there?

"Show me the leaders and I will show you the troops," speaks volumes too!

There are one-hundred-eighty-five cardinals. Not a single cardinal has ever publicly spoken out about the pope's woefully inept handling of the clergy abuse scandal. Neither a cardinal nor a pope has ever removed a bishop from office for his sexual abuse of minors or for protecting priests who have sexually abused minors. This is a travesty of justice as well as a mockery of Jesus Christ and his teachings. Not one cardinal out of 185 cardinals can be called a survivor's advocate. This fact alone confirms the all-encompassing grip evil has on the higher echelons of the church. The triumph of evil is crystal clear at the cardinal level of the Roman Catholic Church.

Worldwide there are roughly five-thousand bishops. Out of the 5,000 bishops, there are only two bishops who are vocal critics of the Roman Catholic Church's handling of the clergy abuse scandal. Both are retired. They are Bishop Thomas Gumbleton of Detroit and Bishop Geoffrey Robinson of Australia. Not only are they public critics, but both are also advocates for victims of clergy abuse. Both been banned from speaking in many dioceses and have suffered numerous other indignities at the hands of cardinals and their fellow bishops. Bishop Robinson said the following about clergy abuse, "Sexual abuse is all about power and sex, so to counter abuse, we must be free to ask serious questions about power and sex in the institution of the church. Without this freedom, we would be attempting to respond to abuse while handcuffed and blindfolded." Noteworthy also is the Archbishop of Dublin, Diarmuid Martin. Not only has he apologized to survivors, but he also demanded the resignations of several bishops steeped in the clergy abuse scandal. Recently, two of the bishops who sent their resignations to Rome had them refused by the pope making the Archbishop look the fool. At the bishop level, evil has triumphed as timid bishops mimic their leaders. Two retired bishops and one active out of 5,000 is an extremely small percentage. Once again evil triumphs because good men do nothing.

However, there is an area of clergy abuse where we can find a larger percentage among bishops. According to BishopAccountability.org in the United States, there are seventeen U.S. bishops credibly accused of sexual abuse. Seventeen out of 425 active and retired bishops is four percent. That number only applies to the bishops in the United States! Is it any wonder why silence is golden when it comes to bishops in the

United States? Not one bishop has ever been laicized and that includes the notorious Bishop Patrick Ziemann who was arrested for having oral sex performed on him, in his car, by a priest who wore a pager in order to be summoned by the bishop for sex. Who protected this bishop? None other than Cardinal Levada, the man appointed by the pope to fill his old position as head of the Congregation for the Doctrine of Faith. Once again evil triumphs!

Show me the leaders and I will show you the troops.

The number of priests worldwide is just over four-hundred-thousand. Of these four hundred thousand priests there are only a handful of well-known outspoken priests who are survivor advocates. Frs. Tom Doyle and Bob Hoatson are the best known both in the United States and globally. Let's say there are in fact 100 vocal priests worldwide. One hundred priests is a miniscule fraction of one percent of the 400,000 priests: .00025 to be exact. Sadly, these are the troops who march to the tune of their bishop who marches to the tune of the cardinals and the pope..

Any human being with even a thread of humanity understands that the rape, sodomization and molestation of children by clergy or anyone are inherently evil acts. Despite the heinous nature of these crimes, despite the outcry from the victims, despite the outcry from Grand Juries and Special Inquiries, there remains a deafening silence among 99.9% of the Roman Catholic Clergy. There has been a great deal of speculation about the cause or causes of this Roman collar silence. We will look at three of these causes of this silence and the arguments supporting them. They are: The Superiority Complex, The Wet Monkey Mentality and a complete and utter Lack of Faith.

The Superiority Complex

Medieval Kings operated on the principle of Divine Right, which is defined as: "the doctrine that kings derive their right to rule directly from God and are not accountable to their subjects; rebellion is the worst of political crimes." Other definitions add this phrase, "any attempt to depose a monarch or to restrict his powers runs contrary to the will of God." Welcome to the centuries-old operating philosophy of the hierarchy of the Roman Catholic Church. Nowhere is this false ideology of Divine Right more clearly stated than in Vehementer Nos an encyclical promulgated by Pius X in 1905.

"It follows that the Church is essentially an unequal society, that is, a society comprising two categories of persons, the Pastors and the flock, those who occupy a rank in the different degrees of the hierarchy and the multitude of the faithful. So distinct are these categories that with the pastoral body only rests the necessary right and authority for promoting the end of the society and directing all its members towards that end; the one duty of the multitude is to allow themselves to be led, and, like a docile flock, to follow the Pastors."

However, Pius X was not alone in his assumption that priests are on a higher level than the laity. Consider the arrogance of this title: Conference of Major Superiors of Men. Who but arrogant, self-serving, elitists would give themselves a title that proclaims them superiors of men? Not to worry, Mother Superiors have their organization too, The Conference of Major Superiors of Women Religious. These groups are made up of all the "Superiors" of the various groups of orders that comprise the religious community other than diocesan priests. One might ask this reasonable question, "Does using the word superior in their title really make them feel superior?" The answer is clear in this passage written about the sexual abuse scandal several years ago by then-director of the Conference of Major Superiors of Men, Fr. Ted Keating.

"The days of the pass or station house adjustment for Father or Brother by the Irish cop or prosecutor are over. Either we will learn to become more comfortable in the gaze of the rude and scoffing multitude (depending on our attitude) or we will be dragged kicking and screaming into a new future for religion and religious life"

There are two things to note in this statement. The first is the unequivocal admission by Fr. Keating that priests, who committed crimes, were not arrested by police. The second is Keating's use of the term *"the rude and scoffing multitude."* Using these words to describe the laity is his tacit acknowledgement of Pius X's statement on superiority of the clergy. This too is an admission that there are those in the priesthood who believe they are superior to mere mortals. This is the height of arrogance and one has to wonder how the laity would react to knowing they were referred to as the *"the rude and scoffing multitude."* The director of the Conference of the Major Superiors of Men has demonstrated by his words that their superiority complex is real.

The irony of the superiority over the rude and scoffing multitude is that is that believers of this warped philosophy lose touch with their humanity. This one sentence "the one duty of the multitude is to allow themselves to be led, and, like a docile flock," explains the utter contempt heaped upon victims of clergy abuse and their families by priests, bishops, cardinals, and yes, even popes. This attitude made it easy for bishops to transfer sexual felons from one parish to another because they had contempt for mere children. This attitude makes it easy for bishops to lie to authorities because civil authorities are, in their minds, beneath them. This ingrained false superiority complex allows bishops to withhold evidence from the civil courts, lie to the world about the extensive nature of clerical sexual abuse and maintain a holier than thou attitude. Slavery cannot exist unless one group believes they are superior to another group and the enslaved group accepts their inferior status. The act of believing one is superior then makes it okay and even easy to use and abuse those however they see fit and treat with utter contempt anyone who would question their decisions. Welcome to the philosophy that has perpetuated clergy sexual abuse over the years.

This fallacious thinking along with the culture that perpetuates it must cease. It will when people realize, of their own accord, that God made them in his image and likeness: Intelligent beings capable of loving, thinking and creating. We were not created to be a "docile flock" led around by our noses by those who purport to speak for God, but who reject his teachings every time the teachings either interfere with or threaten their money and power.

The Wet Monkey Mentality

The Wet Monkey Mentality is the phrase used to describe why some populations act in seemingly irrational ways. The phrase is derived from an experiment where the main objects of study are five monkeys in a cage, with a banana, a set of stairs, and ice water is used as a behavior modification mechanism. Here is a summary of the experiment:

Inside a cage containing five monkeys, a banana was hung from the ceiling and a set of stairs was put under the banana. When one of the monkeys tried to go up the stairs towards the banana the remaining monkeys were sprayed with ice water.

Then another monkey went for the banana with same result: the other monkeys were sprayed with ice cold water. After a while when any monkey tried to climb the stairs, the remaining monkeys prevented him from going to the banana by beating him.

Once this behavior was established, the cold water was stopped and still any monkey going for the banana was beaten by the other monkeys. The one monkey was removed from the cage and replaced with a new one. The new monkey upon seeing the banana wants to climb the stairs and eat it. To his shock, the rest of the monkeys attack him. After another attempt and attack, he knows that if he tries to climb the stairs he will be assaulted.

Each of the five original monkeys were removed one at a time and replaced with a new one. As the newcomer went to the stairs he was attacked. The previous newcomer then took part in the punishment of the next newcomer with as much enthusiasm as the original monkeys. Every time the newest monkey touched the stairs he was viciously attacked.

When all of the original monkeys had been replaced, the new ones having never been punished with ice water continued to beat up any newcomer that went for the banana. Also after receiving a beating for going for the banana, they became active participants in beating up any subsequent monkey introduced to the cage that went for the banana. No monkey ever again got a banana because as soon as he approached the stairs, he was set upon. Why? Because as far as they knew, that was the way it had always been done in there.

If you substitute truth for the banana, this theory provides an excellent explanation for the almost universal silence by the vast majority of the clergy on the subject of the clerical sexual abuse of children. Speak the truth in public and you were viciously beaten. Could this theory explain the incredible lack of support for clergy abuse survivors by all but a miniscule number of clergy? Yes! Does the Wet Monkey Mentality explain the personal attacks on the person of Fr. Tom Doyle, the first outspoken advocate of clergy abuse survivors, who was accused of heresy, fired from his job as an Air Force Chaplain and declared persona non-grata by any number of fellow priests and bishops? Yes! Can it explain why a Pennsylvania bishop went through extraordinary machinations to find the nun behind the non-de-plume Sr. Immaculata; whose letters to the editor chastising bishops and cardinals were carried in newspapers around the United States. Does it account for the terrible things said about and done to Bishop Thomas Gumbleton, who after retiring, spoke out against the church and condemned its role in the cover-up of the clergy abuse scandal? Does it account for Bishop Geoffrey Robinson being forbidden from speaking in any Catholic Church or on any Catholic Church property by bishops and cardinals across the United States?

Yes, the Wet Monkey Mentality explains all of these actions taken by the church against these few and those unnamed who dared to challenge the prevailing norms by speaking the truth about the clerical sexual abuse of children in the Catholic Church. These courageous clergy members Tom Doyle, Tom Gumbleton, and Jeff Robinson as well as others, who spoke out, were pounded relentlessly by those with the Wet Monkey Mentality as a lesson for the rest of the worldwide clergy.

Loss of Faith

Some twenty years ago, while attending a meeting, a young woman told this story. "I have two constant companions, I call them my pets. One is called fear and the other is called faith. Whichever one I feed is the one that grows." I never saw her again, but I have survived and thrived remembering her words and while looking at causes for the deafening silence of good men and women about such an evil issue as child abuse her words came back to me yet again. I maintain that the silence of the clergy is due to their lack of faith in God and the message of compassion in the Gospels. The clergy of the Roman Catholic Church is feeding their fear and not their faith! They fear scandal as if scandal could hurt God. Yet scandal can only hurt men. They fear being found out for the despicable acts they've committed, witnessed and concealed; they fear for their material possessions, their power, their wealth and their false superiority.

If priests, bishops and cardinals had unquestioning faith in God, they would not be afraid to speak out against the evil that has triumphed because of their silence. They would not be afraid of losing their jobs, their pensions, their cushy parish, their shot at purple or red buttons and the biggest prize of all, the white hat. In other words, they would lose their fear of naming evil whether that evil is committed by a bishop, cardinal or pope. Their faith would sustain them if they would just feed it. Fear has frozen the voices of the good men in the priesthood because they have lost their faith in the God. A crash course in the Acts of the Apostles might help the remaining good members of the clergy, who wish to serve God and not their superiors, to find their tongues. We can all pray that the Holy Spirit will once again ignite the flame of faith in Jesus and his teachings.

Only men steeped in fear can keep silent about the travesty of justice and the horrors of sexual abuse that are and have occurred in the Roman Catholic Church. It is almost impossible to believe that out of 5,000 bishops worldwide there are none who remember who they represent. Equally implausible is that there are none who are not appalled by the actions of their fellow bishops, cardinals and the pope relative to the sexual abuse of children by clergy members. The same can be said for the 400,000 priests around the world. There must be more than a handful of priests who want to cleanse the church by driving out the despoilers of our children along with those who protect them.

Those in power have brought the church to the brink of collapse; the triumph of evil. Those that have remained silent have encouraged it! Now is the time to oppose it! Tell the clergy to get some gumption from their boss; the one who died on the cross. Let he who has ears hear!

The Real Impact of the Belgium Raids

Once again, Goliath gets stoned by little David. Belgium ranks thirty-seventh in size out of the fifty-two countries in Europe. Yet it will go down in history as being the only country in the world with the determination to take on the Catholic Church. The Belgium Police have done what the rest of the world should have been doing for years: they have treated the Church just like any other entity involved in a criminal investigation. For that, the global community of clergy abuse survivors owes them a big "Thank You!" The Belgium Police Dept. also deserves applause from all civic minded people who believe no individual or organization is above the law.

What are the repercussions of this dramatic event? There are several. The first, the Belgium Police have set a precedent. The world has witnessed in print, on television, and on the Internet members of the church hierarchy being treated like the alleged criminals they are for aiding and abetting known felons who have raped, sodomized and molested children. No one will be able to remove those images from the minds of those who either watched or read about this historic event. This is a huge step forward and it has struck fear into the hearts of bishops and cardinals around the world who are hiding known sexual offenders.

The truth of this matter is the hierarchy doesn't know where or when this will happen again. Now, anywhere in the world, a police department emboldened by the actions of the Belgium Police may decide that church walls no longer impede criminal investigations. In 2002 a very prophetic priest, Rev. Ted Keating, then director of the Conference of the Major Superiors of Men, (The organization of all priestly orders not diocesan) wrote this in their monthly newsletter.

The days of the *pass* or *station house adjustment* for Father or Brother by the Irish cop or prosecutor are over. Either we will learn to become more comfortable in the gaze of the **rude and scoffing multitude** (depending on our attitude) or we will be dragged *kicking and screaming* into a new future for religion and religious life (Emphasis mine)

Eight years later, that observation has come home to roost in Belgium; the precedent of giving priests and bishops a free pass had a very public ending. The church has finally been dragged kicking and screaming into the twenty-first century.

The world has seen bishops and cardinals sequestered for nine hours in an ongoing criminal investigation and just like they would in any other alleged criminal organization Church computers and files have been confiscated in full public view with no public outcry. The Belgium Police were careful to follow the letter of the law in regard to exercising their legitimately issued search warrants; yet the pope called their actions deplorable.

This brings us to the second aspect of the fallout from this raid. The pope is once again documented as speaking out of both sides of his mouth. Consider these quotes from Pope Benedict XVI over the past year:

In 2009: At the Catholic World Youth Day in Australia Benedict said, "I ask all of you to support and assist your bishops, and to work together with them in combating this evil. Victims should receive compassion and care, and those responsible for these evils must be brought to justice."

In 2010: The Holy Father observed that the "sexual abuse of children and young people is not only a heinous crime, but also a grave sin which offends God."

Benedict out of one side of his mouth tells us that all those who are responsible for these evils must be brought to justice and then when an attempt to do that very thing is made, he calls it deplorable! How things can change in one short year! Benedict called sexual abuse a heinous crime and a couple of months later when the Belgium Police tried to solve some of these heinous crimes, the pope is outraged. One has to wonder where he was being more honest; calling the sexual abuse a heinous crime or calling the actions of the Belgium Police deplorable. Benedict XVI is patently giving lip service to the suffering of the victims of clergy abuse and throwing his full weight behind those that have covered it up.

Herman's Hermits once sang a song called "Kind of a Hush." The words have been changed to reflect the events precipitated by the raid in Belgium.

There's a kind of a hum all over the world, tonight

All over the church you can hear the sounds of shredders at work.

Closer now and you will hear what I mean.

It isn't a dream.

The only sound that you will hear

Is music to your bishop's ear!

Shredding files represents the final fallout from the historic event that took place at the "Palace of the Archbishop of Mechelen-Brussels." The hierarchy of the Catholic Church knows the old ways have ended. The evidence hidden in priest personnel files under the guise of priest-confessor (bishop) relationship is no longer sacrosanct. Thanks to the Belgium Justice System it will henceforth be considered evidence in a criminal investigation. History tells us that the hierarchy will do whatever it takes to keep incriminating evidence out of the hands of the proper civil authorities seeking information in legitimate criminal investigations. Maybe the future will show us that they've learned the white collar isn't a "Get out of Jail Card!" anymore.

* * *

Dateline 5-1-10 Rome

The Vatican announces its decision to change the pope's name to Innocent!

Rooters Vatican Beat: Vinnie Veritas

In a remarkably unprecedented move the Vatican announced early today that the pope will change his name from Benedict XVI to Innocent. The name change can only be described as a divinely inspired flash of genius said Cardinal Spindalie, head of the Congregation for Mutato Nomine. "Benedict is really Innocent!" he said. Citing the global media criticism over clergy abuse, Spindalie said the name change will inspire both Catholics and non-Catholics around the world to call the pope: Innocent. Cardinal Spindalie then confided that the name change wouldn't hurt because of the growing potential for either a deposition or trial by the world court.

Popes are not required to change their name upon taking office; however it has become a tradition in the Roman Catholic Church that a pope, upon being elected, will take the name of a previous pope whose qualities he admired. This name change is extraordinary because Cardinal Ratzinger, a.k.a. Benedict XVI, is five years into his reign. The original Innocent was pope while Rome was sacked by Goths in the fifth century and Benedict like Innocent understands what it feels like to be leading the church into the Dark Ages. More than anything, Benedict desires to be called Innocent.

When asked about Benedict's new found admiration for innocence, Cardinal Spindalie said, "We at the Curia are preparing for the unlikely event that the pope has to go on trial." If there is a trial, the confident cardinal confided, by the time our lawyers are finished with their opening statements, the jury will have heard the word Innocent a thousand times. "How can a jury find anyone guilty whose name is Innocent?" he asked gleefully. They can't, it's an oxymoron, Innocent can't be found guilty regardless of how heinous the crimes!

* * *

We all need to lighten up a bit sometimes, don't we?

Moral Authority, Moral Relativism, Forgiveness, Privilege
And the Roman Catholic Church

They are trying to undermine our moral authority, create a campaign of hate and gossip scream such luminary cardinals as Bertoni, Sodano and Lajolo; who by any standards are accredited Vatican heavyweights. What we might ask of these Johnnies-come-lately to the clerical abuse table is: Where were you when this scandal was brewing and when did you find out that there is a global sexual abuse epidemic among your clergy?"

On the issue of moral authority, the answer is simple. The Roman Catholic Church and the Vatican are bankrupt in the moral authority account. Whatever they once might have had was squandered when, in losing their moral compass, they decided that the reputation of the church was far more sacrosanct than the body and soul of a child; not just a child, countless thousands of children around the globe. Like Adam hiding from God in Eden, the church hierarchy turned away from God and put their church above God, his laws and the lives of children. Having done that, they still have the unmitigated gall to lay claim to moral authority. Their hypocrisy knows no bounds! Jesus told us that a good tree cannot bear bad fruit and if we correctly understand what he was saying, we know today's church, in its current state of governance, is not bearing good fruit.

When Benedict took office, he railed at what he called the "Moral Relativism" endemic throughout Europe and the world. Although the church cannot claim moral authority anymore, they can certainly lay claim to moral relativism. Moral relativism is the concept that the moral standard is set by the times or the culture. It is the pope's contention that there are moral absolutes that hold true for all time. I.e. Sex is only for procreation, using contraceptives of any kind and of course, abortion. However, humanity has some moral absolutes too. I.e. The raping, sodomizing and molesting of children are universally considered taboo. There are laws against it in countries all around the globe and have been since man began making laws. Further underscoring the moral absolute is the U.N. Through its UNICEF organization, it has put together "The Convention on the Rights of the Child." The Vatican was one of the last countries to sign it.

Sexually abusing children is a moral absolute by every standard except for those of the Catholic Church. Either the act of sexually abusing a child is a crime or it isn't. In the document *Crimens Sollicitationis* issued by the Vatican in 1962 and reaffirmed in 2001 by Benedict's own hand, the sexual abuse of children by clerics under Title V of that document is called "The Worst Crime." Therefore, any priest sexually abusing a child is guilty of the "Worst Crime" validating it as a moral absolute. However, the church hierarchy, the bastion of moral absolutes, became the bastion of moral relativism when it came to the sexual abuse of children by the clergy because they did not treat it as a crime.

Another global moral absolute or taboo is incest. Either parent having sex with their children is another ancient taboo. Spiritual incest, Father having sex with his spiritual children, belongs in the same category. Yet neither of the above has been considered a moral absolute for the priests of the Roman Catholic Church.

The question then arises, how can the church consider the sexual abuse of children a crime if there is no penalty for the crime and the offender is not labeled a criminal? Likewise, there is no penalty for the enabler of the abusing priest. Who is more guilty, the animal that seeks prey or the handler who unleashes him upon unsuspecting children? Enter moral relativism. Well, because he's a priest, he's not really a criminal, but a sinner and it is our duty as Christians to hate the sin and love the sinner because we are the church of forgiveness.

Here is where the church thinking became sick, convoluted, twisted and wandered astray. At the crucifixion, Jesus didn't save the repented thief from his legal fate, crucifixion. He said, "This day you will be with me in heaven." He forgave the thief his sins, but he did not stop the prescribed legal punishment for his crimes. Ignoring this truth is the cornerstone of the foul thinking that has permeated the church hierarchy: Forgiveness does not equate to no consequences for the crime. In the eyes of God and man, the sin can be forgiven as Jesus did, but there still has to be a consequence for the crime. If the crime didn't deserve a consequence, Jesus would have spared the good thief his execution. This is a point lost on a hierarchy determined to save their own at any cost.

Along with the above, the church has forgotten a second truth. The priesthood is a privilege. When privileges are violated, they need to be taken away. A driver's license is a privilege for those who can pass the written and road test. If that privilege "the right to drive a car" is abused by speeding or driving under the influence of drugs or alcohol, the privilege to drive is revoked. If a gun owner uses his gun in a reckless manner, his right to gun ownership ceases. His right to freedom in all probability will cease too. The priesthood is a privilege and when that privilege is used to commit crimes as it is when sexually abusing children, it needs to be revoked.

The same holds true for the hierarchy. Becoming a bishop or a cardinal is a privilege given to only a few men of each generation. When that privilege is violated in such a criminal and heinous way as has happened with permitting the sexual abuse of children and then protecting the criminals involved, the privilege of being a bishop or cardinal needs to be revoked. Anything less is moral relativism. Coincidentally, it was Pope Benedict XIV's *Degradatio ab ordine pontificali* (Degradation of a bishop) that created the means to remove a bishop. Hopefully, Benedict XVI will consider using the rite created by his predecessor to excise the existing cancer in the hierarchy.

The *New Advent Catholic Encyclopedia* had this to say about Benedict XIV who wrote these procedures for getting rid of errant bishops: "Benedict XIV is best known to history as a student and a scholar... his enormous application coupled with more than ordinary cleverness of mind made him one of the most erudite men of his time and gave him the distinction of being perhaps the greatest scholar among the popes." The greatest scholar among popes recognized that it was possible for evil to infiltrate the highest reaches of the church and wrote the prescription for removing it. It takes a man of courage and conviction to stand up to evil.

Benedict XVI needs to come to this same conclusion. He needs to clean house starting with the infamous Cardinal Bernie Law, a pubic eyesore as well as monument to moral relativism. The sooner he does this, the sooner he will be able salvage any scraps of moral authority the Roman Catholic Church may still have.

Who Stained the Collar?

Who stained the collar; soiled white?
Savaged our children in the night.
Blame the children, it's in their eyes
They're the culprits telling the lies.

Wanton devils so full of vice
Waiting for a priest to entice.
Such temptation never a break;
Let's burn all children at the stake.

Who stained the collar; soiled white?
Raping our children in the night.

Blame the parents, it's all their fault.
Didn't keep kids locked in a vault.
Parents let their kids go away
Thinking they were learning to pray.
Hearing the truth has turned them pale.
Send the parents, send them to jail!

Who stained the collar; soiled white?
Sodomizing kids in the night.

Blame the lawyers, they're a seedy lot
The thought of money makes them hot.
There are things better left unsaid
They put a gun to the church's head.
What they've done was not very nice
Victim's lawyers, treat them like lice!

Who stained the collar; soiled white
Fondling our children in the night?

Blame the media, it's the press!
They created this damnable mess.
Malcontents, they're atheists all;
Blame them for the collar's fall.
Not their fault, reporting the news.
If all else fails, blame the Jews!

Who stained the collar; soiled white?

Spreading o'er the place like a blight
Blame the laity, blame them all,
They're responsible for the fall.
Turning a blind eye they won't see;
Don't let them keep their dignity.
They are responsible for this mess.
Let's hear a hearty, "I confess."

Who stained the collar; soiled white?
Can't be the priests, it's just not right.

Oh God, Dear God, accept the blame
For all that's been done in your name.
It is your church, you're at the top.
It is with you, the buck must stop.
So pray God let our children be;
Call off your priests and set them free!

Who stained the collar; soiled white?
Priests who wear it day and night!

THE POPE'S LAMENT

Why can't they just go away?
Why can't the laity obey and pray?
Damn this foolish democracy
Bring back a good old theocracy.
Only then can we truly rule
And never be made to look the fool.

Why can't we just have our way?
Why can't the laity obey and pray?

We are priests, given the nod,
Chosen ones, handpicked by God.
With better things to do than jaw
With the ill informed about Canon Law.
We make the rules as we see fit
There's nothing to question, not a bit.

Why don't we hold any sway?
Why can't the laity obey and pray?

Gone are the days when my word was the law
No decent Catholic would point out a flaw.
Gone is the day when they feared my glance
Piercing their hearts like the point of a lance.
Gone is the era when they kissed my ring.
Now I get blamed for every damned thing!

Why can't they see it's us they betray?
Why can't the laity obey and pray?
Who are these victims making demands
About abuse that came by priests' hands?
Don't they realize the harm they're doing
Always complaining and constantly suing?
What happened to sacrifice, offering up pain?
Nowadays everyone's in it for financial gain.

What if a few priests drifted astray?
Why can't the laity obey and pay?

Who is more important a priest or a child?
I can't understand the laity gone wild.
Who's more sacred than an anointed priest?

Of far greater value than a sniveling beast.
How many souls can one child save?
How dare they demand a priest behave!

Why can't my priests get a lay?
Why can't the laity obey and pay?

The Papal Appeal has lost its touch
I feel like a cripple without a crutch.
It'll be hard to maintain my standard of living
Because in the pews they've stopped giving.
But we'll come back; we'll make them wince
Because this is my church and I'm their prince.

Children are part of a priest's buffet
Why can't the laity obey and pay?

Pope Benedict is Firmly Tied to Clergy Abuse

Since the Roman Catholic Clergy Abuse Scandal broke wide open in 2002 it has been the contention of some survivors that the cover up of sexual abuse by priests runs all the way to the top, the pope. Now, thanks to Pope Benedict XVI's failures, it is no longer conjecture.

The facts out to date indicate that as the archbishop of Munich, then Bishop Ratzinger knowingly covered up and sent at least one priest, Father Hullermann, a serial child abuser, back out into the parishes to abuse more children! The NYTimes tells us this happened despite the psychiatrist's warnings and suggested restrictions. Of course, the Vatican (Party) line is that this decision was made without Ratzinger's knowledge. At the eight-year mark since the great Boston scandal, one would think that the Vatican would have given up these tired, well-worn platitudes.

Once again we move from the bishop of the diocese who is responsible for everything that happens, to: there are decisions made in the archdiocese without the bishop's knowledge. This flies in the face of multiple church realities. Note how the Vatican immediately went on the attack to avoid the scandal of having a pope directly tied to sending a pedophile priest back into a parish to abuse again. The culture of the church hasn't changed. It is and has been to avoid scandal at any cost. Now this same scandal-phobic Vatican would ask the world to believe that an opportunity for an extremely grave scandal in Ratzinger's own diocese was unknown to him. As the magician says, "Watch my fingers, they never leave my hands!" Are we to believe someone astute enough in his old age to orchestrate his election to the position of pope, was, in his prime, unaware of what was going on in his own backyard?

The Vatican would have us believe, under pain of excommunication if they could get away with it, that every bishop or cardinal who ever had a child abusing cleric under their auspices never knew or had a say in the disposition of the abusing cleric. Given the obsession the church has with scandal, there are only two words that fit, ad absurdum! The masters of deceit can't have it both ways because bad trees do not bear good fruit and good trees do not bear bad fruit.

This latest revelation of the direct link between the pope and a serial child molester is important because it is a direct link, but it is by far not the only connection. We must consider the global consequences of his failure as the Congregation of the Doctrine of the Faith to create policy to rid the church of abusing clerics. The number of children globally abused because of his abject failure as head of the CDF far outweigh the tragedy he is personally connected with in Germany. The following had a greater impact:

1. As head of the Congregation for the Doctrine of Faith (CDF) for twenty three years, investigating offending priests was his responsibility. Then Cardinal

Ratzinger, now Benedict, knew full well there were priests using their powers to debauch children, but he remained silent and refused to clamp down on the permissiveness that allowed them free reign.

2. In 2001 under his own signature, Cardinal Ratzinger reaffirmed the validity of Crimen Sollicitationis which imposes the "Secrets of the Holy Office" on anyone with knowledge of priests violating the confessional or sexually abusing children, which means they are silenced forever.

3. In 2002, Pope JPII said that there was no room in the priesthood for those that would abuse children. As head of the CDF, then Cardinal Ratzinger disobeyed a very public command made by the pope by not removing offending priests and bishops who enabled them.

4. In 2009: At the Catholic World Youth Day in Australia Benedict said, "I ask all of you to support and assist your bishops, and to work together with them in combating this evil. Victims should receive compassion and care, and those responsible for these evils must be brought to justice." To date, none of the offending bishops or cardinals has been brought to justice by either the church or civil law.

5. In 2010 "The Holy Father observed that the sexual abuse of children and young people is not only a heinous crime, but also a grave sin which offends God." To date, nothing has been done about bringing those responsible for the gross evils committed in Ireland against children.

The Gospels tell us Jesus said, "In time, all will be revealed" So it is with Benedict as his hypocrisy and lies on the subject of child abuse burn brightly before both God and man. Four hundred years before Jesus, Plato had this to say about lies: "False words are not only evil in themselves, but they infect the soul with evil." So it is with the church; the false words of the hierarchy of the Roman Catholic Church have infected the very soul of the church with evil. The following is a paraphrase (replacing only the word State with the word Church and adding the single word religious) from a well known German on the subject of lies: "The lie can be maintained only for such time as the Church can shield the people from the religious, political, and economic consequences of the lie. It thus becomes vitally important for the Church to use all of its powers to repress dissent, for the truth is the mortal enemy of the lie, and thus by extension, the truth is the greatest enemy of the Church": **Joseph Goebbels,** Hitler's Minister of Propaganda. Therefore, Ratzinger needed to reaffirm the validity of Crimen in 2001 and maintain the blanket of silence it throws around any priest caught sexually violating children. The lie had to be protected at all costs.

How ironic or hypocritical in retrospect that upon being appointed Archbishop of Munich and Freising, Cardinal Ratzinger chose as his Episcopal motto: "Cooperators of the truth" He stated that he chose that motto "because in today's world the theme of truth is omitted almost entirely, as something too great for man, and yet everything collapses if the truth is missing" Ratzinger showed that he, like Goebbels, understands the effect truth has on a lie. Knowledge of the importance of the truth or the lack of it, the lie, has the power to bring down churches and governments. Whether Ratzinger was speaking honestly or exhaling hypocritical rhetoric one cannot deny the truth in his words. "The truth is missing!" and the church is collapsing around him.

The big lie is falling apart and with it, the foundations of the Vatican and the Roman Catholic Hierarchy. Is the clergy abuse scandal the big lie? No, it is only the thread that unraveled the cloth which exposed the big lie. The big lie is an equation: The church is greater than God. The equation should read, God is greater than the church, but time and culture and the insatiable appetite for power has long since eroded the original equation. The first commandment states: "I am the Lord thy God, thou shalt not put strange gods before me." And herein lies both the problem and the cornerstone of the house of cards. By assuming the mantle of god, the church had to then present itself and all its priests as being godlike, infallible, able to remain celibate for a lifetime and be above reproach, but being only human, they failed. When they failed, the truth became their biggest enemy and it had to be silenced at all costs as Goebbels so astutely pointed out.

The church as an entity has placed itself above the God it was created to serve. Is this an outrageous statement or one grounded in reality? Consider the following:

1. The clergy abuse scandal. It is *prima facie* evidence that the needs of the church were placed high above the laws of God, the laws of man and the protection of children. Christ used his harshest words in all the Gospels to describe what would happen to those who led children astray.
2. Who but the Catholic Church had the audacity to renumber and change the 10 Commandments from the original ten handed down by God to Moses on Mt. Sinai? If that isn't arrogance, what is?
3. Who violated the first commandment of God given to man at creation "Be fruitful and multiply!" by forcing mandatory celibacy upon their priests one thousand years after Jesus walked the earth?
4. Paul tells us that a bishop must be a good husband because if he can't provide for his family, how can he provide for a flock? The Church ignores this.
5. Christ gave specific instructions saying, "Call no man father because there is only one Father." Perhaps no one in the Vatican has read all the Gospels including the "Holy Father"!
6. With the most astounding arrogance ever witnessed on earth, the church declares the doctrine of Papal Infallibility!
7. If the Vatican had true faith, they would accept Christ's promise that his church would endure forever, and would not be worried about admitting their human frailties.

Examples of the hierarchy putting themselves on par with or above God are too numerous to list here. The seeds of destruction are called secrecy. The darkened wasteland of secrecy is the perfect breeding ground for all sorts of nefarious and malignant growths. It is a cesspool fertilizing the dregs of humanity and creating offspring that are as rotten as the offal from which they spring. Such was the abundance of slime generated by Roman Catholic Church's cesspool born of secrecy that one day it spilled over its banks and ran into the light where it was laid bare to the world. Even now it is still oozing despite the best efforts of all the pope's cardinals and all the pope's bishops and all the pope's priests. They haven't been able to contain it again!

These seeds were sown when the church forgot they were the servants of Christ and assumed the mantle of Christ. Once they declared themselves godlike, no ungodly act could be permitted to stain their imaginary spotless exterior. However, the ungodly acts continued and the church had to protect itself with the big lie. They had to repress the truth in order to perpetuate the big lie. Therefore all cases of the violation of the confessional and child abuse had be wrapped in the "Secrets of the Holy Office" never to be spoken about again. Fortunately for all of us, Jesus has deemed it time to put a stop to these vile acts and secrets. He gave a few survivors the strength they needed to speak up against the oldest multinational religious organization in the world. Once they spoke up, others heard the word and the word spread and the veil of secrecy and filth was lifted for all to see.

Now Benedict must be held accountable for his role in this heresy.

Prophecies Foretold the Current Discord within the Church Hierarchy

In northern Spain in 1961 four teenaged girls received multiple visions from the Blessed Mother over the course of several years. Among the end of time prophecies and other things, there was this prophecy about the hierarchy given in 1965 that is pertinent to the Clergy Abuse Scandal: "Before, the cup was filling up. Now it is flowing over. Many cardinals, many bishops and many priests are on the road to perdition and are taking many souls with them. Less and less importance is being given to the Eucharist." These visions known as the Garabandal prophecies were never fully sanctioned by the church. It isn't hard to figure out why. Here and now in 2010 the church, with diminished power, is still trying to cloak the fact that they are far from perfect. One can only imagine the insult this vision was to a much more powerful church in 1965 preparing for Vatican II."

Several years later, in an unknown convent, in a not so very Catholic part of the world, a Japanese nun began having Marian visions, which lasted from 1973 to the early 1980's. These visions, readily available on the Internet are known as the Akita Prophecies. Among the prophecies that she received was the following:

"The work of the devil will infiltrate even into the Church in such a way that one will see cardinals opposing cardinals, and bishops against other bishops. The priests who venerate me will be scorned and opposed by their Confreres. The Church and altars will be vandalized. The Church will be full of those who accept compromises and the demon will press many priests and consecrated souls to leave the service of the Lord."

Oddly enough, coincidently or prophetically, it was none other than Cardinal Ratzinger, the head of the Congregation of the Doctrine of Faith who gave his blessing to the Bishop of Nugata, Bishop John Shojiro Ito, to declare these visions to be authentic visions or appearances of the Blessed Mother. The irony is too delicious.

More irony comes to us from another Benedict, Pope Benedict XIV. Benedict XIV gave us these two timely presents. He firmly believed that evil could penetrate the highest ranks of the church so he set down the rules for degrading (firing) a bishop and secondly he gave us: the Heroic Virtue, III 144, 150, were he stated: "neither angels nor devils can foretell future events, which are the proper objects of prophecy, unless communicated to them by God. Neither can man of his own nature know the future unless God communicates it to him" Benedict XIV tells us the bottom line is that these visions and prophecies were communicated to us by God.

If, as Benedict says, the above prophecies are from God, they should indeed have merit. Consider the merit of the following statements from this year alone:

- Halifax Archbishop Anthony Mancini says it's time to acknowledge that the Roman Catholic Church is falling apart.

- Internal Catholic Church bickering over the handling of its sexual abuse scandal has escalated to a new level, with one cardinal accusing another of a cover-up.
- Some critics had said the scandal had put the Legionnaires beyond repair and had called for it to be dissolved, but the vacillating pope decided to take a half-way step aimed at restructuring. (See above Akita Prophecy about those who accept compromise)
- Rev. James Scahill called in a sermon last weekend for the pope to resign over the church's sexual abuse scandal.
- Bishop Donal McKeown has said that he and his fellow bishops are being portrayed as "twisted, incompetent old men, well aware of evil actions among some of their colleagues, but saying nothing in order to protect their power".
- At the same time Bishop Drennan made no attempt to disguise a serious disagreement with Archbishop Martin, saying that it was "inappropriate" for the Dublin archbishop to raise questions in public about his conduct.
- Five years after his death, Pope John Paul II's record in office is coming under growing criticism as Vatican officials try to shift the blame for the sex-abuse scandals engulfing the Catholic Church on his leadership.
- Cardinal Christoph Schoenborn also accused Cardinal Angelo Sodano, the retired Vatican secretary of state, of causing "massive harm" to victims when he dismissed claims of clerical abuse as "petty gossip" on Easter Sunday.

Judging from the above, the two aforementioned prophecies are coming true. The following is an excerpt from a letter included in the book "Epistles on Clergy Abuse." The letter was written in 2004. It submits that the global sexual abuse scandal is the fulfillment of Jesus' prophecy and God's will.

"At the risk of sounding like a preacher, I would ask this question, "What makes anyone think that this isn't God's way of cleansing his church?" Meaning, who is to deny that it is not God's plan that the church hits critical mass? If we believe in a righteous God, we should have enough faith in him to believe that he would not let his church go down this path forever. My faith tells me that this whole crisis is his way of cleansing what needs to be cleaned. The new is always built on the ashes of the old. I would use this as prima facia evidence to anyone who argued to the contrary:

Luke 12: 1- 4, He began to say to his disciples first, "Beware of the leaven of the Pharisees, which is hypocrisy. Nothing is covered up that will not be revealed, or hidden that will not be known. Whatever you have said in the dark shall be heard in the light, and what you have whispered in private rooms shall be proclaimed upon the housetops."

Personally, I can't think of a better verse in the whole of the Gospels to describe what is currently transpiring. The dirty laundry is getting aired, the folly grows on a daily basis (Erasmus is laughing up his sleeve) and there is nothing all the church henchmen, bishops, cardinals and pope can do to stop it however hard they might try. This is the beginning of their end.

The court decisions, the penalties, the bankruptcies and continuous exposure of more folly such as Mahony in LA are playing out like a script. The script is authored by God and just like the Pharisees and Scribes of Jesus' time, the current hierarchy is blind to the fact that their days are numbered.
Vinnie"

One could easily assume that the current clergy abuse scandal is the fulfillment of this prophecy, but it is doubtful. As the derision grows between the good and the evil that have coexisted in the Vatican, more shocking revelations and accusations will surface along with the evidence necessary to prove them. Jesus told us all would be made known, the subsequent prophecies were reminders given to the hierarchy. Like their earlier counterparts, the Pharisees and Scribes, these warnings have been totally ignored.

Now the piper has to be paid and Ezekiel's prophecy is unfolding.

Ezekiel 13: 21-23:
Your veils also I will tear off, and deliver my people out of your hand, and they shall be no more in your hand as prey; and you shall know that I am the Lord. Because you have disheartened the righteous falsely, although I have not disheartened him, and you have encouraged the wicked, that he should not turn from his wicked way to save his life; therefore you shall no more see delusive visions nor practice divination; I will deliver my people out of your hand.

Letter to a newspaper

I find it so very sad to watch people argue over abuse. The truth of the matter is that it is a crime whether it is done by a priest or a school teacher. Does a child suffer more at the hands of a priest or a teacher? Probably not although when a child sexually abused by a priest; there is generally no opportunity to seek solace from God.

Another sad part about clergy abuse is that its ramifications are felt by all Catholics. It makes one ashamed to be a Catholic and that causes anger. Unfortunately, the anger is generally misplaced. The term Catholic Bashing is overplayed. People who speak about clergy abuse within the Catholic Church are not criticizing church doctrine, they are not criticizing Jesus; they are criticizing people, bishops. If the anger and energy that goes into arguing about who has more abusers, the church or the school, was concentrated on getting the message to the bishops, there would be no problem. The problem isn't one of faith and it certainly does not contradict anything Jesus said. Matt: 18 tells us that Jesus roundly condemned child abusers in the harshest language used in the Gospels. It is a sin that the bishops don't heed the gospels. Canon Law, specifically, Canon 748, tells us "All are bound to seek the truth in matters which concern God and his church. Therefore writing a letter pointing out the global nature of clergy abuse is in keeping with the above Canon.

For those interested in finding out more about the global scope of clergy abuse, you can go to this website. http://www.catholica.com.au/gc2/vn/001_vn_310808.php.

The Star Tribune ran this story on September 10, 2008 and reported the following: "The Archdiocese of St. Paul and Minneapolis on Wednesday was accused of helping an Ecuadorian priest flee the United States last year after he allegedly molested a 4-year-old girl in Minneapolis..."
What kind of monster sexually abuses a four-year-old girl? Worse still is the person who lets him get away with it and helps him flee the country!

Those who are tired of seeing the stories of abuse in the papers don't need to waste their energy defending their faith; it is not the faith that is the problem. It is the hierarchy that needs to be the focal point of your anger and energies. The letter only points to the truth. Put your anger where it belongs, with the people who have brought this scandal upon the church and by association, the people of the church. The bishops have caused this problem by their failure to obey civil, moral and God's laws.

White hair, White Robes, White Lies and White elephants

In the movie "Chicago," a wife comes home to find her husband in bed with two women and screams, "How could you!" The husband replies, "Are you going to believe me or your eyes!" Today the Vatican is asking us to believe them and not your eyes, heart and mind. The outcries emanating from the Vatican and spreading around the globe give testimony to the big lie. It is déjà vu all over again. We've all heard these tired, lame and intelligence insulting excuses before. Eight years ago, the clergy abuse crisis was simply an "American Problem" caused by the decadent materialism that had become American society.

Once again the church is being picked on. Once again they've rolled out the well worn, clichéd excuses. Look at all the good the church has done! This is a media lynch mob! It is a concerted effort to undermine the church and its teachings! The Catholic Church is being persecuted! Public schools are worse than churches! "What about the clergy abuse occurring in other religions," and the list goes on ad nauseum.

The two main differences between 2002 and now is the knowledge that clergy sexual abuse as a "global blight on the church" and secondly that the cover-up extends all the way up to the white haired, white robed pope. This confirms what was surmised eight years ago, but was never allowed to be put into print. Yet the chain of evidence does reach the pope. Not in one instance, but in several. Also because the pope is directly linked to the cover-up of clergy abuse, the "white" lies have grown and the propaganda has increased a hundred fold with some of the most despicable utterances ever heard from both the Vatican and several bishops trying to either defend the indefensible or score points with their earthly boss.

Two of the most recent and more heinous diatribes are as follows: From New York's own tower of enlightenment Archbishop Dolan, "The accusations against the pope are akin to Jesus' suffering" Matthew: 18, tells us Jesus said those who lead children astray would be better off having a millstone tied around their necks and dropped into the deepest part of the sea. Dolan, ever the intellectual, has not made the connection that Jesus was against child abuse. Of course, one-upmanship being a trademark of the panderer, the Vatican's own Rev. Raniero Cantalamessa, Papal Homilist, chimed in equating of the outrage of the public against the Vatican for covering up unspeakable sexual crimes against children with the persecution of the Jews! Well if that doesn't trigger a gag reflex! Where was this priest when hundreds of thousands of children were being sexually persecuted around the globe? This train of thought is exemplary of the cultural elitism that is so prevalent in the Vatican: "It is okay for us to persecute children, but because we have divine origins, no one can persecute us even if we have committed "The Worst Crime" as defined in the Vatican document: Crimens: Sollicitationis: Title V.

Unlike JPII, Benedict XVI has supporters who will swear that he has done more to eradicate sexually abusive priests than any other pope before him. He doesn't deserve the ill attention he is getting for the cases of Fr. Hullermann of Germany, Fr. Murphy of Wisconsin or Rev. Stephen Kiesle of California. Regardless of these cases which establish a direct papal connection, they are only additional evidence of a white robed pope who is and was thoroughly familiar with the scope of clergy abuse. He is all too familiar with the crime of shuffling pedophiles which has been committed globally by large numbers of the hierarchy. Hullermann and the other cases suggest; that the above includes the white haired white robed pope, which brings us to the white haired, white elephant in the middle of Rome.

The Papal Basilica of Saint Mary Major has as its archpriest (manager) the notorious white haired Cardinal Bernie Law of Boston infamy. He is the "White Haired White Elephant" of Rome. True, JPII officially gave Law the job, but Ratzinger's influence over the dying pope cannot be denied. He probably blessed it and regardless of his role in the appointment, Benedict has allowed Law to keep the job for the past five years. This is the fact which belies Benedict's true feelings for prelates who have prized protecting the church over the lives of children. The scourge of Boston whose purposeful transferring of pedophile priests led to the rape, sodomization and molestation of hundreds of children still sits in a seat of power. There in the middle of Rome this aberration of a man stands as a mirror to all that is wrong with the church.

What is the white haired, white robed pope to do with this white elephant in his back yard? Build Basilicas all over Rome to accommodate every cardinal guilty of playing shuffle the sexual abuser? Even the Vatican can't afford such an ambitious building binge. Yet Law is there. No one mentions him anymore, but he will always stand at the head of the line with Boston as the starting point for the global spread of the clergy abuse scandal. Such is his legacy.

Law, this white haired red robed white elephant is the reason that the white haired white robed pope is powerless to reprimand or remove other Cardinal criminals. Cardinal Egan of New York, Cardinal George of Chicago, Cardinal Mahony of Los Angeles, Cardinal Brady of Ireland and of course himself as Cardinal Ratzinger are all guilty of enabling sexual predators. It has been fascinating to follow the verbiage as the white haired white robed pope has toned down his rhetoric. He went from holding all those responsible for abusing children to the current: We will rid the church of abusing priests. One has to surmise that the hierarchy like the church is sacrosanct!

So like the Coliseum of Rome, a reminder of a coarse vulgar time when people were slaughtered for the amusement of the masses, Rome also has Benedict's white elephant, Cardinal Law a living testimony to a hierarchy who worshipped the church more than the founding God and His principles.

Until such time as the white haired white robed pope removes his white elephant along with the cadre of hierarchal enablers, the white robes will continue to be stained.

Jesus Gave us the Beatitudes, Benedict Delivers Platitudes

"A man of words and not of deeds is like a garden filled with weeds." wrote the poet Rod McKuen. How applicable is this to today's response to the decades old blind eye given to the rape sodomization and molestation of countless children in Ireland given by the current pontiff. It is also applicable to the last pope who held a summit eerily familiar to the Irish bishops meeting with the current pope which took place eight years ago with the bishops from the United States. There are two common threads: Sexual abuse and Cardinal Ratzinger who was responsible for investigating clergy abuse then, now Pope Benedict. For eight consecutive years, we have had nothing but platitudes from the Vatican.

2001: As Cardinal Ratzinger, Benedict reaffirms the validity of Crimen Sollicitationis which imposes the "Secrets of the Holy Office" on anyone with knowledge of priests violating the confessional or sexually abusing children, which means they are silenced forever.

April 2002: Pope JP II calls clergy abuse Mysterium Iniquitous.

April 2002: "There is no room in the priesthood for those who would abuse children" Pope JP II

April, 2008: "I am deeply ashamed." The words uttered by Benedict on the plane ride over to the United States.

July, 2009: At the Catholic World Youth Day in Australia Benedict said, "I ask all of you to support and assist your bishops, and to work together with them in combating this evil. Victims should receive compassion and care, and those responsible for these evils must be brought to justice."

December, 2009: Pope Benedict said today after meeting with Irish bishops at the Vatican that he was "deeply disturbed and distressed" and would write a pastoral letter to the people of Ireland

February, 2010: "The Holy Father observed that the sexual abuse of children and young people is not only a heinous crime, but also a grave sin which offends God."

After hearing these platitudes, we must now ask what adjectives of solace Benedict will offer to the people of Germany when their smoldering clergy abuse scandal burns brightly. Will it be: aghast, appalled, baffled, bewildered, chagrinned, confused...? Because it involves the Jesuits, will he return to the Latin of his predecessor by labeling clergy abuse Mysterium Iniquitous?

No need to ask what Jesus would say, He's already said it!

Jesus said: "You hypocrites! Well did Isaiah prophecy of you, when he said: This people honors me with their lips, But their heart is far from me; In vain do they worship me; teaching as doctrines the precepts of man". Matt: 15:7-9,

Such is the stuff of platitudes!

Benedict's own words betray him for what he is! Before God and man the infallible pope has shown himself a hypocrite. His predecessor JP II said, "There is no room in the church for those who would abuse children." Reporting to Pope John Paul as head of the Congregation for the Doctrine of Faith, the office that handled all clergy abuse accusations, then Cardinal Ratzinger's record on clergy abuse was abysmal. As a cardinal, he disobeyed and broke his sacred vow to obey the pope in all matters. Cardinal Ratzinger, by ignoring JP II's proclamation, proclaimed to the world that there is room in the priesthood for those who would abuse children by failing to rid the global priesthood of those who did in fact abuse children and those that enabled them.

Benedict, in dealing with Ireland, reneged on his own words spoken as pope before God and man when he said, "Those responsible for these evils must be brought to justice." The tragedy, disgrace, and grave scandal that is known as the Irish Clergy Abuse Scandal was an opportunity for the pope to prove himself a man of God as well as a man of his word. By his own words and lack of deeds he has proven to the world he is neither. Therein lies the rub. If he performs the rites of degradation so richly deserved upon certain Irish bishops, then he himself must step down because he too is steeped in the blood of innocent children by his omissions.

The Catechism tells us the following:

2326: Scandal is a grave offense when by deed or omission it deliberately leads others to sin gravely.

2287: Anyone who uses the power at his disposal in such a way that it leads others to do wrong becomes guilty of scandal and responsible for the evil that he has directly or indirectly encouraged. "Temptations to sin are sure to come; but woe to him by whom they come!"

Canon Law tells us this:

Can. 1369: A person is to be punished with a just penalty, who, at a public event or assembly, or in a published writing, or by otherwise using the means of social communication, utters blasphemy, or gravely harms public morals, or rails at or excites hatred of or contempt for religion or the Church.

Has Benedict by his commissions and omissions when dealing with the Clergy Abuse Scandal gravely harmed public morals and excited hatred of and contempt for the Church?

Can. 1389 § 1: A person who abuses ecclesiastical power or an office, is to be punished according to the gravity of the act or the omission, not excluding by deprivation of the office, unless a penalty for that abuse is already established by law or precept.

§ 2 A person who, through culpable negligence, unlawfully and with harm to another, performs or omits an act of ecclesiastical power or ministry or office, is to be punished with a just penalty.

Common sense tells us that by failing to exercise his ecclesiastical power in refusing to remove the Irish bishops who prolonged the misery of Irish children, the pope has brought immeasurable scandal down upon the church and therefore violated Canon Law.

Pity the Catholic laity for having a pope who has brought scandal down upon their church. Pity the Catholic laity for not being able to do anything about it. In the United States, Catholics held hope out; First for the bishops to do the right thing, then for the Cardinals to do the right thing and then for the pope to do the right thing. Catholics around the globe have been waiting and waiting and waiting. The Irish like the Americans and the Canadians and the Australians before them have just found out that nothing is going to happen to those who permitted wolves in collars to prey on the most defenseless of our society, the children.

The Catholics of Ireland have just received their Platitudes.

One can only imagine how difficult it must be for Catholics to have a pope devoid of personal integrity. A shameless leader who will tell one audience that those who are responsible must be brought to justice and then tell another audience that he is deeply disturbed with no reference to justice and then to tell yet another that it is a lapse in the morals of the times completely ignoring the fifteen hundred year written church history documenting clergy abuse.

What is a good Catholic to do? Find solace in the words of the Savior

Luke 12: 1- 4: "He began to say to his disciples first, "Beware of the leaven of the Pharisees, which is hypocrisy. Nothing is covered up that will not be revealed, or hidden that will not be known. Whatever you have said in the dark shall be heard in the light, and what you have whispered in private rooms shall be proclaimed upon the housetops."

Is there a better passage in all the Gospels than this to describe the Irish Clergy Abuse Scandal? Testimony before Inquiries has come to light. Cover-ups have come to light, complicity has come to light, the rape, sodomization and molestation of children have come to light. The culture of deceit has come to light. This is the fulfillment of the words of Gospel. It is Revelations; those marked with stain of children are the same ones who are marked with the sign of evil.

It is time for all to remember that Jesus and his teachings neither abide in pomp and circumstance nor in bricks and mortar, but in the hearts of men and women.

The Survivor's Dream

I have a dream that one day the pain of clergy abuse survivors will be recognized by the Roman Catholic Church and the laity will grasp the immense harm done to all the victims of clerical abuse.

I have a dream that one day the red hats of the hierarchy will openly admit the length and breadth of the clergy abuse without having the courts impose their will upon the church.

I have a dream that one day even the Vatican, a state sweltering with the heat of injustice, sweltering with the heat of oppression, will be transformed into an oasis of freedom and justice in the path of the Lord.

I have a dream where all little children will one day be allowed to grow up without having to fear sexual abuse. Where children are not looked upon as baubles or sex objects to be used and discarded by so called "men of God," but respected as the human beings they are.

I have a dream today!

I have a dream that one day, in the Vatican, with its vast hypocrisy, with its pope having his lips dripping with the words of "We didn't know" and "I'm deeply disturbed" — one day right there in the Vatican survivors, men and women, will be able to join hands and be recognized for the living hell the church put them through.

I have a dream today!

I have a dream that one day truth and justice shall be exalted, and every participant responsible for clergy abuse shall be laid low, the extent of their hypocrisy made plain, and the crooked crosiers will be made straight; and the glory of the Lord shall be revealed and the flesh of all children will be safe from predators.

And in my dream, Dr. King said, "Amen"

Machiavelli and the Irish Clergy Abuse Scandal

Four bishops is a good start, but its right out of the Machiavelli playbook. In chapter XIX: Essential to Avoid being Hated or Despised, Machiavelli advising the prince on how to maintain power, he says, "thus if it was in those days necessary to satisfy the soldiers (bishops) rather the people, this was because the soldiers (bishops) were more powerful than the people. Nowadays, princes must satisfy the people, for they are more powerful than the soldiers (bishops).Consider the following passage: "To this end he (the Prince) appointed Messer Remiro d'Orco, a cruel and energetic man, as governor giving him full powers. This official, to his own great renown, soon made the province peaceful and united" The Duke fully aware of the hatred that Messer d'Orco was inspiring rode in and promptly executed him, which brought the Duke instant acclaim from all the people.

The hierarchy of the Roman Catholic Church is feudal in nature. Every bishop and cardinal has to swear a most sacred oath of fealty to the Holy Father including his life if necessary. So what if four bishops have fallen on their croziers? Does a department store change its culture by replacing the dummies in their windows? There are hundreds of Irish priests standing in line with bated breath ready to assume the title and power that goes with being appointed bishop. Is Diarmuid Martin the pope's version of d'Orco? Was Martin given the authority to chop heads? If so he is using that authority well.

The danger is, as pointed out in The Prince, that it is in the best interest of both the pope and the church to have a man like Martin in place. Will the abrupt forced resignation of a few bishops after the obligatory protests of innocence appease the masses or will the laity demand more? How far is Martin and his Prince prepared to go to appease the masses?

And what of the Cardinal Emeritus Desmond Connell? Will the Irish laity forget that he appointed the now disgraced Eamonn Walsh as his senior secretary while Archbishop of Dublin? Was that appointment tantamount to pronouncing Walsh as his heir apparent? Will the laity forget that Connell was shamed into dropping his request to withhold 5,000 documents regarding clerical abuse from the commission even as he was Cardinal Emeritus; this despite those same documents being handed over to the commission by Archbishop Martin? Was that Connell's final embarrassment leading to a capitulation of the power and papal authority wielded by Martin?

Will Martin be rewarded for slaying his fellow bishops with an elevation to the rank of cardinal and be given a shot at the white hat? Most assuredly so, but the biggest question is the following: "Will anything change within the church?" Sadly the answer to that is a resounding no unless the laity gets deeply involved. Why, because the Prince is still in power and the Prince is still calling the shots and no Prince will never voluntarily relinquish power.

What is the difference between the Vatican and the Great Pyramids of Egypt?

The pyramids are along side the Nile, the Vatican is deep in denial. To wit, this is the statement that was quoted in the Irish Examiner today about the acceptance of the resignation of Bishop Murray.

> A statement from the Vatican on the resignation did not mention clerical abuse but said the Pope had accepted Bishop Murray's resignation according to a clause of Canon Law that calls on bishops to quit if they cannot fulfill their duties for a "serious reason".

Without mentioning crimes like willful neglect, depraved indifference, aiding and abetting in the commission of felonies and probably breaking a host of other laws, the Vatican remains mute on the subject of accepting Murray's resignation for the real reasons it was tendered. We must remember, of course, that the Vatican is country and that Murray is a citizen of that city-state, which has proven over and over again that they don't abide by the civil laws of any country.

One might then ask, "What about God and Church Law?" The answer here is that the Vatican flaunts God's Law: Scripture, the Catechism and Canon Law as easily as it flaunts Civil Law.

Don't take my word for it; it is here in the teachings of the church.

Scripture:

Matt. 18:6: "But whoever causes one of these little ones who believe in me to sin, it would be better for him to have a great millstone fastened round his neck and to be drowned in the depth of the sea."

Matthew, Mark and Luke all quote Jesus as directly speaking these words. However, only Matthew and Luke speak of a virginal birth and their descriptions are not direct quotes from Jesus but rather the narrative form. In the Magisterium, the spoken word of Jesus takes precedence over the narrative form. Therefore, the violation of children as an offense against God should be held in higher regard than the Virginal Birth. If that had been the case, these scandals would have never arisen.

Luke 12: 1- 4: He began to say to his disciples first, "Beware of the leaven of the Pharisees, which is hypocrisy. Nothing is covered up that will not be revealed, or hidden that will not be known. Whatever you have said in the dark shall be heard in the light, and what you have whispered in private rooms shall be proclaimed upon the housetops."

Is there any better passage in all the Gospels than this to describe the Clergy Sexual Abuse Scandal? Secret testimony before Inquiries has come to light. Cover-ups have come to light, complicity has come to light, the rape, sodomization and molestation of children has come to light. The culture of deceit has come to light. **This is not church bashing**; it is the fulfillment of the words of Gospel. The Vatican defends these hypocrites and now we know it.

Paul to the Corinthians:

This is St. Paul talking straight from his letters, straight from the New Testament, straight from the heart, straight from God or so we are told until the verse conflicts with the Vatican's objectives.

 1. Corinthians 1, 5: 1-2, It is actually reported that there is immortality among you, and of a kind that is not found even among pagans; for a man is living with his father's wife. And you are arrogant! Ought you not rather to mourn? **Let this be removed from you**.

 2. Corinthians 1, 5: 6-8, Your boasting is not good. Do you not know that a little leaven leavens the whole lump? **Cleanse out the old leaven** that you may be a new lump, as you really are unleavened.

 3. Corinthians 1, 5: 11-13, But rather I wrote to you not to associate with anyone who bears the name of brother if he is guilty of immorality or greed, or is an idolater, reviler, drunkard, or robber-not even to eat with such a one. For what have I to do with judging outsiders? Is it not those inside the church whom you are to judge? God judges those outside, **"Drive out the wicked person from among you."**

 4. Corinthians 1, 15: 33, Do not be deceived: **"Bad company ruins good morals."**

 Even without my emphasis, a blind man could see the exhortation here is to get rid of the evil within the ranks. We have been taught that there is indeed a family or Body of Christ and priests are the spiritual fathers; have we not? Well, there is spiritual incest in the family of Christ and the Vatican has fought long and hard against ending it.

 The above are scriptural admonitions for removing offending bishops and we didn't even get past Paul's first letter to the Corinthians. The word of God takes precedence over the word of man, yet the Vatican refuses to abide by the word of God. Did that change as the church changed from a spiritual entity to its current status of a bureaucracy? Is giving a back seat to Scripture a heresy? Paul speaks to that too.

 Paul: **Galatians 1: 9, "As we have said before, so now I say again, If anyone is preaching to you a gospel contrary to that which you received, let him be cursed."**

168

But what if Scripture are not the only thing being given a back seat by the Vatican? There are still church laws which provide for the removal of offending bishops. Let's examine what the Catechism has to say about the behavior of the bishops

Catechism

The dictionary definition of scandal: "a disgraceful event." These are the Catechism definitions:

2326: Scandal is a grave offense when by deed or omission it deliberately leads others to sin gravely.

Sounds like a duck!

2287: Anyone who uses the power at his disposal in such a way that it leads others to do wrong becomes guilty of scandal and responsible for the evil that he has directly or indirectly encouraged. "Temptations to sin are sure to come; but woe to him by whom they come!"

Walks like a duck!

2353: Fornication is carnal union between an unmarried man and an unmarried woman. It is gravely contrary to the dignity of persons and of human sexuality which is naturally ordered to the good of spouses and the generation and education of children. Moreover, it is a grave scandal when there is corruption of the young.

Talks like a duck!

So the acts of raping, sodomizing and molesting children, allowing it to continue and then covering it up can safely be assumed to be manifestly a grave scandal. Is it possible that the Vatican doesn't know these rules applied to cardinals, bishops and priests? This is what Canon Law has to say about the rules applying to bishops.

Canon Law

Can. 212 1: Priests and Bishops are also bound by this obedience, in fact more so since they are responsible for passing on to the faithful genuine Catholic teaching. In other words, a Bishop or Priest who dissents from Church teachings is not to be obeyed in that matter, rather all must obey the Magisterium at all times, as Vatican II states.

Hypocrisy in the Highest! The rules apply whether you wear a berretta up to a zucchetto.

Can. 1369: A person is to be punished with a just penalty, who, at a public event or assembly, or in a published writing, or by otherwise using the means of social communication, utters blasphemy, or gravely harms public morals, or rails at or excites hatred of or contempt for religion or the Church.

Has the Clergy Abuse Scandal gravely harm public morals and excite hatred of and contempt for the Church? Is a courtroom a pubic event? How about a press conference? Do either the Ferns Report or the Dublin Report qualify as a public event?

Can. 1389 § 1: A person who abuses ecclesiastical power or an office, is to be punished according to the gravity of the act or the omission, not excluding by deprivation of the office, unless a penalty for that abuse is already established by law or precept.

§ 2: A person who, through culpable negligence, unlawfully and with harm to another, performs or omits and act of ecclesiastical power or ministry or office, is to be punished with a just penalty.

Hypocrisy

Zephaniah 3:3-4: Her officials within her are lions; her judges are evening wolves that leave nothing till the morning, Her prophets are wanton, faithless men; *her priests profane what is sacred, they do violence to the law!*

Matt: 15:7-9: You hypocrites! Well did Isaiah prophecy of you, when he said: This people honors me with their lips, But their heart is far from me; In vain do they worship me; teaching as doctrines the precepts of man.

Matt 23: 25-28: Woe to you, you hypocrites! for you clean the outside of the cup and the dish, but inside they are full of greed and self-indulgence...Woe to you, you hypocrites! for you are like whitewashed graves, which appear beautiful on the outside, but are full of death and corruption. In the same way, you outwardly appear righteous, but inside you are full of hypocrisy and wickedness...Woe to you, you hypocrites! because you build tombs for the prophets, and decorate the graves of the righteous, and say, "If we had lived in the days of our fathers, we would not have shared with them in the blood of the prophets". But you are the descendants of those who murdered the prophets...You snakes, you brood of vipers, how will you escape being condemned to hell?

Conclusion

There is nothing wrong with the scriptures, the Catechism or Canon Law. Each prohibits the very fundamental issues of clergy sexual abuse. What is wrong is the hierarchal culture that has lost sight of the Word of God and its meaning. What is wrong is the culture of power, superiority and depraved indifference that infects today's hierarchy has no regard for the members of the Body of Christ. Evil has permeated the culture of the hierarchy. Ignorance is not an excuse. Church history contains admonitions against sexually abusing children that go back fifteen hundred years to the Council of Elvira. The hierarchy has become very much like the Pharisees, self-centered, overbearing and a burden upon the church. That burden has to be lifted.

Catholics all over the world have the right to expect an honest church. Dealing with human beings we can always expect flawed personalities, but as outlined above, when we find them, we have to be able to use the tools given to us rid the church of them.

Ireland, Another Papal Act of Attrition

In Ireland like the United States, Australia and a host of other countries, the Roman Catholic Church has adopted a policy of attrition. They will speak their platitudes, beat their chests and scream their mea culpas, but in the end nothing will have changed. Almost eight years have passed since the Boston Clergy Abuse Scandal burst upon the scene and not one member of the hierarchy has paid the price for their crimes or their sins.

In 2002, there was the Boston Clergy abuse scandal and the American church survived. Cardinal Bernie Law, the poster boy for the criminal neglect that led to hundreds of Boston area children being abused, is at the forefront of the storm. Pope John Paul II calls the major American Church leaders to Rome. After he meets with the American cardinals and bishops, Pope John Paul II declared that "there is no place in the priesthood and religious life for those who would harm the young" Has any member of the hierarchy responsible for the Boston debacle been forced to retire or get laicized for their criminal actions? No, Cardinal Law instead is whisked away to the Vatican and given a cushy job as the manager of one of Rome's most famous Basilicas. As a member of the Vatican, he has diplomatic immunity and escapes any justice that could have been meted out in the United States. So much for the phrase, "There is no place in the priesthood and religious life for those who would harm the young."

Pope John Paul II called the cardinals to Rome. The whole world watched as these white-haired men in their red robes donned their most solemn faces for this meeting. It proved to be a charade at best. Cardinal George fresh from the meeting told astonished reporters that there was a big difference between a repugnant predator like Fr. John Goeghan and a priest who after having a drink too many responded to an underage girl's advances. This was the first public indication that nothing had changed.

Then the joke that was to become known as the Dallas Charter came into existence. Later that same year in Dallas, Texas, all the bishops from around the country met with the same solemn plastic face. They created national drama vowing a new openness, compassion for the victims, cooperation with civil authorities and swift disciplining of offending priests. Anyone looking for confirmation that this document was nothing more than clerical wallpaper, need only to familiarize themselves with these two examples: 1. Cardinal Mahony's multiyear court battle to keep the names of priests who have sexually abused children a secret and 2. Cardinal George's handling of the Fr. McCormack case in Chicago. George and Mahony are the ranking cardinals in the United States and therefore, they set the example for the rest of the hierarchy.

About the same time in New York, the soon to be Cardinal Egan has the church clean up his past with a multimillion dollar settlement to victims of the Bridgeport Diocese. This is an effort to make him look squeaky clean to New Yorkers. A failed attempt at best. While cardinal, Egan fought tooth and nail legal battles to keep his horrid depositions a state secret. After seven years, the Supreme Court finally forced the courts to release the transcripts. So much for the openness declared in the Dallas Charter. During Egan's tenure, the two grand juries were convened, one on Long Island and one in Westchester County. The findings of both Grand Juries were the same, they found the church failed to supervise and prevent pedophile priests from being removed or charged for their criminal actions.

In Philadelphia, Pennsylvania, during 2005, yet another Grand Jury was report was released. Their findings, in over 500 pages, documented 50 years of sexual abuse by priests and harshly criticized the hierarchy for their failure to protect children. Similar results were found in in Grand Jury reports from Los Angeles to Boston. In each case, just as in Ireland with the Ferns and Dublin reports, the hierarchy of the church was universally condemned for their abysmal failure to protect children and the extremes they went to in order to protect their priests

In 2008 Pope Benedict XVI visited the United States. Before going on about that visit, it must be stated that before becoming pope, Pope Benedict was Cardinal Joseph Ratzinger, the Prefect of the Congregation for the Doctrine of the Faith formerly known as the Office of the Inquisition. It was his duty to handle all cases brought to the attention of Rome regarding sexually abusive priests. In April of 2008, while on the plane over to the United States, Benedict XVI said, "I am deeply ashamed" while referring to the Clergy Sex Abuse Scandal. How ashamed was he? He was so ashamed that he appointed Cardinal Levada formerly of California to take over his position as head of the Congregation for the Doctrine of Faith. How ashamed was he? He was so ashamed that he appointed Archbishop Raymond Burke of St. Louis to head the Vatican's highest court, which would be dealing with the most extreme cases of abuse. Anyone wishing to know the non-stellar record of these men on the issue of clergy abuse merely has to go to bishopaccountability.org and type in their names.

Later that same year, the pope visited Australia and had this to say to the Australians:

> "These misdeeds, which constitute so grave a betrayal of trust, deserve unequivocal condemnation...
> "I ask all of you to support and assist your bishops, and to work together with them in combating this evil. Victims should receive compassion and care, and those responsible for these evils must be brought to justice"

Once again bishops have been summoned to the Vatican, but this time it was the Irish bishops. The names had changed, but unfortunately, the attitudes remained the same. One thing had changed though, Benedict XVI had definitively reduced the tone of his rhetoric. Instead of demanding those responsible for these evils be brought to justice, he only said he was disturbed and distressed. Irish Catholics should be deeply insulted over this slight. Oh, the shock of it all to find out that in the world's most Catholic country, Ireland, priests were raping sodomizing and molesting young boys and girls. How distressed could the pope have been if he couldn't even muster the same kind of pseudo anger that he expressed in Australia? He is a disturbed enough individual however to realize that if he made a comment that was even close to what he said in Australia, he would might have to live up to his lip service.

Where does that leave Ireland? It leaves the Irish in the same boat as the Americans and the Australians. They are left facing a church that excels in the art of stonewalling. They are left facing a church that knows if they wait long enough and stall long enough, they will win the war of attrition. The Irish are left facing men who aren't human enough to recognize their own lack of humanity, for any man claiming to be part of humanity cannot in conscience permit the rape, sodomization and molestation of children.

 Now is the time for the Irish Catholics to shine. American, Australian, Canadian and Catholics from other countries have failed to hold their leadership accountable. The more time that passes after the release of the Dublin and Ferns reports, the less there will be done. If nothing is done, the church wins and goes on its merry way until the next time a clergy sexual abuse scandal rears its ugly head, which will be South America. There again, the war of attrition will be waged against the laity. If they too fail to prosecute, hundreds of thousands of children worldwide will continue to suffer the horrors of sexual abuse for centuries to come just as hundreds of thousands have suffered in centuries past.

 May St. Patrick give the Irish the strength to resist the war of attrition and throw the rest of the snakes out of the Ireland.

The Pope Soars to new Heights of Hypocrisy!

Is it politically correct to call the Pontiff a liar? Doing that would surely raise the ire of good Catholics all over the world eliciting both anger and hate from them. Questions are asked like, "Don't you know the pope is appointed by God?" This would then be followed by these worn down platitudes: The Catholic Church is no worse than any other church, the RCC has done so much good, the RCC doesn't even compare to the public schools etc., ad nauseum.

How do you get the masses to change their mind about their leader? How does one tell a person that has lived their life according to Catholic Rules that their leader doesn't follow them? How do change deeply embedded beliefs that are, in this day and age, groundless.

You start by showing people the truth, the facts!

The Irish Clergy Abuse Scandal is making Papal hypocrisy legendary. Last July, in Australia, oddly enough, for World Youth Day, the pope made the following statement:

> "These misdeeds, which constitute so grave a betrayal of trust, deserve unequivocal condemnation.

> "I ask all of you to support and assist your bishops, and to work together with them in combating this evil. Victims should receive compassion and care, and those responsible for these evils must be brought to justice.[1]"

It was a rousing speech that was carried in papers around the world. The pope sounded tough on clergy abuse, but was he really? He said, "Those responsible for these evils must be brought to justice." To date, not one bishop has been brought to justice. Have we seen anything near as profound from the pope about the events in Ireland which are by all accounts a hundred times worse? No, all we have heard is that he is deeply disturbed. No doubt, because only a deeply disturbed man could let such heinous crimes go unpunished. Since civil authorities across the globe are reluctant to pursue justice, the pope is the only one who has the power authority to administer justice to those bishops and cardinals responsible for perpetuating the evil of sexual abuse of children.

One has the right to ask this question of the pope, "How can you, Benedict XVI say those responsible must be brought to justice when you as the head of the RCC have steadfastly refused to hold even one bishop accountable for their criminal acts?" This is especially true after the pontiff has told us that their misdeeds deserve "unequivocal condemnation?" This year in Ireland as last year in Australia, the pontiff has yet to unequivocally condemn even the most flagrant enablers of sexually abusing priests.

The incredible hypocrisy of his statement becomes greatly amplified when you consider two things: 1. That it was made in front of the attendees at World Youth Day and 2. It was issued in the presence of Cardinal George Pell. How are we to reconcile the above with this story, which was all over the Australian media a week before the pope's visit?

> Australia's ABC television network revealed on July 7 that Cardinal Pell had written to an alleged victim of sexual abuse, telling him that there had been no other complaints against the priest he accused, on the same day that the prelate wrote another letter acknowledging assaults by the same priest.

Does the pope really think the laity is so stupid as not to recognize this blatant hypocrisy? Where are those condemnations now? Will the pope fire a bishop, a cardinal? How is the pope going to bring justice to Ireland? No, not just Ireland, justice to the world, because the clergy abuse scandal is global problem with documented cases in over 28 countries around the world. If one wants to familiarize themselves with the reasons the pope can't and won't, read the unifying theory of sexual abuse on this site at http://reform-network.net/?p=2408. Then wait, watch and see if anything is changed in Ireland. They can't do it because it will break the solidarity (glue) that holds the organization together.

Yet in the face of all this hypocrisy, where are laity? Where are the good priests? Where is the global sense of outrage against the murder, rape, sodomization and molestation of children by men of the cloth? Sinead O'Connor, is the only public figure in Ireland to call for the pope to step down. Only when the global church falls in lockstep behind that call will changes be made. To alter a quote of Daniel Patrick Moynihan, "A church that loses its sense of outrage is doomed to extinction."

At the Root of Clerical Sexual Abuse Are Celibacy, Power, Silence and Dehumanization Caused by Cultural Inbreeding

Dehumanization

Starving, gassing, burning, hacking, bombing and mutilating on a large scale are all well documented crimes against humanity. In each case humanity reflects on how inhuman man can be to his fellow man, decries and tries to destroy the offending dictators or regimes and puts up a memorial in the hope it doesn't happen again. The travesties generally last no longer than the time span of the despot's rule: I.e. Hitler, Pol Pot, Idi Amin etc. There is however, one very notable exception. That exception is the rape, sodomization and molestation of children by the clergy of the Roman Catholic Church. There is ample documentation showing this carnage has been carried out unabated for centuries!

The focal point of this essay is not the pedophile priest, for we know what he is. He is a sick twisted deviant who relishes despoiling innocence. He is the predator. An animal who exists for his next meal: despoiling an innocent child. Like the jackal, he preys on the weak and vulnerable in order to feed his sick insatiable appetite. This examination will focus on the following: How the pederast became an integral part of the clergy, why their handlers, the bishops, allow these jackals free reign to prey on children, and the causes for the utter silence of the priesthood at large on the subject of the sexual abuse of children by priests.

What do you call a man who knowingly allows a malevolent individual to prey on children? What term can be coined for a man who upon finding out that a perverted priest has violated a child, moves said priest to new hunting grounds? How do you address someone who knowingly sends a serial child molester into a parish with an elementary school? What term can accurately describe a man who sends a child raping priest out of his country to prey upon the children of poor indigent people; whose only hope in life is an afterlife in heaven? Sadly, there is one answer to all of these questions, you call him bishop!

Any man worthy of the name man, with merely a meager amount of humanity, would run and hide in deep shame at the thought of allowing innocent children to be sexually abused, but not a bishop. Any father, who understands what it means to have, hold, raise and love a child, would cringe at the thought of putting any child in the path of a sexual predator, but not a bishop. If a man's son or daughter runs afoul of a sexual predator, he cries and berates himself for years burdened with the guilt of thinking he has failed his child, but not a bishop. If the child commits suicide as a direct effect of the abuse, that man takes his burden to the grave, but not a bishop! A bishop will defend his logic for allowing children to be raped by a priest from a pulpit, in front of cameras and even under oath in written depositions. Normal human beings just don't do that!

Normal people are simply not capable of casually allowing children as young as four years old to be raped, sodomized or molested. This is not a character trait found in the general public! Why, then, does it exist in the hierarchy of the Catholic Church? Societies as well as cultures around the world have stringent laws against sexually abusing children. Interpol has the prevention of sexual abuse of children as one of its main goals. The U.N. through its UNICEF organization has put together "The Convention on the Rights of the Child," which states a child has the right to grow up unmolested. It has been signed by most of the civilized countries of the world with one major exception, the Vatican.

There is no love in and even less humanity in any person who moves sexually abusing priests among parishes as easily as he would move a chess piece across a board. Men such as this can't possibly stake a claim to humanity or to the teachings of Jesus. Therefore, the imperative question is, "What caused these men: priests, bishops and cardinals, to shed their humanity and act in ways that defy human dignity?"

Cultural Inbreeding

The answer, for all who care to look, lies in the history of Catholic Church. Much has been written about the term culture. Culture is something that defines an individual or groups of individuals. It includes things like, beliefs, foods, language, dances, music, etc. Cultures also have traditions some of which can date back hundreds or even thousands of years. Rites of passage into manhood have long been a cultural tradition. Circumcision is a good example. It goes back millennia. So it is safe to assume that if the same thing continuously occurs within the same group over hundreds or even thousands of years, it is deeply embedded in that culture. So let it be known that history tells us that the sexual abuse of children is a longstanding part of the culture of the clergy in the Roman Catholic Church.

The following are historical examples of this malevolent cultural practice recorded over a sixteen-hundred year period.

The Fourth Century
From the Council of Elvira 306: There were a host of Canons, internal church laws, which came out of this Ecumenical Council. Here are just two of many that speak to the subject of sexual abuse.[1]

18.   Bishops, presbyters, and deacons, once they have taken their place in the ministry, shall not be given communion even at the time of death if they are guilty of sexual immorality. Such scandal is a serious offense.
71.   Those who sexually abuse boys may not commune even when death approaches.

Laws are not written to protect children from things that don't occur and if the church enforced these laws today, the number of clerics receiving communion the world over would drop significantly.

The Eleventh Century: St. Peter Damian's Letter 31, the Book of Gomorrah (Liber Gomorrhianus), Randy Engel says it is "the most extensive treatment and condemnation by any Church Father of clerical pederasty and homosexual practices. [2] His manly discourse on the vice of sodomy in general and clerical homosexuality and pederasty in particular, is written in a plain and forthright style that makes it quite readable and easy to understand." [2]

Pierre J. Prayer translated Peter Damian's work and in his introduction, he makes this comment: "One of his consistent themes was an attack on the sexual immorality of the clergy and the laxness of the superiors who refused to take a strong hand against it." [3]

We can take away two things from this book. 1. The problem of sexual immorality had to be so widespread that Damian deemed it necessary to write this treatise in a time when writing was a tedious job done with quill and ink on very expensive paper. 2. If the Church Fathers had disagreed with Peter Damian, his treatise the on sexual immorality of the clergy would have never survived and he would never have attained sainthood.

The Seventeenth Century
From Karen Liebreich's book Fallen Order: "One of Fr. Calasanz's recruits in particular, Father Stephano Cherubini, was to prove a disaster. Cherubini was dogged throughout his career by allegations of inappropriate behaviour with pupils, but his powerful family ties and connections with the Inquisition made Calasanz wary of expelling him. Instead, he invented that staple of the Catholic church in subsequent centuries when faced with paedophile priests – he promoted him, writing to the priest he charged with clearing this up: "I want you to know that your reverence's sole aim is to *cover up this great shame* in order that it does not come to the notice of our superiors"[4]

The Twenty-First Century:
From the Boston Globe referring to Cardinal Law: "He knew about allegations that John J. Geoghan, the now-convicted child molester, had been attacking little boys and returned him to parish work nevertheless.

Law knew that the Rev. Peter J. Frost was an admitted sex addict and child abuser and still held open the prospect of future ministry for him." [5]

Author's note: There are numerous books such as <u>Sons of Perdition</u> by Jay Nelson or <u>Sex, Priests, and Secret Codes: The Catholic Church's 2,000</u>

Year Paper Trail of Sexual Abuse by Doyle, Sipe, and Wal dedicated to chronicling clerical sexual abuse both over its long and sordid history as well as during specific periods.

We can therefore deduce the following about the culture of the church regarding clerical sexual abuse:

1. Any member of the hierarchy who even attempts to claim ignorance of clerical sexual abuse or its history in the church is either a liar or an ignoramus.

2. Celibacy and complete Chastity are unattainable myths. If the combined force, intelligence and fear of God commanded by the church over a millennium cannot teach priests to adhere to their vows, the vow is impossible to keep.

3. It is said that is repeatedly doing the same thing over and over again for centuries and expecting a different outcome is insanity. Celibacy and chastity belong under this definition.

4. Clerical child abuse has been going on uninterrupted in the RCC for a millennium and a half. These are not new crimes; just old ones getting new publicity.

5. For the last thousand years, the tradition has been to gloss over and cover up the existence of violations of both celibacy and the sexual abuse of children.

6. The hierarchy of the Catholic Church has passed the tradition of protecting priests at all costs down through the ages to where it has become a cultural policy.

The Depths of Depravity: Dehumanizing Actions

The culture of the RCC has been to totally ignore their victim's pain and suffering. There is not a shred of historical information that proves otherwise. The RCC has steadfastly refused to promote the healing and well being of children who have fallen victim to predator priests. Even to this day, the church fights tooth and nail in their attempts to ignore their victims. Are these the acts of an organization with humanitarian goals or one that has been dehumanized? Certainly they do not follow the precepts of Jesus.

The too obvious questions are: "What kind of men would allow heinous crimes against the bodies and souls of children to go unpunished?" What kind of men would then leave these children to suffer in silence? Never once has a bishop said that he considered the children when transferring sexually abusing priests to a new parish. Heartless is a kind moniker. Inhumane is a better one. The less obvious and more important question is why would men allow these same crimes against humanity to persist over centuries? To really understand that question, you have to first understand the depths of depravity reached by priests committing these crimes before you can truly appreciate the inhuman actions of person that lets them continue unabated.

The detachment molesting priests are capable of borders on sociopathic; meaning there is no remorse for even the most monstrous of crimes. The following stories are true and the reader must remember these are not the worst. Propriety and respect for the reader prohibit going into graphic detail regarding the sordid crimes priests have committed upon the bodies of children. However, for those seeking verification, a quick search of the Internet reveals over three quarters of a million entries on the subject of clergy abuse. The query "survivor stories of clergy abuse" produces almost ninety thousand entries.

> The Archdiocese of St. Paul and Minneapolis was accused of helping an Ecuadorian priest flee the United States in November of 2008 after he allegedly molested a 4-year-old girl in Minneapolis.[6]

> A woman goes to her parish priest for counseling. She tells the priest that she wants to be a good Catholic, but is having a hard time because she was sexually assaulted by a priest as a young girl. This priest gains her confidence and uses her needs to get to her twin boys and sexually abuses both of them. One of the boys, as a result of the abuse, attempts suicide. As he lay in his hospital bed hovering between life and death with his mom at his side, who comes to her offering prayers and consolation? None other than her counselor, her parish priest, and her son's abuser, the same man whose sexual abuse drove the boy to attempt suicide in the first place!

Behavior like that defies any connection with either a conscience or humanity, yet it happened. Worse still is the abusing priest who has the unbridled audacity to say the funeral mass for one of his victims that succeeded in committing suicide. This behavior strongly mirrors that of the arsonist who delights in watching his flames devour a building.

Just as twisted as the above but on a different level is the priest who while buttoning the cassock of the young altar boy fondles the boy's genitals. Ten minutes later, he is using those same fingers to lift and consecrate a host. In yet another few minutes, he is using those same fingers to place the host on the tongues of adoring parishioners seeking communion with Jesus. He moves blithely from one despicable act to the next with no remorse, no conscience or one so suppressed as not to exist.

He has no fear, not even the wrath of God. His abominable sacrilege and desecration of children and the host continues Sunday after Sunday.

How can anyone claiming ties to humanity perpetuate these acts by moving offending priests from parish to parish? Yet, bishops, cardinals and popes have done it as routinely as saying mass. First they ignored the complaints. Then, when the complaints grew too loud, they simply moved the priest to another unsuspecting parish, with unsuspecting parents and vulnerable children. With a fifteen hundred year history of sexually abusing children, the RCC can hardly expect us to believe they **"Didn't know!"** Bishops knew children were being raped, sodomized and molested, but simply did not care. Behavior such as this is both heartless and inhuman. For centuries, bishops have knowingly tossed children to predator priests as easily as throwing peanuts to an elephant. Consider the following: In Canada, there are over 50,000 aboriginal children missing. They either died or were murdered in residential schools across the country.

> "An international tribunal found the government and several churches guilty of the crime of genocide. Ever since June, 1998, when an international tribunal in Vancouver found your government, the RCMP, and the Catholic, United, Anglican, and Presbyterian churches guilty of acts of Genocide against native people, the world has waited to see if your government and the churches in question would respond to the charges brought against you by survivors of the residential schools. Your government and these churches have shown by your silence that you do not dispute the charges of mass murder and Genocide being made against you.[7]"

The story from Ireland is just as bad.

> In Ireland, several commissions on Clergy Sexual Abuse have filed their reports over the past few years and each report from the Ferns Report to the most recent Dublin Report unequivocally condemns the Roman Catholic Church for their dismal failure in dealing with priests who abuse. The reports deal with the thousands of Irish children abused while the bishops of the church in Ireland did nothing to put a halt to it.

Why is it that bishops have no fear? There are a couple of possibilities: either they know there is no God, think they are gods or they believe they will suffer no consequences because they were appointed by God. The first one is difficult to prove, but there is a plethora of evidence for the latter two. Defying criminal law, while hiding behind a false interpretation of "separation of church and state," bishops believe they are the only ones who can censure the criminal acts of a priest. Believing they are appointed by God, they act horrified when anyone has the effrontery to cast aspersions on their character and they have history on their side because of the thousands of cases where bishops knowingly shuffled pedophiles, to date not one has been jailed. Not one bishop has paid the consequences for the most egregious crimes against humanity dating back a thousand years.

Somewhere during the first thousand years, after the Council of Elvira, the hierarchy realized there could be no such thing as a celibate priest and the stringent rules were relaxed. Concurrent with this knowledge, men in the hierarchy have lost touch with both their humanity and the teachings of Jesus.

The Culture of Power and Hubris

Cultural clerical inbreeding has wed the "god complex" with hubris. A person who is said to have a "god complex" does not believe he is God, but acts so arrogantly that he might as well believe he is a god or that he was appointed to act by a god" and hubris applies to any outrageous act or exhibition of pride or disregard for basic moral laws."

Hubris or the outrageous acts and total disregard for moral laws displayed by today's hierarchy are readily explained by the above. Now compare the definitions above to the passage below. It was written to the members of an organization known as the Conference of the Major Superiors of Men by their then Executive Director. These words, written shortly after Boston's sex scandal broke were truly prophetic. The organization's name alone should give the reader a preview of how high they hold themselves in their own esteem. The CMSM represents all the religious orders of priests. Behold the words of those who believe themselves the divinely appointed betters of the human race.

> "The days of the *pass* or *station house adjustment* for Father or Brother by the Irish cop or prosecutor are over. Either we will learn to become more comfortable in the gaze of the ***rude and scoffing multitude*** (depending on our attitude) or we will be dragged ***kicking and screaming*** into a new future for religion and religious life"[8](italics are the author's emphasis)

The thought processes that allow priests to refer to the laity as the "**rude and scoffing multitude**" are the same ones that allow and even encourage priests to use children as sex objects. "Less than" is the operative concept; it allows the children to be treated as though they are mere baubles to be used, abused and discarded. This is the dehumanized effect: those who believe they are "better than" humanity are the ones who, in reality, lose their humanity. They suffer "the disconnect" of being separated from humanity by their vows so they had to conjure up a rationale to compensate for that disconnect. Nowhere is this false ideology more clearly stated than in Vehementer Nos an encyclical promulgated by Pius X in 1905.

> "It follows that the Church is essentially an unequal society, that is, a society comprising two categories of persons, the Pastors and the flock,

those who occupy a rank in the different degrees of the hierarchy and the multitude of the faithful. So distinct are these categories that with the pastoral body only rests the necessary right and authority for promoting the end of the society and directing all its members towards that end; the one duty of the multitude is to allow themselves to be led, and, like a docile flock, to follow the Pastors."[9]

Being chosen by God to lead sinners into the light goes a long way to rationalizing their separation from and superiority over humanity. But it only goes so far because it never satisfies the true itch..

In Genesis 2, God says, referring to Adam, "It is not good that the man should be alone." In Matt. 19:5 Jesus said, "Have you not read that he who made them from the beginning made them male and female, and said, "For this reason a man shall leave his father and mother and be joined to his wife, and the two shall become one flesh?" Leave it to the Catholic Church to countermand both the Father and the Son just as they have done in Matthew 18 where Jesus uses his harshest language to describe the fate of child abusers. Then again in Matt: 23: 9 where Jesus says: "And call no man your father on earth, for you have one Father, who is in heaven." Isn't it about time someone read this passage to the "Holy Father"? Hubris?

Much has been written about the need human beings have for intimacy. Studies have found that human babies need physical and emotional contact in order to thrive. The operative word here is thrive. More than that, recent studies prove the need for intimacy continues into adulthood and those who are not afforded intimacy generally turn to addictions of all sorts. God instilled in man and woman the need for intimacy. The only organization that has refused to recognize this concept is the Roman Catholic Church. The Eastern Orthodox Church came to grips with it a long time ago.

The lack of intimacy created by the unfounded and unproven beliefs of the Roman Catholic Church about celibacy has created a unique brand of both hetero and homosexuality. The clerics that rule the church have created an institution of men and women, who because of their vows, can only indulge in unfulfilling sex. Whether with one another, one night stands, prostitutes, sexual abuse of children, adults, or pornography; they are all classic symptoms of those who lack intimacy in their lives. Contrary to what the church would have us believe, being married to the church doesn't fill that void. God put two sexes on the earth so man and woman would fulfill each other. Louise Hagget's Bingo Report [10] sites loneliness as the primary reason for breaking vows and what is loneliness but the lack of intimacy.

A prominent psychiatrist who worked for the church had this to say:

In fact, statements by Dr. Jay Feierman support a link between sexual repression and pedophilia. As a psychiatrist who has met with hundreds of pedophilic priests at a Catholic treatment center in New Mexico, Feierman is in a position to recognize the connection.

Feierman says celibacy is not "a natural state for humans to be in." Pointing to the celibacy requirement as a cause of clergy abuse of children, he explains: "If you tell a man that he's not allowed to have particular friends, he's not allowed to be affectionate, he's not allowed to be in love, he's not allowed to be a sexual being, you shouldn't be surprised at anything that happens."[11]

"You shouldn't be surprised at anything that happens" and the RCC isn't, because it is the oldest continuous enclave for hetero and homosexual men seeking all forms of self gratifying sex. There is no other institution in the world with a longer, well documented, continuous history of the sexual abuse of children than the RCC. Their own records stand in testimony to this fact.

In either hetero or homosexual relationships where there is intimacy or the expectation of it, there is a commitment. A homosexual couple raising a child would be just as outraged at having their son or daughter defiled by a priest as would a heterosexual couple. Why, because they have what priests lack, a commitment, intimacy and love. By their very nature, human intimacy and a priest's commitment to his vows are mutually exclusive. Therefore attempts to seek intimacy through sexual gratification always fall short leaving the sex unfulfilling and the priest unfulfilled.

This failure, on a grand scale, to adhere to celibacy mandated that a rationale be concocted to excuse breaking the vow. Celibacy itself became one of the chief rationales; the excuse used for allowing exceptions. "Oh, you a good priest and it is so hard to keep your vows; say your confession and try not to do it again." The biggest coup in history for the hierarchy was the laity swallowing it hook, line and sinker. How many Catholics have said, "A priest is entitled to break a vow once in a while, after all they are only human." Cardinal George gave us the best known public example of this type of exemption in this quote:

Cardinal George said, "There is a difference between a moral monster like Geoghan," who preys in serial fashion, and an individual who, "perhaps under the influence of alcohol," engages in inappropriate behavior with "a 16- or 17-year-old young woman who returns his affections."[12]

Even this rationale couldn't soothe the conscience of the clerics. And so a grand philosophy had to be constructed; one that would forever blind or bind the conscience of priests and bishops. Enter the scion of the marriage between the God Complex and Hubris: the Dehumanizing Effect. This stated that all who received Holy Orders were called directly by God. The act of being selected directly by God made priests better than the rest. The myth of celibacy was the linchpin that proved priests were the betters of man. *Ipso facto*, the rude and scoffing multitude could be used and abused without penalty. (If anyone really thought God was calling these perverts to serve in the priesthood, they would all be running for the exit doors.) The irony is that this myth of being better than the rest is precisely why the hierarchy has been rendered soulless.

For centuries the hierarchy has had an ingrained attitude that there is nothing wrong with habitual dalliances by members of their priesthood with men, women and children. This thought process became a clerical tradition and the tradition became church policy. It readily explains the process by which the hierarchy lost any semblance of humanity when dealing with children being raped, sodomized or molested by their priests. It took a proclamation by the pope in the sixteenth century to declare that Native Americans had a soul. Hitler referred to his idea of sub-humans as mud people. American slave owners declared slaves property. Religious orders call them, "the rude and scoffing multitude." Whoever the abuser, they all see their victims as: "less than," which makes any crime against them palatable.

Do priests really consider themselves to be divinely selected? Proof of the god complex theory comes to us from the surveys done to gather information for Louise Haggett's *Bingo Report*.[13] According to the survey, a full third of priests surveyed said they either agreed or strongly agreed with this statement: "I believe in priestly divinity" an additional 10% said they neither agreed nor disagreed with the statement.

A Different Hypothesis:

The late, great, erudite New York Senator and Catholic, Daniel Patrick Moynihan wrote an essay titled: Defining Deviance Down.[14] His premise was that society keeps lowering the bar by which they define deviant behavior. If he were alive, he would certainly understand how his work applies to the RCC especially this paragraph.

> "In this pattern, a growth in deviancy makes possible a transfer of resources, including prestige, to those who control the deviant population. This control would be jeopardized if any serious effort were made to reduce the deviancy in question. This leads to assorted strategies for re-defining the behavior in question as not all that deviant, really."[15]

Moynihan's observations lead to a completely new perspective on the permissiveness of the Roman Catholic Church. The permissiveness pervasive in the church now has a purpose behind it: The bishop's control would be seriously jeopardized if any attempt were made to eliminate sexual deviants from the ranks of the priesthood. The greater the deviance allowed in the priesthood, (a virtual feudal system) the greater control and power the hierarchy exerts over its priests. This would certainly explain the unprecedented inhumanity exhibited by bishops towards children. Sexual abuse was redefined from a crime to a sin. Ephebophilia was split off from pedophilia to make sex crimes with post-pubescent boys a few degrees more palatable since a teenager is not a prepubescent boy or girl. (Defining deviance down as if there were a distinction in abuse) That distinction with post-pubescent boys was made to place the blame squarely on homosexual community within the priesthood totally ignoring the sexual abuse of teenage girls by priests. The bishop's had a very clear choice, their power or children's lives. The bishops opted to keep their power by tightening their power over this group.

The hierarchy has an incredibly strong hold on its priests. Marketing 101 has the 4P's: Product, Price, Packaging and Promotion. The hierarchy of the RCC has its four P's for absolute power: Placement, Promotion, Penance and Pension. All four are controlled exclusively by either the bishop or the order's superior. The 4P's are strong enough strings to make most priests dance. It is the difference between being stationed in the inner city or a country club parish. The four P's are real power and very real control. Anyone of these strings when pulled by a superior can affect behavior. When all four are controlled by the same person, it is a recipe for total control. The four P's of hierarchical power explain a great deal of the global priestly silence, but they can't explain it all away. Enter Moynihan's theory of defining deviance down in order to maintain control.

Combine the 4P's of power with the concept of deviant control and you seal lips forever. Take an abusing priest of either homo or heterosexual nature. How much stronger is that priest's allegiance when the priest knows his bishop or cardinal will protect him? Defend him by every means available? Will keep him out of jail, out of site and then ship him to a new parish, a.k.a. hunting grounds, where he can once again ply his immoral trade?

The Code of Silence Testifies to These Truths

Edmond Burke said," All that is necessary for the triumph of evil is for good men to do nothing." This could be the motto of the Roman Catholic Church. One of the most astonishing and disturbing facts of the Clergy Abuse Scandal is the singular solidarity of both priests and bishops in refusing to speak out against their brothers who have abused children. This silence is a condemnation of the entire church and its leadership. Out of forty thousand priests in the United States, only a handful have ever publicly spoken out against clergy abuse. Only a handful have ever aided victims in their quest for justice. The only internationally known priest advocate for survivors is Fr. Tom Doyle. The silence of the priesthood is not only about the abuse, it also applies to the outrageous crimes committed by the hierarchy in their handling of clergy abuse cases. The bishops have brought down great scandal upon themselves, their priests and the church yet the majority of "good" priests remain silent.

The question begs itself, why this deafening silence from men of god? Crimes as heinous as the rape, sodomization and molestation of children should inspire outrage, yet there was and is only silence. The cover-ups by the hierarchy should have resulted in calls for removal, yet there was and is only silence. The monumental scandal and shame brought down upon the church should have brought screams of anguish from every pulpit, yet there was and is only silence. Has every priest, like their bishops, lost every spark of humanity, been so dehumanized as to be indifferent? Are we to believe that in the thousands of rectories across the United States not one good priest is upset about this? What compels men of God to maintain their wholesale silence?

As striking as the silence of the priests is regarding clerical sexual abuse, it is just as striking on the subject of homosexuality. The RCC is one of the most vocal anti-homosexual religions in the world. The tirades let loose from the pope on down to the pulpit on the evils of homosexuality are legendary. They are strong, inciting, inflammatory and resolute in their condemnation. Yet at the same time, the website Religious Tolerance [16] offers, from a wide variety of sources, various projections (anywhere from 15% to 75%) on the number of homosexual men in the priesthood. Their conclusion is that about a third of the priests in the United States are homosexual. Is that anything new? I refer the reader to the church's own history mentioned earlier.

How must these priests of the homosexual persuasion suffer listening to the constant tirades streaming down from a hierarchy whose own ranks are replete with homosexuals? How does the hierarchy tie the tongues of good men and why do good men allow their tongues to be tied? Fear and shame are the names of the game.

These Facts Underscore the Truth

Scientists, in order to test a theory, keep looking for the one thing which will disprove their theory. If none of the known facts refute the theory, it is considered a truth until such time as proof is offered to the contrary. So let it be with the following statements:

1. The RCC has known about priestly sexual abuse within its ranks and has actively covered it up for over one thousand years.

2. The RCC is the only organization in the Western World that has had men living with men on a continuous basis for fifteen hundred years.

3. The RCC has had some of the world's most brilliant minds working on their behalf during the last fifteen hundred years as priestly philosophers, scientists and writers, yet none of them have figured out how to make celibacy work.

4. The priesthood of the RCC has had active heterosexuals, homosexuals and child abusers in the clergy for over a thousand years. At varying times in their history, the size and scandal of one or more of the above groups has reached epidemic proportions.

5. At various times in church history, there has been a public rebellion against the clerical decadence that became pervasive. We are currently in one of these periods.

The RCC knows more than any other organization in history about trying to keep men celibate during the last millennium. Yet they still fail. God's design is too strong for church doctrine. Judging by the fact that celibacy and chastity are still vows, it is obvious that there exists another reason to keep unholy vows. Knowing full well these vows can't be kept by normal people, why does the RCC keep them as well as the sordid sexual perversions they have produced. The new hypothesis is the RCC has kept chastity and celibacy as vows for no other reason than to exert control over the members of the priesthood as in the manner stated by Moynihan in <u>Defining Decadence Down</u>.[17]

This is the foundation of mutual protection as evidenced in Crimens Solicitationis,[18] (the crime of soliciting) which turns all reported sexual abuse into a "Secret of the Holy Office," the pope essentially gags everyone who has knowledge of the crime under the penalty of excommunication. How far will members of the hierarchy go to protect sexually abusing priests? Up until now, Cardinal Law had been the poster boy, but he has been replaced by Cardinal Roger Mahony who has been fighting for a dozen years to keep the names of predator priests a secret. We've already discussed the moral turpitude of a man who knowingly protects child abusers. This is a sterling example of the lengths the cardinal has gone to prevent the names of abusive priests from being made public. It is an excerpt from a motion filed by the archdiocese of Los Angeles to squirm out of a commitment it made to survivors when they settled the sexual abuse claims against it

> The relationship between a Roman Catholic priest and his employer, the Archdiocese in this case, is a uniquely close, all-encompassing one, in which the employer is also the direct spiritual superior of the employee, and between them there can be no secrets."[19]

Therefore, as per the words of the cardinal himself, all bishops and cardinals have tacit knowledge of all the actions of sexually abusive priests in their employ. Once again, the often repeated words of the hierarchy, **"I didn't know!"** ring hollower by the moment.

The child abusers only account for a minority of priests. What about the rest of the priests, does deviance bind them to the bishop in the same manner? Yes, but the deviance is not child abuse, it is the deviation from their vows. The bishops know who is philandering with whom and their sexual preferences, which places the majority in the same boat as the minority. Once you compromise yourself each and every deviance has to be accepted. The bishops have to protect everyone including those with the most egregious sexual appetites. The price for this protection is the priest's absolute silence regardless of the shame attached. Appointing a confessor further guarantees the silence under the seal of confession.

The Real Threat of Homosexual Priests to the Church

This also explains why homosexual priests stay in an organization that openly condemns them? What buys their silence? The same 4P's plus the deviant control and the fear of being exposed as a homosexual? How does a good hardworking homosexual priest feel living and working among parishioners who have been conditioned to believe that homosexuality is either an abomination or an aberration? How painful is it for them to read that a bishop has refused communion to supporters of homosexuals with no more cause than an identifying ribbon? How painful is it to know that the opportunistic sex homosexual priests are forced to partake in, because of celibacy, carries greater risks such as a higher incidence of AIDS than the general population? This is high price to pay for an attempt at intimacy.

Has anyone wondered why the church is so adamantly opposed to legitimizing homosexual unions through marriage? One very real possibility is that homosexual marriages present a genuine threat to the priesthood and therefore the church itself. Over the past twenty years, homosexuality has integrated into the mainstream. It is shunned by a few, tolerated by some and accepted by most of the general population. Since Vatican II, many heterosexual priests have left the priesthood to get married. They left for the intimacy that was designed into their beings and fulfilled their natural needs.

When homosexual priests realize that they too can live a shameless life with a lifetime partner, a commitment, and intimacy among the general public, the priesthood will lose its appeal as a safe haven for homosexuals. This bears repeating: the priesthood will lose its appeal as a safe haven for homosexual men. When homosexual priests start to leave the priesthood for committed relationships outside the priesthood, they will leave the church in critical condition. Along with that, the number of homosexual men needing refuge in the priesthood will drop too.

Behavior no longer considered deviant, equates with no more power. The RCC is pulling out all the stops to prevent the legalization of homosexual marriages because its future depends on it. If it doesn't succeed, it is doomed to atrophy. Their recent bid to attract Anglican priests upset by the ordination of homosexuals is nothing more than attempt to shore up their dwindling clerical numbers. Without homosexual priests, the church will deteriorate at an even faster pace spurred on by an extremely critical shortage of priests.

Portends for the Future

Someone once said, "Hope springs eternal." In the case of the RCC, we have to have serious doubts. Despite fifteen hundred years of evidence to the contrary, celibacy and chastity are still required as means of assuring control of the priesthood. The inhumanity that it has created has been catastrophic. The following is your assurance that nothing will change in the near future.

The pope was head of the Congregation for the Doctrine of Faith for some twenty odd years and during those years maintained the culture's status quo. He says he was horrified by the stories he read as head of the CDF. As pope, he has assured the maintenance of the status quo by appointing Archbishop Levada to his former post. Jesus predicted this well when he said, "Woe to you, scribes and Pharisees, **hypocrites**! for you traverse sea and land to make a single proselyte, and when he becomes a proselyte, you make him twice as much a child of hell as yourselves."

Since past behavior is pretty much indicative of future behavior, we need to look at Levada's record regarding sexual abuse to determine if he is a party to the culture that has dominated and perverted the Catholic Church over the past thousand years. Let's start and end with the case of Bishop Ziemann which defines the depths to which Cardinal Levada will sink. Ziemann combines the elitist culture with the lack of humanity we've been discussing. Bishop Ziemann was arrested while receiving oral sex from a priest in his own car. To make matters worse, Ziemann forced this priest wear a pager so that he could be summoned for sex at the Ziemann's whim. According to the priest's testimony, Bishop Ziemann had twice given him Venereal Disease infections. When Ziemann left the diocese of Santa Rosa, he left it sixteen million dollars in the red. Consider the following from the San Francisco Weekly.

> "He has been protected by and remains intimately connected with three influential fellow hierarchs, including San Francisco Archbishop William J. Levada. It was Levada who presided over Ziemann's skipping away from Santa Rosa with criminal impunity after church officials refused to fully cooperate with authorities. Ziemann's mentor and chief patron is Los Angeles Cardinal Roger M. Mahony, whose problems with pedophile priests rival the scandal-plagued Boston archdiocese's. The other member of the troika is Manuel Moreno, who until his surprise resignation this month for health reasons, was bishop of Tucson, Ariz., and in whose diocese Ziemann was given refuge at the Holy Trinity Monastery... Moreno has a long and tawdry record in covering up for pedophile priests...
>
> At a time when someone else might have tossed him to the wolves, Levada lauded Ziemann to the bitter end in Santa Rosa. The day Ziemann resigned, shortly after a lurid audiotape surfaced exposing the bishop's illicit relationship with the priest, Levada extolled his friend as someone who had done much to help the diocese. It didn't seem to matter that, right up until the revelation of the bishop's tape-recorded apology to Father Jorge Hume Salas for forcing him to engage in sex, Ziemann's personal attorney proclaimed him to be "a very holy man" and the bishop steadfastly denied any misconduct."[20]

Bishop Ziemann recently passed away retaining all his faculties.

Why did Benedict XVI pick Lavada to replace him as head of the CDF? His unwavering loyalty, no matter how disgraceful, to a brother bishop and the church seems like the most logical answer. Silence is the golden rule. Levada has publicly proven the depths to which he is willing to sink in order to protect a fellow bishop from criminal prosecution. His is a sterling quality, a la Bernie Law, which is obviously deeply appreciated by the Pope. When handling future accusations of sexual abuse against priests and bishops, Levada has already shown how low he can be expected to drop the deviance bar. With Levada at the helm of the CDF, the culturally embedded concept that bishops have the right and obligation to cover-up for abusers will carry on into the future.

Not being satisfied with Levada and Law, the pope has recently given Bishop Raymond Burke a slot at the Vatican. This is a man who handed out excommunications like pedophiles hand out candy. Like the queen of hearts in Alice and Wonderland, he ran around yelling, "To hell with your souls!" Burke is noted for his ability to silence victims as noted here.

> But some members of Raymond Burke's former flock paint a far different portrait of the erstwhile bishop of La Crosse. If cases of clergy sex abuse were few and far between, they say, it was because Burke was a master at keeping a lid on them. Several victims who claim they were abused by priests in La Crosse tell Riverfront Times they were stonewalled by Burke, who declined to report their allegations to local authorities. And while some of his fellow church officials nationwide were reaching hefty settlements with victims, Raymond Burke was unyielding in his refusal to negotiate with victims' rights groups. He declined to make public the names of priests who were known to have been abusive, and he denied requests to set up a victims' fund. Most strikingly, Riverfront Times has learned, while bishop in La Crosse Burke allowed at least three priests to remain clerics in good standing long after allegations of their sexual misconduct had been proven — to the church, to the courts and, finally, to Burke himself.[21]

Burke has recently been appointed by the pope to an office that will handle the worst cases of the clergy sexual abuse as the prefect of the Supreme Tribunal of the Apostolic Signatura. Once again, we have the pope planning for the future and insuring the status quo. What chance is there of change with men like these in positions of power?

Conclusion

We have seen how men, supposedly good men, are so hypocritical in their nature, that they can one day preach justice and morality before a packed cathedral and the next day transfer a serial rapist to another parish. This is not only the pinnacle of hypocrisy, but it is so much more than that. It is about a totally corrupted system that not only trains men to behave in this manner, but which has become the only quality that will ensure promotion.

And what of the Catholic laity? Ashamed, embarrassed, angry, distraught, hurt, victims of a culture that uses fear and human sexuality to maintain control; what is to become of them? They have been trained well to pay, pray, and obey. Those that wake up to hypocrisy will leave discontented, others will pray for change, some will try to affect it, and the rest will pray and pay regardless of how outrageous the acts of the hierarchy become because more than anything else in the world, they want to go to heaven. It is thus fitting to close with a line from <u>Defining Deviance Down</u>. "A society that loses its sense of outrage is doomed to extinction."[22] So is a church!

Reference

1. From: The Council of Elvira, ca. 306, retrieved November 26, 2009
http://faculty.cua.edu/pennington/Canon%20Law/ElviraCanons.htm

2. Engel, Randy. St. Peter Damian's Book of Gomorrah:A Moral Blueprint for Our Times – Part I Nov. 26, 2009 Retrieved from: http://www.ourladyswarriors.org/articles/damian1.htm

3. Damian, Peter. The book of Gomorah an Eleventh Century Treatise Against Clerical Homosexual Practices. Translated by Pierre J. Payer. November 26, 2009 Retrieved from:
http://books.google.com/books?id=hr4VAAAAMAAJ&pg=PA11&lpg=PA11&dq=eleventh+century+clerical
+abuse&source=web&ots=kBcxq4YpkG&sig=PwlMgSfUtRxys6KqhwrSJNf4GSE&hl=en&sa=X&oi=book_res
ult&resnum=1&ct=result#PPA12,M1

4. Liebreich, Karen. Fallen Order – November 27, 2009 Retrieved from:
http://www.liebreich.com/LDC/HTML/Books/FallenOrder.html

5. Farragher, Thomas. Admission of awareness damning for Law. Nov. 26, 2009.
http://www.boston.com/globe/spotlight/abuse/stories3/121402_admission.htm

6. Estrada, Herón. Archdiocese helped priest flee, suit says. Nov. 26, 2009
http://www.startribune.com/local/stpaul/28150429.html?elr=KArks:DCiUnP::DE8c7PiUiD3aPc:_Y
yc:aUU

7. Annett, Kevin. Open letter, Nov. 26, 2009 Retrieved from: http://signatoryindian.tripod.com/id80.html

8. Keating, Ted, From the Executive Director. July/August Bulletin, 2002 Retrieved from:
http://www.cmsm.org/index.shtml Author's note, site is no longer open to public.

9. Pious X. Vehementer Nos. (encyclical on the French law of separation) 1905, retrieved from:
http://jingalls.com/holy_father/pius_x/encyclicals/documents/hf_p-x_enc_11021906_vehementer-
nos_en.html   Nov. 26, 2009

10. Hagget, L. The Bingo Report, Mandatory Celibacy and the Clergy. CSRI Books (October 20, 2005)

11. Sommer, J. Clerical Celibacy and Pedophilic Priests. Nov. 27, 2009
http://www.humanismbyjoe.com/clerical_celibacy_and_pedophilic.htm

12. Wilgoren, J. Scandals in the Church: The Lay Members; In Chicago, Group Urges A Suspension of Donations. NYTimes, Published: Saturday, April 27, 2002,
http://query.nytimes.com/gst/fullpage.html?res=940DEEDA103EF934A15757C0A9649C8B63&partner=rss
nyt&emc=rss

13. Ibid, 9

14. Moynihan, D. P. Defining Deviancy Down. *American Scholar* (Winter 1993) Retrieved from:
http://www2.sunysuffolk.edu/formans/DefiningDeviancy.htm

194

15. Ibid,

16. Homosexual orientation among Roman Catholic priests. Nov. 27, 2009. Retrieved from:
http://www.religioustolerance.org/hom_rcc.htm

17. Ibid, 14

18. Wikipedia, Crimens Sollicictations. Retrieved from
http://en.wikipedia.org/wiki/Crimen_sollicitationis_%28document%29 Nov. 26, 2009

19. City of Angels Blog, October 1, 2008 Retrieved from:
http://cityofangels13.blogspot.com/2008/10/objection-to-transfer-of-personnel.html

20. Russell, R. Bishop Bad Boy. San Francisco Weekly, March 19, 2003 Retrieved from: www.bishop-accountability.org/news/2003_03_19_Russell_BishopBad.htm

21. Gay, M. Immaculate Deception. Riverfront Times, August 25, 2004, Retrieved from:
http://www.bishop-accountability.org/news3/2004_08_25_Gay_ImmaculateDeception_Raymond_Bornbach_etc.htm

22. Ibid, 14

The Irish Litany

The Irish Church is a big disgrace
Blood and semen all over the place.

We will, we will out you!
We will, we will out you!

Christian Brothers losing face
Why doesn't the government make a case?

Singing: We will, we will out you!
We will, we will out you!

Crying poverty like a welfare case
Hiding your money without a trace

Singing: We will, we will out you!
We will, we will out you!

Sisters of Mercy morals misplaced
What terrible torture young girls faced

Singing: We will, we will out you!
We will, we will out you!

Brothers and Sisters so debase
Could've been maggots from outer space

Singing: We will, we will out you!
We will, we will out you!

But now you're undone
The children paid for your fun

We will, we will shun you!
We will, we will shun you!

Your dirty laundry basks in the sun
The beginning of the end has begun.

We will, we will shun you!
We will, we will shun you!

What is that smell
Where evil does dwell?

We will, we will leave you!
We will, we will leave you!

That Irish church we know so well.
Clerical souls journeying to hell.

We will, we will leave you!
We will, we will leave you!

Dateline Vatican City
Satiricus Acerbus Diernum
Vicente Veritas reporting.

Vatican announces draft for Catholic children

The Vatican announced today that it is instituting the first Catholic draft since the Children's Crusade several hundred years ago. The draft is in response to a recent Vatican symposium on pedophilia and the sexual abuse of minors by priests. After examining the 220 page report ushered in after the symposium entitled "Sexual Abuse in the Catholic Church" the Vatican finds it necessary bring back the Children's draft. It was determined that the draft was needed when experts in the field of mental illness (and they are all in the field because they are blooming idiots) called the zero tolerance policy on priests that sexually abuse children both barbaric and a disaster waiting to happen. Outraged that priests should be subject to criminal law for the rape, sodomization and molestation of children, it was unanimously decided that priests are better off in the rectory than in jail. The Vatican doesn't believe priests should go to jail for criminal acts because they are responsible to a higher power. Jailed priests, it was noted, are a poor reflection on the church as well as causing considerable angst for the incarcerated priests.

Cardinal Amplus Derriere, the red cheeked Vice President of Pontificating, made the announcement standing alongside the renowned German priest/psychiatrist Heso Fulluvit. Derriere pronounced, "This is only a first step. For the benefit of all those who have suffered due to sexual abuse and for the good of priests, other steps will be taken," but he failed to elaborate.

Derriere said the church was faced with a conundrum. (Not to be confused with a condom) On one hand survivors are calling for zero tolerance and on the other, the Vatican's hand picked experts are calling for patience and an opportunity to treat and cure the incurable. Therefore they are initiating the one strike rule for children, which will treat the problem without having to embarrass the church. The most any child can be abused with the draft is one time. This will keep priests out of jail and ease the responsibility on the larger society (tax dollars pay for jails) by keeping priests out of jail. The church will be asking all Catholic families to sign their children up for the draft in the army of Christ.

The draft rules are as follows:

1. All children upon being baptized will be signed up and eligible to be called for duty until they reach the legal age of consent.

2. Each year in every parish a lottery will be held where the names of two eligible parish children will drawn, one boy and one girl.

3. Each of these children will be housed in a rectory for a period of one year when the next lottery will take place.

4. Once having served their year, the child's commitment is over.

5. Only one child per family can serve in any given year.

6. The first children to be selected for the draft are from parents who have told victims, "get over it and get a life!" for they are true Christians. The second group to be selected from are children whose parents have expressed a willingness to forgive and forget the crimes of their priest who is only human for they too are only human. The third group is the children of parents who remained silent on the subject for silence is golden.

7. Survivors can claim conscientious objector status for their children and their children's children only.

The Rules

If at any point a child living in a rectory is abused, the incident is to be immediately reported to the Blooming Idiot Brigade (BIB) founded by Fulluvit who will immediately hear the priest's confession. This will prohibit anyone from disclosing the facts to the civil authorities. Next in an effort to modify this sinful behavior, the following techniques will be used: counsel the priest on the error of his ways, use all forms of drugs including chemical castration, psychoanalysis, and cognitive behavioral techniques combined with spiritual counseling. The molested child, having served their purpose, will be sent home and a special lottery will be held to replace him/her. Fulluvit said, "Only by replacing the molested child with a new one, will the BIB's be able to judge the effectiveness of the treatment selected and then modify it, if need be, thereby insuring the misguided priest leads a normal healthy life in the service of God."

Dr. Fulluvit is a renown researcher who has conducted several earth shattering studies in the field of human behavior. His most famous was the $100 million survey which examined the causes behind why incarerated criminals attempt prison breaks. Second was his study into why notorious art thieves choose the works of old masters to steal.

Fulluvit has recently completed a monumental and unparalleled study commissioned by the Vatican. Though the cost is undisclosed unnamed sources say it was worth every million. Fulluvit's psychiatrists, psychologists and psychotherapists have made a startling discovery. They determined that a priest was less likely to either confess his sins or notify his superiors of his sexual deviancies and associated crimes if he knew that he could be defrocked and sent to jail.

Therefore, Fulluvit delighted in the Vatican's decision to draft children. Cardinal Derriere shook his head in agreement saying that drafting children for service in the rectory allowed the entire church to share the burden of sexual abuse. Furthermore, it was a just and Christian solution as the one strike rule would assure no child would suffer abuse more than once. Better than that it would provide for an open and honest relationship between perverted priests, their superiors and their therapists.

You may reach Vinnie Veritas at eccum spiri 220.

The creative juices of Veritas Vinnie (also known as Vinnie Nauheimer) have been stimulated into high gear by the recent letter Bishop William Murphy of Rockville Centre, New York, sent to Treasury Secretary Paulson and four principal leaders of Congress, asking these leaders to apply 5 key moral principles to the nation's financial crisis. Voice from the Desert previously carried the bishop's letter as it appeared in the Long Island Catholic, the Rockville Centre diocese's official newspaper. Vinnie joins Dick Regan in finding the bishop's letter fertile ground for creative teaching about the bishops' failure to apply Christian principles in addressing the ongoing Catholic Church clerical sex abuse crisis. Dick rewrote Bishop Murphy's letter, also carried on Voice from the Desert recently, so that it addressed the Catholic Church clerical sex abuse scandal rather than the nation's financial crisis. Early email and YahooGroup reviews of Dick's rewrite are highly laudatory.

Here is Veritas Vinnie's spoof on Bishop Murphy's letter.

* * *

Dear Secretary Paulson, Majority Leader Reid, Minority Leader McConnell, Speaker Pelosi and Minority Leader Boehner:

The sexual abuse crisis facing our nation is both terribly disturbing and enormously complicated. I write to remind you of the rights of the U.S. Catholic Bishops and express the concerns of our Conference as you face the difficult choices on how to limit the financial damage to our church and urge you to use prudence and justice so we can maintain our status quo. As charlatans and purveyors of abuse, my brother bishops and I bring over one thousand years of technical expertise to these complicated matters. However, we believe our faith and immoral principles can help guide the search for just and effective responses to the economic turmoil threatening our church.

Human and Moral Dimensions: This crisis involves far more than just economic or clerical matters, but has enormous human impact. The clear ethical dimensions which should be at the center of this debate are the church's right to exist and the guaranteed secrecy of our personnel files. Families are filing suits because we destroyed their homes. Retirement pensions for priests are at risk. Priests are losing their jobs and benefits. Economic arrangements, structures and remedies should take into consideration the rights of the church to serve. We have as a fundamental purpose the safeguarding human life and dignity. The scandalous search for excessive payouts in civil lawsuits has gotten out of hand to the point that dangerously high settlements have exacerbated our pain and losses. One of the more egregious examples is the survivor that places economic gain above all other values. This totally ignores the economic impact of the cash awards on the lives of our bishops as well as the ethical dimension of the choices we will be forced to make with fewer priests. Not to mention the moral responsibility we have for defending our priests, bishops and cardinals. Los Angeles is a prime example, which has cost us untold millions in legal fees alone.

Responsibility and Accountability: Clearly, effective measures are required which address and alter the behaviors, practices, and misjudgments of the civil courts that led to our financial crisis. Sadly, greed, revenge, and exploitation of vulnerable priests by dishonest practices helped to bring about this serious situation. Many blameless and vulnerable priests have been and will be harmed. Those who directly contributed to this crisis by attempting to profit from their abuse should not be rewarded or escape accountability for the harm they have done to the church. Any response of government ought to seek greater safety and minimal awards in both economic and disclosure awards to protect the church.

Advantages and Limitations of Abuse: Pope John Paul II pointed out that the "forgiveness is the most efficient instrument for effectively responding to the needs of the abused. But there are many survivors who find no solace in forgiveness and are not in the market to forgive. It is a strict duty of justice and truth not to allow fundamental human needs to remain unsatisfied." Both the media and civil courts have failed in responding to fundamental human needs of Catholic priests. A new sense of responsibility on the part of all should include a renewal of the instruments of the separation of church and state thereby preventing economic distress to the institution known as the Roman Catholic Church. The financial preservation as well as effective public regulation and protection for the church may be clearly necessary.

Solidarity and the Common Good: The principle of solidarity reminds us that we are in this together. We have the cash and the power to elect officials. We warn you that concern for narrow interests (survivors) alone can make things worse. The principle of solidarity commits us to the pursuit of the common goals, not the search for victim's gain or economic advantage. Protection of the vulnerable priests, bishops, and cardinals must be included in the commitment to protect religious institutions. As Church leaders we ask that you give proper priority to the priests and the most venerable.

Subsidiarity: Subsidiarity places a responsibility on the private deals we make to accept each other's own obligations. If we do not do so, then larger lawsuits will be filed. The government will have to step in to do what our private lawyers have failed to do: reduce the size of the monetary judgments that the church is being forced to pay. This is a challenging time for our church. Everyone who carries responsibility should exercise it according to their respective roles and with a great sensitivity to reforming practices and setting forth new guidelines that will preserve our money for the common good of all religious institutions. This includes not just the leaders of our courts. It means the political leaders and all those whose own expertise can contribute to a resolution of the current situation.

Our Catholic tradition calls for a "society of sex, abuse, and embezzlement" which "is not directed against the politicians, but demands that the laity be appropriately controlled by the forces of religion and by the state to assure that the basic needs of the church are satisfied" (Centesimus Animus). These words of John Paul II should be adopted as a standard for all those who carry this responsibility for our church, the priests, and the common till.

Sincerely,

Most Reverend William F. Murky
Bishop of Rockbottom Central
Chairman, Committee on Domestic Injustice and Inhumane Development

The letter spoofed

Dear Secretary Paulson, Majority Leader Reid, Minority Leader McConnell, Speaker Pelosi and Minority Leader Boehner:

The economic crisis facing our nation is both terribly disturbing and enormously complicated. I write to offer the prayers of the U.S. Catholic Bishops and express the concerns of our Conference as you face difficult choices on how to limit the damage and move forward with prudence and justice. As pastors and teachers, my brother bishops and I do not bring technical expertise to these complicated matters. However, we believe our faith and moral principles can help guide the search for just and effective responses to the economic turmoil threatening our people.

Human and Moral Dimensions: This crisis involves far more than just economic or technical matters, but has enormous human impact and clear ethical dimensions which should be at the center of debate and decisions on how to move forward. Families are losing their homes. Retirement savings are at risk. People are losing jobs and benefits. Economic arrangements, structures and remedies should have as a fundamental purpose safeguarding human life and dignity. The scandalous search for excessive economic rewards even to the point of dangerous speculation that exacerbates the pain and losses of the more vulnerable are egregious examples of an economic ethic that places economic gain above all other values. This ignores the impact of economic decisions on the lives of real people as well as the ethical dimension of the choices we make and the moral responsibility we have for their effect on people.

Responsibility and Accountability: Clearly, effective measures are required which address and alter the behaviors, practices and misjudgments that led to this crisis. Sadly, greed, speculation, exploitation of vulnerable people and dishonest practices helped to bring about this serious situation. Many blameless and vulnerable people have been and will be harmed. Those who directly contributed to this crisis or profited from it should not be rewarded or escape accountability for the harm they have done. Any response of government ought to seek greater responsibility, accountability and transparency in both economic and public life.

Advantages and Limitations of the Market: Pope John Paul II pointed out that the "free market is the most efficient instrument for utilizing resources and effectively responding to needs. But there are many human needs which find no place on the market. It is a strict duty of justice and truth not to allow fundamental human needs to remain unsatisfied." Both public and private institutions have failed in responding to fundamental human needs. A new sense of responsibility on the part of all should include a renewal of instruments of monitoring and correction within economic institutions and the financial industry as well as effective public regulation and protection to the extent this may be clearly necessary.

Solidarity and the Common Good: The principle of solidarity reminds us that we are in this together and warns us that concern for narrow interests alone can make things worse. The principle of solidarity commits us to the pursuit of the common good, not the search for partisan gain or economic advantage. Protection of the vulnerable, workers, business owners, homeowners, renters, and stockholders must be included in the commitment to protect economic institutions. As Church leaders we ask that you give proper priority to the poor and the most vulnerable.

Subsidiarity: Subsidiarity places a responsibility on the private actors and institutions to accept their own obligations. If they do not do so, then the larger entities, including the government, will have to step in to do what private institutions will have failed to do. This is a challenging time for our nation. Everyone who carries responsibility should exercise it according to their respective roles and with a great sensitivity to reforming practices and setting forth new guidelines that will serve all people, all institutions of the economy and the common good of the people as a nation. This includes not just the leaders of the economic life of our country. It means the political leaders and all those whose own expertise can contribute to a resolution of the current situation.
Our Catholic tradition calls for a "society of work, enterprise and participation" which "is not directed against the market, but demands that the market be appropriately controlled by the forces of society and by the state to assure that the basic needs of the whole society are satisfied" (Centesimus Annus). These words of John Paul II should be adopted as a standard for all those who carry this responsibility for our nation, the world and the common good of all.

Sincerely,

Most Reverend William F. Murphy
Bishop of Rockville Centre
Chairman, Committee on Domestic Justice and Human Development

An Ill Wind Blows for Children of Chicago Catholics

Where would you look to find the church's most skilled buck passer, second only to the pope? Where would you look to find the master of denial with a straight face, who arguably sports the best razor sharp convenient memory in all of Chicago? You have to go no farther than Chicago's own Cardinal George. Like the pope, he would have us believe that he was never consciously in the business of hiding sexually abusive priests. He deserves special attention not only because of his condescending and despicable attitude towards children, civil law, church law and God, but because he is also the president of the United States Conference of Catholic Bishops whose stated purpose is:

> The purpose of the Conference is to promote the greater good which the Church offers humankind, especially through forms and programs of the apostolate fittingly adapted to the circumstances of time and place.[1]

As such, Cardinal George will be responsible for policy in the United States for the next three years and his minions will do the same into the foreseeable future.

Cardinal George has proven himself particularly adept at fittingly adapting things to fit the circumstances of his view on clerical sexual abuse. The USCCB is the august body that created the very superficial and now legless Dallas Charter of 2002. It has subsequently been trampled upon by the Cardinal. How ironic is it that George led the delegation to Rome to receive the Vatican's stamp of approval for the Dallas Charter?

> Cardinal Francis George of Chicago, who led the U.S. delegation, reported the completion of the task to Bishop Wilton Gregory, October 29, from Rome.
>
> "The four U.S. Bishops representing the Conference in the Mixed Commission will report to their brother Bishops during the November meeting in Washington, D.C. We believe that the goals of the Dallas decision, i.e. to protect minors and to reach out to victims, have been preserved and that the Dallas documents have been completed in elaborating normative procedures that respect the rights of priests who have been accused," he said.
>
> Other members of the delegation from the United States in addition to Cardinal George, included Archbishop William Levada of San Francisco, Bishop Thomas Doran of Rockford, Illinois, and Bishop William Lori of Bridgeport, Connecticut.[2]

This is the pledge Cardinal George along with the other bishops made concerning the Dallas Charter.

It is with reliance on prayer and penance that we renew the pledges which we made in the original *Charter*:

We pledge most solemnly to one another and to you, God's people, that we will work to our utmost for the protection of children and youth.[3]

Isn't it fascinating that Catholic bishops would forget to pledge to God or Jesus, their savior, in a pledge to protect children! Coincidence hardly, it's more like children crossing their fingers behind their back before making a promise they know they will never keep.

Here we have Cardinal George leading the delegation to the Vatican to get approval of the Dallas Charter and then making a pledge (not to God) to do his utmost for the protection of children. It is impossible to reconcile Cardinal George's actions with either his pledge or the Dallas Charter. That is, of course, unless you believe him to be a feeble minded idiot. Oh that it was that easy to dismiss him and his criminal acts. Hypocrite yes, feeble minded no!

There is no excuse for allowing anyone to rape, sodomize and molest children. Just as there is no excuse for protecting criminals who have committed these heinous acts against children. Only a scurrilous miscreant consumed by evil would put predators back on the street to prey again upon the bodies and souls of innocent children. Those who do the above are nothing but criminals protecting criminals.

The transcripts from Cardinal George's deposition have just been released. If they are nothing else, they are a testimony to the monstrous evil that resides in his soul. They also speak to a well defined mindset which places perverted priests with wanton desires ahead of innocent children. What manner of man condemns children to a lifetime of pain and agony so that a criminal can continue to say mass? Only an arrogant, loathsome, vile, despicable individual without a conscience can perform such an evil act. The following are excerpts from the deposition given by Cardinal George; the hypocrite who led a delegation to Rome seeking approval of the Dallas Charter and once obtaining it, made a personal pledge to protect children.

Fr. Bennett

-The cardinal says that allegations against another priest, Joseph R. Bennett, first surfaced in 2002, but the archdiocese did not act to remove him from his church until 2006, despite the earlier urging of its Review Board to do so. By the time Bennett was review, more than a dozen allegations had surfaced against him (p. 181 ff).

-After allegations surfaced against Bennett, and against the recommendations of his own hand-picked abuse panel, the cardinal let

Bennett to be "supervised" by Bennett's good buddy, Father Leonard Dubi. Dubi and Bennett owned property together (p. 158)

-The cardinal says (and along with other documents) reveal the Father Edward Grace, the archdiocese's Vicar for Priests, helped to coach predator clergy in denying allegations. In November 2005, Grace told Bennett a note from a dermatologist suggesting that "freckles" on his scrotum identified by a victim might, in fact, be aging marks that couldn't have been there at the time of the abuse (p. 196 ff).

Fr. McCormack

The cardinal says that he didn't follow the archdiocese's Review Board recommendation in October 2005 that McCormack be removed from ministry (p. 81). "They gave me that advice, yes....I thought they had not finished the case investigation."

The cardinal says he thought McCormack was being "supervised" adequately after his first arrest (p. 43). "The one egregious time when the protections of children failed to our great shame was the McCormack case where I thought he was being supervised and it wasn't adequate." (McCormack was, in fact, continuing to molest kids "on an almost daily" according to prosecutors.) The cardinal says he thought McCormack was being "supervised" adequately after his first arrest (p. 43).[4]

The saddest sentence in this essay is from the above paragraph: "McCormack was, in fact, continuing to molest kids "on an almost daily" according to prosecutors." What does that make Cardinal George? If George had adhered to his pledge to uphold the Dallas Charter, or listened to his Review Board, no more children would have been sacrificed to feed the sexual appetites of a perverted priest. This is the relevant passage from the Dallas Charter.

> The diocesan/eparchial bishop is to exercise his power of governance, within the parameters of the universal law of the Church, to ensure that any priest or deacon subject to his governance who has committed even one act of sexual abuse of a minor as described below shall not continue in ministry.[5]

Cardinal George on two occasions overrode the decisions of his own Review Board. Then in a clear violation of the Dallas Charter put predators back on the street. And what does Cardinal George say, he says I'm sorry, I didn't know! It was a breakdown in communications. If you believe that, then you will believe George was just exercising his

Christian love by writing letters to get a convicted serial child molester out of jail as evidenced in another part his deposition.

> -The cardinal admits that he and archdiocese officials repeatedly tried to reduce Maday's sentence, even though the priest was a serial child molester.[6]

Cardinal George has proven through his actions that he believes priests have a God given right to sexually abuse anyone they see fit without penalty. Who can forget this sick pronouncement uttered by the Cardinal, before the world, upon returning from a meeting with the pope to discuss the Clergy Abuse Crisis in 2002?

> Cardinal George said, "There is a difference between a moral monster like Geoghan," who preys in serial fashion, and an individual who, "perhaps under the influence of alcohol," engages in inappropriate behavior with "a 16- or 17-year-old young woman who returns his affections."[7]

Cardinal George, if anything, has been consistent over the years in his opinion that priests should not be held responsible for their criminal acts with children. He knows full well what a moral monster looks like; he sees one every time he sees his reflection. The above paints a vivid picture of Cardinal George's unbridled arrogance as well as his disdain for children. What follows below confirms it.

1. He defied the recommendations of his own Review Board on two separate occasions, which resulted in additional lives being shattered.
2. He defied the Dallas Charter; a charter he pledged to uphold.
3. He mocks Pope John Paul II whose condemnation is in the Dallas Charter: "There is no room in the priesthood for those that would abuse children."
4. He defies the Canon Law which demands he hold sexual abusers accountable.
5. He defies Civil Law which holds the rape, sodomy and molestation of children is a criminal act.
6. He tramples on the very concept of morality
7. He defies Scripture
8. He defies the words of Jesus Christ!

Any man, clergy or otherwise, who allows the souls of children to be murdered and their bodies ripped asunder for the sole purpose of a priest's pleasure is neither a proponent Jesus Christ nor his teachings. He is the epitome of the Anti-Christ, evil.

> Matt. 15:7-9
>
> You hypocrites! Well did Isaiah prophesy of you, when he said: "This people honors me with their lips, but their heart is far from me; in vain do they worship me, teaching as doctrines the precepts of men.'"

Shakespeare rightly noted in his play Julius Caesar that the evil men do oft lives after them. So too it will be with Cardinal George. He is the current president of the USCCB and his term runs for the next three years. During this time, he will be responsible for shaping Catholic policy in the United States. The thought of this is probably sending thrills down to the scrotums of every aberrant priest while at the same time sending chills through the hearts of all decent people. Even the most ardent defenders of Catholicism having either children or grandchildren should be running for the exit signs.

Will it end when George retires or dies? No, because those who've been appointed by George and those of his ilk will take over in his stead. Jesus predicted this when he said, "Woe to you, scribes and Pharisees, **hypocrites**! for you traverse sea and land to make a single proselyte, and when he becomes a proselyte, you make him twice as much a child of hell as yourselves."

Example 1.

> The cardinal says he that knowing now that McCormack was accused of sexual misconduct with a minor and two of his peers while in seminary, he would never have ordained him (p. 95-96; 98.) One of the seminary officials at the time, Gerald Kicanas, (now bishop of Tucson and vice president of the U.S. Conference of Catholic Bishops), told the Chicago Sun-Times that it would have been "grossly unfair not to ordain him."[8]

With Kicanas as vice president, next in line to be president, George's evil will be the dominant mindset of the USCCB for the next six years! It's enough to scare anyone, but a sexual predator.

Example 2.

> Auxiliary Bishop Thomas Paprocki, a civil and canon lawyer and one of Cardinal Francis George's six active deputies, recently suggested in a homily to Catholic lawyers and judges that decisions to award large sums to victims of clergy abuse place an excessive burden on the free exercise of religion for American Catholics.
>
> "This burden needs to be lifted," Paprocki said during a special mass for judges and attorneys in Grand Rapids, Mich., last month.[9]

This is tantamount to admitting that there will be more priests raping, sodomizing and molesting children in the future, for which Paprocki doesn't want the church to pay. Paprocki is asking lawyers and jurists to make the cost of these aberrant flings as painless as possible for the church so they can continue on their merry way without upsetting the applecart.

Paprocki asks for this with total disregard for the lifetime of agony abused children are put through. He does so with full knowledge that the only positive changes made to church policy regarding the sexual abuse of children have been forced upon them because of large settlements. If change had anything to do with Jesus Christ or his teachings, the hierarchy would have put an end to the sexual abuse of children centuries ago. Paprocki, like George and a host of others in the hierarchy have no regard for Jesus. Their well-documented actions and words speak louder than any protest they can muster. The sad truth is Cardinal George and the hierarchy of the Roman Catholic Church didn't move one inch towards protecting children until it cost them too many dollars. Therefore, whether they admit it or not, their actions prove beyond the shadow of a doubt that they worship at the altar of dead presidents; For Money Is Their God!

Cardinal George is living in the past; a past where bishops and cardinals were never questioned regardless of how ghastly the nature of the crime. His hubris is a function of his age for he was bred in a closed society and hasn't the wherewithal to function in an open one. He and his minions have not realized, as most of the priesthood hasn't, that their flaws, criminal acts and indiscretions are now subject to global scrutiny thanks to the Internet. The evidence presented in this essay was retrieved with just a few keystrokes.

This phenomenon hasn't been addressed anywhere more eloquently than in the following paragraph written by a Marist priest named Ted Keating in his capacity as Executive Director of Conference of the Major Superiors of Men. His words were truly prophetic. The name of this organization in and of itself gives readers a preview of how high they hold themselves in their own esteem. The CMSM represents all the orders of priests outside of diocesan fold. Behold the words of those who see themselves as the betters of the human race!

> "The days of the *pass* or *station house adjustment* for Father or Brother by the Irish cop or prosecutor are over. Either we will learn to become more comfortable in the gaze of the ***rude and scoffing multitude*** (depending on our attitude) or we will be dragged ***kicking and screaming*** into a new future for religion and religious life"[10](italics are the author's emphasis)

The current hierarchy is being dragged kicking and screaming into the present by the rude and scoffing multitude. They are old men, dinosaurs living in the twenty first century reminiscent of the pathetic Matthew Harrison Brady character portrayed by Fredric March in *Inherit the Wind*. In their day, they got all the station house passes they wanted and received them in silence. Cardinals like George cannot accept the new reality. So they take it upon themselves to say and do inane things like rejecting the advice of their hand picked Review Board; still trying to preserve their power even as it slips through their fingers.

However, the old dinosaurs have left their minions in positions of authority poised to take over upon the death or retirement of the current lot. The new guard, seeds of the old, will have to find new ways to maintain control. No finer description of this process comes to mind than this paragraph from the Devils of Louden written by Aldous Huxley in 1952.

"In order to justify their behavior, they turn their theories into dogmas, their bylaws into First Principles, their political bosses into Gods and all those who disagree with them into incarnate devils. This idolatrous transformation of the relative into the Absolute and the all too human into the Divine, makes it possible for them to indulge their ugliest passions with a clear conscience and in the certainty that they are working for the Highest Good. And when the current beliefs come, in their turn, to look silly, a new set will be invented, so that the immemorial madness may continue to wear its customary mask of legality, idealism, and true religion."[11]

And what is to become of the "rude and scoffing multitude?" They walk around like the Tin Man looking for something already in their possession: the key to salvation. Like the Tin Man they have fallen prey to Oz. The rude and scoffing multitude pulled back the curtain of awe and mystery only to find very human old men in red dresses who maintain power through fear. Fear created by professing themselves to be the gateway to salvation and the fear created by the threat of withholding said prized salvation. The hierarchy never imagined this happening. The flock never imagined what they found. Much to their surprise, what they found was much too human, arrogant, condescending, hypocritical, and criminal.

Such is the legacy of Cardinal George.

References

1. http://www.usccb.org/whoweare.shtml

2. http://www.usccb.org/comm/archives/2002/02-216.shtml

3. http://www.usccb.org/ocyp/charter.shtml

4. http://reform-network.net/?p=1910

5. http://www.usccb.org/ocyp/charter.shtml

6. http://reform-network.net/?p=1910

7.http://query.nytimes.com/gst/fullpage.html?res=940DEEDA103EF934A15757C0A9649C8B63&partner=rssnyt&emc=rss

8. http://reform-network.net/?p=1910

9. http://reform-network.net/?p=1127

10. This paragraph was taken from an editorial in the monthly bulletin posted on the website of Major Superiors of Men. Shortly after I sent Fr. Keating my thoughts on his editorial, they stopped posting bulletins publicly and restricted access to their past bulletins. The reason in my opinion was that one too many of the "rude and scoffing multitude" found their ideas rude and scoffing.

11. Aldous Huxley, *The Devils of Loudun*, 1952, Harper and Brothers, NY, NY.

Who Changed the Church?

Survivors, parents of survivors, and parents of clerically abused children who committed suicide are the ones who have changed the way the hierarchy does business. Anyone telling you different is lying. The courts are the arbiters of last resort in this county and thank God that the founding fathers had the sense to protect our court system from religion. The following scenario played out a thousand times with the same results: Fr. Fingers was found molesting children. The parents, who believed their children (not all the victims of clerical abuse were fortunate enough to have parents who believed them) went to the archdiocese. The archdiocese acted properly shocked and dismayed promising to take care of the problem "in house." The dyed-in-the-wool Catholic parents went home thinking that they had done a good thing for both their child and the church. Only when Fr. Fingers showed up again in the next parish or made the front page did the parents wake up to the fact that they had been bamboozled. It became quite clear to survivors and parent of survivors that the hierarchy could not be trusted. (They still cannot be trusted, which is a fact that is still lost on most Catholics including members of VOTF) That is when the lawsuits started, the press coverage began. and the shit hit the fan. These things were also the amniotic fluid that nurtured VOTF.

The sense of betrayal is enormous. You tell another priest. He urges you not to do anything. You go to the monsignor, you hear the same. You go to the Vicar of Priest Personnel, the bishop and then the cardinal. Each step of the way, you are sure someone will right this egregious wrong. Oh we'll take care of it, this is the first we've heard about and on and on *ad nauseum*. They all lie to you and in some instances make concerted efforts from the pulpit, in the media and with legal tactics to discredit and disgrace you. Grappling with the concept of members of the hierarchy lying to your face is incredibly hard to wrap your mind around; especially if you're a dyed-in-the-wool Catholic. Then it sinks in that there exists a criminal conspiracy to keep Fr. Fingers from being held accountable. In the depths of your heart, you realize that the people you are dealing with don't give a rat's ass about you, the Gospels, or Jesus Christ! They are really all about themselves. That's the mind blowing experience which makes legal action against the church possible. Enough people came to that conclusion to seek the courts as a means of changing an institution that was incapable of changing itself and it worked!

About five years ago, I spoke to two VOTF groups. They were comprised of Baby Boomers and Senior Citizens. I congratulated them for showing up to hear me, but I also told them their showing up meant nothing unless they took action. They were appalled by the truth, but they were more frightened of writing a forceful letter to their bishop. When a person gets older and the concept of dying begins to take on reality, the thought of losing heaven weighs heavily either consciously or unconsciously. Getting a cradle to grave Catholic to go against the hierarchy (the church) and thereby risk losing salvation is an awesome task. (Such is the effectiveness of Catholic indoctrination) It takes a life changing, gut wrenching decision after believing for so long to say so long or to demand change. That is why most in-house Catholics will never stand up and be counted in the war to reclaim their church.

The concept of "when a person declares him or herself and ex-Catholic, he or she loses a great deal of influence among Catholics themselves." is synonymous with "Ex-Catholics should not be sponsoring petitions" which is synonymous with "If you don't like the way the church does business, find another church!" The main idea of these three statements is that the only people capable of rectifying what is wrong with the church are Catholics inside the church. Balderdash! The only people who have brought significant changes to the way the hierarchy handles things are people who for the most part have left the church! The ones on the inside don't have the nerve to call a bishop or cardinal anything but "your eminence." You will know them by their fruits, but don't take my word for it.

Matt 7: 15-20
"Beware of false prophets, who come to you in sheep's clothing but inwardly are ravenous wolves. You will know them by their fruits. Are grapes gathered from thorns, or figs from thistles? So, every sound tree bears good fruit, but the bad tree bears evil fruit. A sound tree cannot bear evil fruit, nor can a bad tree bear good fruit. Every tree that does not bear good fruit is cut down and thrown into the fire. Thus you will know them by their fruits.

Women and the Church

Women, fruit of your womb was Jesus Christ
Your true place in His church, part of a heist
By supposed men of God without ears
Who've lied and manipulated for years.

If men and women are equal in God's eyes
Then priests and bishops tell fallacious lies.
Woman nurtured Christ, He suckled her breast.
Why then can't loving women do the rest?

Priests have named her Holy Mother Church
But all God's women are left in a lurch.
If God trusted woman with his Son's life
Why not consecrate a host without strife?

Was it Magdalene or Peter, who lied
That terrible day when Jesus Christ died?
Who was with Him at the foot of the cross
Women or the bishops who think they're boss?

Hiding in that upstairs room like fossils
There were found the eleven apostles.
Were the men or women first at His tomb?
Women who brought Jesus forth from the womb!

Now's the time for women to take their place,
Recognizing that they are full of grace.
There's no evil that church men haven't done
It's time for women to shine in the sun.

That's the story; it doesn't take a sleuth
To read the bible and find out the truth!
A woman shall crush the head of the snake.
This prophecy causes bishops to quake.

The Saddest Story Ever Told

An injured child lies in the street and cries.
A passerby ignores the cries; the child dies.
Depraved indifference in anyone's eyes.
In the face of reason, this indifference flies!
Is there any excuse for the gravity of this depravity?

A pedophile priest children enslaves
Seeking the illicit sex he craves.
Creating wounds children take to their graves
He's a sexual predator, that's how he behaves.

They never see the gravity of their depravity.

Bishops had knowledge of these horrific acts;
They chose to ignore all the grotesque facts.
To contain the damage, they shuffled priests
Sacrificing more children to feed these beasts.

They never accepted the gravity of the depravity.

Predator priests left children bloodied and gored
The plight of their victims completely ignored
How could they deny a sexually abused child?
These violations should have driven the laity wild.

They never understood the gravity of their depravity.

The depth of their depravity knew no bounds.
It sprang forth straight from hell's hounds.
Not satisfied with leaving children strewn about;
Bishops crucified any who tried to speak out.

They hid well the gravity of their depravity.

Abusive tactics, gag orders and even shame
Were all gambits employed in an ugly game
To keep wounded children alone and at bay
So no one would notice a church full of decay.

They knew well the gravity of their depravity.

In two thousand two the whole scandal blew.
Bishops and cardinals denied all they knew
About abusive clergy they'd shuffled about
As the media and church used their clout.

Forsaking truth defines the gravity of their depravity.

It was all about them; they didn't know!
Bishops and cardinals, what a convincing show!
Now they recoil at being called depraved
Still making excuses for the way they behaved.

Thus they denied the gravity of their depravity.

The pope called the cardinals to his home.
Old men in red dresses gathered in Rome
To hear the cause: "mysterium iniquitous!"
The pontiff feigned ignorance too, fortuitous!

A mystery, the gravity of their depravity!

"There is no room in the priesthood," he said,
"For those who abuse children," his face red.
Hollow words rang hollow under St. Peter's dome
After which, the cardinals solemnly headed home.

Let's declare an end to the gravity of this depravity.

The bishops drew up the Dallas Charter
To the man, they played the martyr
Furiously debating one strike or two
As if one wouldn't give the devil his due!

We must protect all our priests, even the beasts!
Bernie Law elevated priests above his God
And with a vulgar smile gave them a nod.
Depraved indifference was the essence of Law
How many children had he sent to hell's door?

Victims cried out with a roar, "Up yours Bernie Law!"

He resigned steeped in humiliating disgrace,
But good old J.P. found him an honored place;
The reward for cardinal sins: a Basilica in Rome.

Out of the court's reach, his lavish new home!

Christ was betrayed in this remarkable charade,

Hierarchal duplicity soared to new heights
Stomping on victims in the name of priest's rights.
There wasn't a legal venue they didn't thwart
In their Herculean efforts to stay out of court.

Fighting tooth and nail to keep molesters out of jail!

Monstrous was their deft use of deceit
Making the carnage of children complete.
Doing nothing while a child's soul dies
Is Depraved Indifference in anyone's eyes!

Who could imagine the hypocrisy of this theocracy?

Feigning concern, they commissioned a survey
From an honorable institution called John Jay
On the numbers of priests gone sexually astray
And then paraded the findings like a bad toupee!

So much dung flung from many a forked tongue.

The bishops created a National Review Board
Whose every request was then patently ignored
By a hierarchy who only answered to the Lord
Ask Frank Keating, who struck the wrong chord.

What a disgrace; it backfired in the bishop's face.

"The hierarchy used mafia tactics," said Keating.
Speaking the truth, earned him a verbal beating.
Cardinals and bishops demanded his resignation,
Which he gladly tendered out of sheer frustration.

If the truth is spoken aloud; put the speaker in a shroud.

Grand Juries all reached the same conclusion
Honesty from church leaders was just an illusion
They came away with the same recommendations
There must be changes to the Statute of Limitations.

They will have to address the flaws if we change the laws!

Victims come to terms with abuse later on in life.
The Statutes deny justice, creating more strife.
Bishops used the statutes as a legal solution
Whereby criminal priests escaped prosecution.

How could this be? Policy from the Holy See!

They spoke of sorrow, forgiveness, and grace
While hiring legions of lawyers without a face
To forestall any changes from taking place
To the Statutes of Limitations and further disgrace.

Sons of the Pharisee, they have nothing on thee!

And what of the priests sworn to God's law
The majority, it seems, were made out of straw.
Never speaking out against the evil they saw
Child abuse, hypocrisy and breaking the law.

Serving their human boss, not Christ on the cross.

All the spin about prayerful healing;
Just a sham to cover their double dealing.
They're full of contrition for getting caught;
Not for the untold damage they've wrought.

The children's plight was never in their sight.

The pope speaks often of human rights,
Evoking peals of laughter as we recall the fights
To conceal the scandal of their own making
Which left countless children alone and aching.

Limitless is the hypocrisy of this theocracy.

Illusions of their grandeur fill their eyes
Blind to the truth, they can't see their lies.
From which side of their mouth have they spoken?
The side giving the impression nothing's broken
.
The men in red have the devil wed.

Years from now they will speak of the day
When a corrupt hierarchy had their way.
A once mighty edifice flew out of control
Because the bricks and mortar lacked a soul.

Our children became toys for grownup boys.

We can't say if this is the church's demise
That's for future generations to surmise.
But the beginning of the end is no surprise
For the church that lies eventually dies!

The price of the gravity of their depravity.

March 16, 2008

Dear Editor,

Gary Stern's article "The church needs more priests" left out one important impediment to men wanting to become priests, moral authority! Groucho Marx is famous for saying he would never become a member of any club that would have him for a member. Rephrasing that, we would have to ask, "Who would want to be a member of a church whose leadership protects child abusers?" The church has lost its moral authority and is steeped in hypocrisy. The four largest dioceses in the country are Los Angeles, Boston, Chicago, and New York. Three of the four are headed by cardinals whose hands are deeply stained with child abuse. The ex-cardinal of Boston, Law, arguably the worst, sits upon the throne of a Basilica in Rome. Across the country, there are numerous bishops equally befouled with the stench of clergy abuse. Why would any normal, healthy man want to be part of an organization whose management protects child molesters and persecutes their victims?

The last part of this story talks about an ad campaign for real men. That is the saddest line in the entire story. Real men do not sexually abuse children. Real men stand up for what is right. Real men don't play "shuffle the pedophile." But most of all, real men don't work for people who do these things. They stand up against injustice when they see it, even if the source is their boss.

Many of the current election campaign ads are tagged: "My name is: and I have approved this message." My name is Pope Benedict and I have tacitly approved the actions of my cardinals and bishops because no matter how grievous their actions, I have left them in place. Real men don't operate that way and won't work for those that do!

Vincent J. Nauheimer

Why won't charges be brought against American Bishops and Cardinals under Canon Law?

Several years ago my family was disparaged from the pulpit by the Vicar of Priest Personnel after we filed a lawsuit against a predator priest. The Vicar got up and from the pulpit declared that ours was the first complaint of this type against the priest and told the parishioners that the suit was all about money. He made that statement even though he had been in the parish quietly fixing a similar incident with another family a year earlier before vehemently decrying our accusations. In short, this man lied from the pulpit. This is all part of the public record of the Westchester Grand Jury Report investigating clergy abuse.

Being in a state of shock and too naïve at the time to file a slander suit, we did nothing. However, public humiliation and abuse of that magnitude is not easily forgotten. It seemed to me that a bureaucracy like the Catholic Church that has laws for everything, should have some condemning behavior like this. So with justice in mind, I acquired a copy of Canon Law and the Catechism and went to work reading. I found the following:

From the Catechism:

2326 Scandal is a grave offense when by deed or omission it deliberately leads others to sin gravely.

2287 Anyone who uses the power at his disposal in such a way that it leads others to do wrong becomes guilty of scandal and responsible for the evil that he has directly or indirectly encouraged. "Temptations to sin are sure to come; but woe to him by whom they come!"

2353 Fornication is carnal union between an unmarried man and an unmarried woman. It is gravely contrary to the dignity of persons and of human sexuality which is naturally ordered to the good of spouses and the generation and education of children. Moreover, it is a grave scandal when there is corruption of the young. (My emphasis)

From Canon Law:

Can. 1369 A person is to be punished with a just penalty, who, at a public event or assembly, or in a published writing, or by otherwise using the means of social communication, utters blasphemy, or gravely harms public morals, or rails at or excites hatred of or contempt for religion or the Church.

Can. 1389 § 1 A person who abuses ecclesiastical power or an office, is to be punished according to the gravity of the act or the omission, not excluding by deprivation of the office, unless a penalty for that abuse is already established by law or precept.

§ 2 A person who, through culpable negligence, unlawfully and with harm to another, performs or omits and act of ecclesiastical power or ministry or office, is to be punished with a just penalty.

Can. 212 1, Priests and Bishops are also bound by this obedience, in fact more so since they are responsible for passing on to the faithful genuine Catholic teaching. In other words, a Bishop or Priest who dissents from Church teachings is not to be obeyed in that matter, rather all must obey the Magisterium at all times, as Vatican II states.

Bishops and Cardinals have been in clear violation of the above since before the Clergy Abuse Scandal was blown wide open. After it became public, they only served to create greater scandal and incited incredible hatred and humiliation of the Roman Catholic Church. The burning question is, "Why won't charges be brought under Canon Law against the cardinals and bishops who are the most egregious offenders?" Court proceedings, newspaper and personal accounts of their transgressions are numerous, sadly too numerous. Yet no one, even those who profess a desire to clean up the church, will file charges against those who have grievously wounded the Catholic Church. Why is that?

The answer, of course, is obvious. No member of the hierarchy will file charges, no matter how just, against another member of the hierarchy. Doing so would expose to the world to the extensive hypocrisy and corruption existing in today's hierarchy. The hierarchy, all the way to the Vatican, would have to put their peers on trial and judge them for all the violations that the public already knows they have committed. Canon Law demands just penalties, but is there a bishop with enough spine to mete out a just punishment for such horrific sins against God, children and the church?

Bishop Accountability.org tells us that there are some thirteen or more credibly accused bishops. However, not one of them has ever been laicized nor proceedings begun to laicize. They have all been allowed to retire. Bishop Tom Gumbleton has the distinct privilege of the being the only bishop to stand up for survivors and he was immediately forced to retire. That speaks volumes for the collective will of the brotherhood of the red hat.

Surely, there must be a way for the laity to file charges under Canon Law and somewhere in this world at least one Canon Lawyer willing to take on this onerous task to save his or her church.

Confession

Bless me Eminence for I have sinned.
The fat Cardinal smiled and grinned.

Who was it you did hurt?
A young girl, I lifted her skirt.
It's not of very much I speak
I just took a little peek.

Are her parents, a good touch?
Nah, they don't contribute much.

How goes your favorite new toy?
Oh you mean that new altar boy?
Things are going well all right
I'm taking him away Friday night.

Tell me of the Cardinal's Appeal
Are you parishioners giving for real?

From the pulpit I throw abuses
At all those who offer excuses
On why they hide and refuse to tithe.
I do my best to make them writhe.

Ah my son you're a good priest
At the Lord's Table you'll have a feast.

Little old ladies still open their purses,
I'm busy chasing children and nurses.
It's such a wonderful life we lead
Thank God for planting this seed.

I don't hear anything requiring a solution
How about I give you absolution?

Let me get down upon my knees
And show intent for forgiveness please.
To set an example for those who sin
After all we don't want the devil to win!

The world is wicked, full of hate.
Just remember the collection plate!

FORTY THESES AGAINST CLERGY SEXUAL ABUSE

Protect children, Heal Survivors, Reform the Church©

By Vinnie Nauheimer

Dear Bishop: _____

Almost five hundred years ago on October 31, 1517, Dr. Martin Luther posted his 95 Theses on the door of the Cathedral of Wittenberg. At the turn of the second millennium the church once more finds itself in dire need of major reform. St. Paul admonishes us in Cortinthians 1: 5-6 "Do you not know that a little leaven leavens the whole lump? Cleanse out the old leaven that you may be a new lump." The survivors of Clergy Sexual Abuse, their families, friends and the Catholic laity demand change, justice and reform. These are the Forty Theses of Clergy Sexual Abuse and we demand their immediate adoption by the Roman Catholic Church. We urge you and all members of the Roman Catholic clergy to forward these to the Vatican. Without the immediate implementation of these Forty Theses by the Roman Catholic Church neither the victims of clergy abuse nor the church can move forward.

FORTY THESES OF CLERGY ABUSE

1.   The Pope must immediately release and open for public inspection all secret files contained in dioceses throughout the world including the Vatican that have information relating to the abuse of children.

2.   The Catholic Church must release and make public the names of all priests, bishops, and cardinals who have had credible accusations of sexual abuse made against them, their current status as well as their current location.

3.   The pope must, in writing, free all those survivors from their confidentiality agreements "Gag Clauses" with any dioceses around the world in order to let victims of clergy abuse speak freely.

4. The Vatican should demand of all clergy, as applicable, that as an act of atonement, they will, in writing, declare null and void all private confidentiality agreements made between them and their victims.

5. The Pope and the Vatican must release and forever disavow keeping any secrets of the "Holy Office" related to clergy or any other form of abuse perpetrated by the clergy.

6. All secret letters and instructions issued to cardinals and bishops worldwide such as "Crimen Sollicitationis" are to be declared null and void.

7. The hierarchy of the Catholic Church must change its policy on clerical abusers to demand under penalty that they report cases of abuse to their local civil authorities.

8. The pope will issue a Papal Bull reconfirming the love of Jesus for children and that none should be harmed as they, and not the clergy are our greatest treasure.

9. The hierarchy of the Catholic Church must recognize that the children are our future and if the church is to have one, their future too.

10. The hierarchy of the Catholic Church must recognize that all children have the inalienable right to grow up without fear of being sexually abused by any cleric or lay minister.

11. The hierarchy of the Catholic Church must acknowledge that children have the right to attend mass, serve on the altar and attend church functions without being molested.

12. The Church must acknowledge that parents have the right to expect that their children will not be sexually abused, molested or otherwise harmed by priests, nuns or deacons while engaged in church activities.

13. The Church must declare in the plainest of terms that the sexual abuse of children is against God's Law, Natural Law, and publicly restate that abuse is against both Canon Law and the proscription of the Catechism.

14. The church must admit that in the past, when it came to sexual abuse of children by clergy, there have historically been no rules, no order, no discipline, no desire to change, and make a sacred vow to erase this mentality from their clerical culture.

15. Having recognized the above to be true, they must take the actions necessary to enforce these changes listed in thesis' one through fourteen.

16. All members of the Catholic Church have the right to expect exemplary behavior out of those who would answer the call of ordination and the right to receive justice when the clergy falls short.

17. The hierarchy of the Catholic Church will accept the fact that the priesthood is comprised of men who are mere mortals some of whom have a penchant for evil

18. The hierarchy of the Catholic Church must remove any such men quickly and decisively when their behavior endangers the safety and welfare of any child.

19. The hierarchy of the Catholic Church must acknowledge that the priesthood is a "privilege" and not a "right." Privileges can and should be revoked when abused.

20. The hierarchy of the Catholic Church must understand that the privilege of serving as a priest must be revoked when the actions of a priest endangers the welfare of children.

21. The hierarchy of the Catholic Church must publicly acknowledge the many types of abuse being committed by their clergy.

22. The hierarchy of the Catholic Church must stop trying to make clergy abuse a homosexual issue. It is not necessarily true with pedophiles and is certainly not true in the global cases of abuse committed against female children and teens.

23. The hierarchy of the Catholic Church must admit that female children, teens and adults are abused as often as their male counterparts.

24. It is incumbent on the Catholic Church to recognize and accept the equality of men and women in the eyes of man and God in all matters, not only sexual abuse.

25. The hierarchy of the Catholic Church must join the world in recognizing the sexual abuse of children as a criminal act.

26. As a criminal act it is incumbent upon the Catholic Church to report criminal activities to the proper civil authorities and not to hinder their reporting.

27. The Catholic Church must recognize that the criminal activities of errant priests can in no way benefit the well-being or future of the church.

28. The church must beg for forgiveness, not expect it.

29. The church must make amends to all those that have been sexually abused by its clergy.

30. The church must make amends to all those who have suffered at the hands of the church because of their efforts to expose these grievous criminal actions.

31. The Catholic Church must recognize the rights of all victims of sexual abuse and their families to be hurt and angry.

32. The Catholic Church must recognize their moral and spiritual obligation to help victims and their families work through the anger and pain caused by clerical abuse and the churches indifference toward predatory priests.

33. The hierarchy and all clerics must adhere to the wishes of the current Holy Father who said, ""All bishops must carry out their pastoral ministry with utmost care in order to help foster the protection of minors, and they will be held accountable," and his two predecessors: Pope Benedict XVI, who said: "Victims should receive compassion and care, and those responsible for these evils must be brought to justice." And John Paul II who said, "There is no place in the priesthood or religious life for those who would harm the young."

34. All members of the hierarchy of the Catholic Church who were themselves abusers, covered-up for abusers or shuffled abusers should immediately tender their resignations in order to abide by the wishes of the current pope and the last two; all of whom are and have been Spiritual leaders and representative of Jesus Christ here on earth

35. If the hierarchy of the Catholic Church who covered up and shuffled predator priests causing considerable harm to the young do not resign, it is incumbent upon the pope to force them out or forever more be known as a hypocrite. Those of the hierarchy who ignore the explicit words of these three popes will forever more be known as heretics who deny Jesus Christ and the church he founded.

36. The church must admit full accountability for the Clergy Abuse Scandal. No accountability is the equivalent of no belief in judgment from the higher power to whom they ascribe their faith.

37. Pride is one of the seven deadly sins. Secrecy, when used to hide failings is pride in disguise. A church keeping secrets becomes a darkened wasteland. Secrets create the perfect breeding ground for all sorts of nefarious and malignant growths. Secrecy is a cesspool fertilizing the dregs of humanity and creating offspring that are as rotten as the offal from which they spring. The abundance of slime generated by the Roman Catholic Church's cesspool became so large it spilled over its banks and ran into the light where it was laid bare to the world. The culture of secrecy regarding sexual abuse must end!

38. The Catechism of the Roman Catholic Church
     #2326 tells us: "Scandal is a grave offense when by deed or omission it deliberately leads others to sin gravely." There is hardly a more apt statement against either clergy abuse or bishops moving pedophiles.
     #2287 tells us: Anyone who uses the power at his disposal in such a way that it

leads others to do wrong becomes guilty of scandal and responsible for the evil that he has directly or indirectly encouraged. "Temptations to sin are sure to come; but woe to him by whom they come!"
The hierarchy has brought grave scandal down upon their church and a just penalty is demanded for those who facilitated this scandal.

39.   Recognizing the shame, scandal and scorn that the hierarchy of the Catholic Church has brought down upon the global church, the number of good Catholics that they have driven from the church by their blatant lies and the generations that the hierarchy has lost for the church: an appropriate penance is demanded.

40.   Create a day of Holy Obligation making it mandatory for all members of the clergy to attend a mass once a year which is to be dedicated to remembering all the victims of clergy abuse who have suffered at the hands of the church, the damage done by scandal to the church and to pray that a scourge like this never again plagues the church or any other organization.

By conveying to you this copy of these Forty Theses, I affirm my support of them and urge you to forward them on to the Vatican and Holy See.

Sincerely

_____   _____
Name   Date

Directions for emailing the Forty Theses

Go to: http://www.catholic-hierarchy.org/bishop/lla.html where you will find a list of all the living bishops. Click on your local bishop's name and it will give you information about him. In the second row in the left box it will say, contact the bishop through the diocese. Click on the diocese and upon getting to the diocese, look to right for general information and click the official website. Once at the diocese official website, you can click on "Contact us" and you will find the bishop's email address along with the addresses of other diocesan leaders. You can send the 40 Theses to as many of their clerics as they have listed. Either copy and paste it in the email or send it as an attachment or, preferably both. If stamps are not an issue, by all means print and mail a hard copy.

I would anyone who has read this book to this point send a copy of these Forty Theses Against Clergy Abuse to their local priest, bishop and cardinal.

The Tenth Circle

While heading back to his office from lunch, Charlie took notice of the truck making a delivery to Joe's Deli. Not because it was out of the ordinary, but because there were several boxes precariously perched on the edge of the side door and they were swaying in the strong March breeze. The next thing Charlie saw was a young boy about five or six years old walking past him. The kid was doing a balancing act while walking along the edge of the curb. Just as the boy walked under the boxes, a strong gust of wind blew and the boxes started on their descent to the sidewalk.

Charlie acted on instinct as he knew the potential outcome. He darted toward the curb, snatched the boy out from under the falling boxes, and slipped while trying to avoid a head on collision with a parking meter. Charlie managed to set the boy down as his momentum propelled him towards the sidewalk. He tried to break his fall with an outstretched hand, but his momentum was too great for his hand to function as a brake. For this heroic effort he received a scratched palm, bruised knee and a ruined suit. Once again, in trying to do the right thing, Charlie found himself in pain. Worse was the fact that no one witnessed the event. By the time he had gotten up and inspected the damage to his knee, the child was gone. Run off to play no doubt and probably totally oblivious to what could have happened. The only thing the truck driver saw was Charlie getting up alongside the boxes scattered on the sidewalk. His only concern was about getting sued.

Charlie lay in bed praying for sleep that evening. The pain shooting from his knee and hand were reminders of the day's events, just like the pain in his heart reminded him of this past year's troubles. "Who was that kid anyhow?" he asked himself. Then he told himself it didn't make a difference because the kid didn't get hurt.

After reliving the day's events, Charlie's mind turned to what was had been eating at him for months: his son's molestation at the hands of their parish priest. He prayed as he prayed every night lately, "Please God! Let me know that going public wasn't a futile gesture on my part. Tell me my sense of righteousness didn't get in the way of my better judgment. Tell me that the publicity surrounding this suit won't make things worse for my son. Let me know there is a purpose to this mortifying charade that has torn my family, my community and me apart. Most of all, Lord, let me that my son will be all right." These were the same prayers that Charlie recited so many times during the past few months as he lay in bed desperately wanting the escape only a deep sleep could provide.

Once again, as he lay staring at the ceiling, the litany of whys started in his head: Why was his son chosen as a victim? Why was the Archdiocese protecting this pedophile priest who wronged not only his son, but others? Why did they keep this priest on as pastor in spite of the overwhelming evidence against him? Why did the Archdiocese attack me and my family as if we were the guilty parties? Why have some of my friends, neighbors, community and church members turned against me? Why was this happening to me and my family? Tired of no answers to these questions, Charlie faced the onerous task of telling his mind to shut up so he could sleep. Finally, Charlie prayed for sleep. God was prepared to grant his wish this night.

Charlie tossed and turned trying to find a comfortable position for his swollen knee. When at last he found one, the mantle of sleep quickly enveloped him. Moments later, his consciousness was transported to a strange and beautiful place where peace and tranquility seemed to permeate the very air. As he walked about lush vegetation he felt the serenity that he had been seeking all his life. Walking down a path towards him was the same young boy from the truck incident earlier in the day. Charlie smiled at the boy and the boy smiled back saying, "My name is Innocence."

Charlie felt an overwhelming sense of calm as the boy neared him. "Come," said the boy as he reached for Charlie's hand. He held it like any child would hold his own father's. At once Charlie felt the unconditional love that emanated from the child's hand as it surged through him. Charlie asked in a matter of fact manner, "Where are we going?" The child just pointed in a direction and they started to walk. Innocence led Charlie to a beautiful glen filled with people radiating love. As Charlie and Innocence entered their midst, they gathered round and applauded. Two of the group walked up to Charlie and somehow, he instinctively knew who they were.

"You're Virgil and you're Dante aren't you? Charlie asked.

"Yes we are," was the reply.

"What am I doing here?" asked Charlie surprised at the calmness of his voice.

Dante said, "The Lord has seen fit to answer your prayers and ease your pain. You will learn shortly that there is a special place for those who use God and his church to desecrate children. For the Lord holds children close to his heart. Woe upon the man who masquerades as a priest in order to fill his own lusty desires with children. He has a special place in hell as do all those who aid him in his crimes. Innocence has brought you to us so that we may put your mind at ease."

"Will I learn exactly what becomes of these monsters and more importantly, to those who allow it to continue?" asked Charlie.

Dante told Charlie that it was God's will that his question be answered and the time was near. Virgil cautioned him to hold onto Innocence's hand for only Innocence could protect him from the horror he was about to witness. Charlie looked down at Innocence and patted the little hand that rested snugly in his own. At the same time, he felt the incredible strength that flowed from the child to him. Suddenly Charlie and his guides were in the depths of hell. Without being told, Charlie knew they were in the ninth circle. The Circle reserved for the souls who were fraudulent against those to whom they were given a special trust.

"It is here that we will find the priests who have violated children over the centuries", said Dante.

"Why weren't they mentioned in the Inferno?" asked Charlie.

Dante replied, "It wasn't time. The Comedy was written to legitimize the church, not offend it"

As Charlie took in the surreal view of the ninth circle before him, he saw Satan seated in the middle on his great throne with Legion at his side. Then looking over the souls before him encapsulated in ice, he saw a great many priests immersed in the ice up to their collars.

"Is this where the abusers go?" asked Charlie.

"No," said Virgil, "this is too good for them! Then he turned and commanded Satan, "In the name of God most high and holy I command you move aside and let us see the most prized of your souls."

Charlie whispered to Dante, "Why are they the most prized of his souls?"

Dante replied, "Because their acts were such abominations that next to Satan himself, no single group has driven more people from God than sexually abusive clergy.

Satan boomed, "Who is it that wishes to see my pets?"

Virgil replied, "Someone who is trying to thwart their work on earth and it is heaven's desire that he see the punishment which lies in wait for those who commit these atrocities. The Lord wishes man to know that regardless of the outcome of the earthly courts, there is one court of justice that cannot be escaped."

With that, Satan waved his hand and the great throne he was seated on slid back revealing the tenth circle of hell. This circle was reserved exclusively for clergy who sexually abused children and those who enabled them. This level was ten times that of the largest football stadium Charlie had ever seen. It contained four concentric rings; each one was a different level reflecting varying degrees of punishment. The innermost and bottom ring radiated various shades of red. Charlie knew that the bottom ring contained the worst of them all.

On the first ring were those clergy who inflicted harm with lecherous touches. Each priest was surrounded by devils who had taken the form of every victim the priest had abused; victims who had been demeaned by the touching and fondling of the priest. These devils turned children looked pure and innocent. The kind of children molesters would drool over. Some priests were surrounded by only girls, some only by boys and still others by boys and girls. Each priest was in his own enclosure along with the replicas of his victims. It was bounded by walls, but no ceiling and the children were gathered around the priest in a circle. Some circles were very large and others were small, but in each circle, the same scenario was unfolding. As the perverted priest reached out to passionately touch and caress one of these children, his hand or hands would instantly ignite in a bright flame. Then the hands would turn to ash and the priest would let out such a sorrowful cry as not to be described.

Charlie held his hands to his ears as his eyes remained riveted on the spectacle before him. And one by one in turn, the priest went round the circle trying to touch each of his victims again and again with the same result. And after the attempted touch, the once beautiful child would return to its hideous hell form. The priest continued until all of the children that he had molested were touched and returned to their hideous hell forms. Then all the demons attacked the priest tearing him asunder and the cries from the priest and his tormentors bespoke the agony of their eternal suffering. Then the cycle repeated itself with all the demons returning to their childlike forms while the priest once again tried to molest them. It was a scene that was to play out for all eternity giving Charlie his first insight into the true essence of hell.

Next they viewed the second ring containing the priests who had penetrated children. They too were surrounded by devils in the form of the priest's earthly victims. Again, some were surrounded by only boys, some only girls and others by both. Some priests had several victims, others had hundreds. The childlike demons were completely naked, innocent looking, and appearing with the features most craved by their abuser. Charlie stood in horror at what he saw next. The priests in this ring grabbed each child in turn looking to relieve their visibly aroused state, but they couldn't because there were no orifices to penetrate. Try as they may from every conceivable position with each child, these feverish priests could not penetrate one child. Frustrated they moved from one to the next. As the aroused priest tried each child in turn; his frustration grew a hundred fold. He cursed, screamed, begged and pleaded for relief, but none was to be found.

When the priest reached the last child, all the children returned to their demonic forms, circled and turned on the priest. One at a time, they recited Matthew 5, "If your right eye causes you to sin then gouge it out." Then a demon would pluck out the priest's eye and each demon in the group in turn took a piece of that priest saving the genitals for last. When the priest was totally dismembered and the genitals were removed, the priest returned whole and the process started again and would continue for eternity.

There were some exceptions though; a certain number of these priests would leave the second ring to go down to the third ring. There they would go through a different cycle before returning to the second level. Their eternity would be spent going back and forth between two kinds of hell one worse than the other.

The third ring was horrific and at the same time heartbreaking for it contained devils in the guise of children who had committed suicide. Charlie cringed at a thought which raced to his mind, but Innocence squeezed his hand and the awful thought passed. There before each priest were the children who took their own lives because the sexual abuse suffered at the hands of that priest. These deviant priests had shattered their will to live. These were the faces of victims who could not cope with the ultimate betrayal. They were betrayed by priests from whom they sought solace. Abuse at the hands of a priest was the last straw and the final confirmation that life was hopeless. These children suffered the ultimate betrayal. They were the victims who had been sent to priests for help, be it bereavement counseling, divorce, parental alcoholism and various forms of abuse. The priests, who were supposed to help them, sexually abused them. The victims of these priests shared the common thread of ultimate betrayal, which leads to total despair.

The eyes of these victims reflected their absence of hope; they were dull and lifeless. Their movements were slow and mechanical. Each had with them the means of their own end and was seated in a row in front of their abuser. Some of the girls had razor blades or pills, some boys had ropes or guns and there were a few without anything. Charlie watched the horror; his eyes riveted on the unearthly scene as each victim gave the priest the means of his or her demise. As each victim handed the priest the means of their death, they watched the priest use it upon himself.

Charlie saw the blood flow as one priest slit his wrists and he instinctively knew the priest was experiencing the pain of the life flowing out of him while being mocked by the child turned demon again. Another priest took a rope, put his head in the noose and stepped off a stool. Charlie heard the snap as his neck broke and watched him writhe in agony as his face swelled while the ever-tightening coil slowly choked the life out of him. Charlie was startled as one boy stood up and an instant later, out of nowhere, a train smashed into the priest. Some priests had only one child in front of them while others had several and more. Those that had multiple children in front of them had to experience each death in turn by whatever means their victim had used. Then the priest was returned to the second ring.

Charlie's attention then turned to the innermost and bottom ring. On this level were the enablers, the pastors, monsignors, vicars, bishops, cardinals and popes who allowed perverted priests to continue in their evil ways. These were the hypocrites who turned a blind eye to the rape, sodomization and molestations committed by the priests in the outer circles. They may or may not have partaken themselves, but they were responsible by their commissions and omissions, for the foul deeds of others. They were the hierarchy of the church; the men who were supposed to be emulating Jesus. This august group, who denied the existence of clerical sexual abuse, lied from the pulpit, railed against innocent victims and allowed the carnage to continue unabated. They used every trick in the book to deny, belittle or vilify victims to save their status quo. A variation of the color red emanated from each member of the hierarchy in the inner circle and it spread out encompassing all the predator priests they had enabled. Some were responsible for only a few while others could have filled a church with those they let run amok.

In the innermost ring each member of the enabling hierarchy was seated in front of a large mirror. The mirror reflected their atrocities. First they watched themselves defend the actions of pedophile priests to their victims, then to the victim's parents, then to the parishioners and finally to themselves. Next, the prelate was forced to watch the acts of each individual predator he let loose upon unsuspecting children. One by one the prelate watched these acts in all their lurid detail. Next, the mirror showed how a predator, upon being promoted to the hierarchy, allowed even more abusers to run rampant and in turn promoted some of them. Charlie immediately realized that some of these links went on for generations: pederast in power empowering more of the same.

When the images stopped, the prelate stood at a pulpit and addressed the multitude of Satan's legions in his defense, "But I did this to save the church! The church is more important than a few children! I was doing God's work! I didn't know they were serial molesters. Think of the scandal! It was consensual! You don't understand how difficult a priest's life is! Children of Satan were seducing my priests! Priests are only human! Think of all the money I saved the church, and think of all the good I have done with that money!"

The speech was suddenly interrupted by peals of laughter emanating from Satan himself. He said as he slapped Legions back, "This is my favorite part; I just love the good intentions speech!" Then as the speaker continued, one by one the members of Satan's army started throwing coins at the speaker, and each coin tore a piece of the speaker's body off. Not a large piece, but a small piece and piece by piece the speaker was flayed alive until only his tongue was left flapping in his skeleton. Then when the last coin hit the tongue, Satan burst forth from it saying, "Thank you my friends for destroying the innocence of children. You've planted the seeds of fear and distrust in their hearts. For with fear and distrust burned into a heart, it is almost impossible to accept the idea of a loving God."

It was at that moment that Charlie understood the true nature of sexual abuse. He knew that the true violation was the stripping of innocence from children. By using them as objects, the abuser destroyed the fundamental building block of relationships, which is trust. Without trust, the victim can never truly love. In addition to destroying trust, the perpetrators created shame. Shame based behavior combined with the inability to trust wreaks havoc and spreads misery. Abusive priests were creating conditions that if not treated could or would last a lifetime. The defilement of a body was bad enough, but being defiled by God's representative on earth generally closed the victim's heart to friends, family and God.

Satan, aware of Charlie's new found knowledge, flew at him in a rage and inflated himself until Charlie recoiled in fear at the immeasurable evil hovering above him. At that same moment, he felt strength surging from that little hand in his. The more the strength flowed from Innocence, the smaller Satan's stature became until it disappeared. Then the whole scene faded and Charlie drifted off into a long awaited peaceful sleep.

The next morning Charlie awoke feeling well rested in spite of the vivid memory of his dream. As he slowly walked from his car to his storefront office, Charlie was shocked to see the new mannequin in the clothing store window next to his. It looked remarkably like Innocence and as he took note of it, the mannequin winked at him. Charlie winked back as a broad smile crossed his face and a new spring entered his step.

www.ingramcontent.com/pod-product-compliance
Lightning Source LLC
Chambersburg PA
CBHW060234050426
42448CB00009B/1437